WINTER CLIMBS

BEN NEVIS AND GLEN COE

About the Author

Having climbed on Ben Nevis and in Glen Coe for 15 years, IFMGA Mike Pescod has an in-depth knowledge of the climbs, the weather and the conditions you can experience here. Working full time as a mountain guide in the region for ten years, Mike has been on Ben Nevis over a thousand times and regularly spends up to a hundred days climbing each winter, both professionally and recreationally.

Mike has been on climbing trips right across Europe as well as to Russia, Tajikistan, Nepal, East Africa and Peru, but it is the unique quality of the climbing in Scotland that gives him the most enjoyment and satisfaction.

With his wife, Louise, he runs a mountain guiding and instruction company and has every intention of climbing in the hills here for many years to come.

WINTER CLIMBS

BEN NEVIS AND GLEN COE

by
Mike Pescod

CICERONE

2 POLICE SQUARE, MILNTHORPE, CUMBRIA LA7 7PY
www.cicerone.co.uk

© Mike Pescod 2010

Seventh edition 2010
ISBN: 978 1 85284 620 6

Sixth edition (by Alan Kimber) 2002   Third edition (by Ed Grindley) 1981
Fifth edition (by Alan Kimber) 1994   Second edition (revised by H MacInnes) 1974
Fourth edition (by Alan Kimber) 1991 First edition (by IS Clough) 1969

Printed by mccgraphics, Spain

A catalogue record for this book is available from the British Library.

All photographs are by the author unless otherwise stated.

Rea… …nors to ensure
the … …occur during
the … …ok's page on
the … …your trip. We
wou… …s as transport,
acc… …e altered over
time… …ncies between
a gu… …fo@cicerone.
co.u… …7PY, UK.

Warning

Mountain climbing can be a dangerous activity carrying a risk of personal injury or death. It should be undertaken only by those with a full understanding of the risks and with the training and experience to evaluate them. While every care and effort has been taken in the preparation of this guide, the user should be aware that conditions can be highly variable and can change quickly, materially affecting the seriousness of a mountain walk. Therefore, except for any liability which cannot be excluded by law, neither Cicerone nor the author accept liability for damage of any nature (including damage to property, personal injury or death) arising directly or indirectly from the information in this book.

To call out the Mountain Rescue, ring 999 or the international emergency number 112: this will connect you via any available network. Once connected to the emergency operator, ask for the police.

Front cover: Dave MacLeod climbing Orion Direct on the 50th anniversary of its first ascent (photo: Paul Diffley)

CONTENTS

LIST OF DIAGRAMS

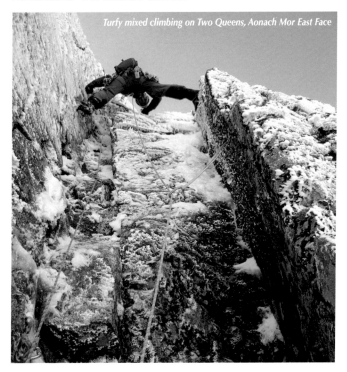

Turfy mixed climbing on Two Queens, Aonach Mor East Face

PREFACE

Moving on...

It's time for a change. In 1990 Ed Grindley generously handed me the opportunity to author this important Scottish winter guidebook. After 20 years, and with three editions under my belt, I'm handing over to Mike Pescod, another Fort William-based mountain guide. In doing so, both Mike and I wish to dedicate this guide to Ed's memory, as he sadly passed away after a short struggle with illness earlier this year. We miss you Ed.

Ed Grindley

Ed and I arrived in Lochaber at an interesting time for Scottish winter climbing. Fortunately (?) we both missed the step-cutting era. Hamish McInnes, John Cunningham and Yvon Chouinard were experimenting with ice daggers, and bent and drooped picks from the mid-60s onwards, many of which were forged in workshops or sheds from Glen Coe to Clydeside and California to Llanberis. We have the fertile minds of these iconic climbers to thank for our funky modern gear that allows for safer and faster climbing.

Grades have also changed in the 40 years I have spent in Fort William. The Hamish McInnes 'Bumper fun-book' of Scottish winter climbing used adjectival grades for winter climbs. Thus, Point Five Gully was described in 1971 as Very Severe, SERIOUS, 8–12 hours. In summer it received an alpine grade of V+. In a later Cicerone guidebook Ed Grindley was the first to introduce the winter grade of VI and allied grades to recommended times in a similar fashion to alpine route descriptions.

The old classic V's are now well-trodden paths, and climbers can often be seen to leave rucksacks at the foot of routes. Being 'old school' I still prefer to carry my salvation on my back in the face of a potential west coast storm. Many of us have been convinced of leashless climbing, albeit attached by a thin umbilical to our harness. The harness attachment is not at all new, by the way, as it provided instant protection following a footslip in 1970, as it still does today! I cannot, however, recall casually hanging my pick over my shoulder whilst making a rock-climbing move or placing protection. More likely, the tool was hanging off of my wrist as I struggled to climb a difficult pitch!

The new author of this guide has a depth of knowledge and ability in this area, and has introduced winter crag photo-diagrams to help depict the location of routes. However, as is usual in winter, the conditions will dictate whether or not a route is visible (or viable) on the day.

Thanks for taking the guide on, Mike. I'm sure it's in safe hands.

Alan Kimber
Fort William, 2010

Best foot forward

With nearly 1000 routes and two new climbing areas, this new edition of *Winter Climbs – Ben Nevis and Glen Coe* will keep even the most active climbers busy for many years. All the most popular areas are described, and now depicted on photo-diagrams for maximum clarity. For a definitive list of routes covering this area, readers are advised to consult the Scottish Mountaineering Club's series of comprehensive guidebooks and the yearly *Scottish Mountaineering Club Journal*, which contains details of new routes.

Although I have climbed hundreds of different routes and visited nearly all the crags in this guide, I have certainly not climbed all of them. The basis of this guide goes back to Iain Clough and Hamish MacInnes. It is interesting to see the use of photo-diagrams in some of MacInnes's guidebooks from the mid-1970s, and to compare them to the photo-diagrams in this edition. We all owe Alan Kimber our thanks for his work on three successive editions, keeping us informed and up to date with current climbs. My thanks go to Alan for considering me to continue work on the guide, and I feel honoured to be part of the list of esteemed authors. Much help was drawn from first ascentionists and active climbers, especially in identifying the lines on the photo-diagrams. Particular thanks are due to Donald King, Blair Fyffe, Iain Small, Dave MacLeod, Paul Diffley, Jamie Hageman and Rob Jarvis.

Winter climbing in Scotland is all about adventure. We are never quite sure what to expect each time we venture into the hills, and variations in conditions and weather make every day unique. This uncertainty of outcome is what makes winter climbing so rewarding. The route descriptions in this guide should be taken on this basis; they are sufficient to follow the line of the climb, but climbers will be required to make decisions for themselves while on the route.

Your feedback is welcome. Descriptions are always evolving, and your comments will be gratefully received.

Good climbing.

Mike Pescod, IFMGA Mountain Guide
Fort William, 2010

INTRODUCTION

Scottish winter climbing is world renowned for its adventure and quality of experience. Nowhere is it better than on Ben Nevis, the peaks of Glen Coe and the surrounding mountains. So popular and well known is Ben Nevis that climbers from all parts of the globe can be heard calling to each other while enjoying the unique style of climbing found here.

The traditional approach to climbing is strongly maintained here, and the history of the climbs is well remembered. Modern ice climbing was developed here, and that heritage adds greatly to the modern-day climbing experience.

In the winter of 1960 Jimmy Marshall and Robin Smith completed the most significant week of climbing ever achieved in Scotland. Orion Direct, Smith's Route, Minus Two Gully and the first single-day free ascent of Point Five Gully were amongst the seven climbs they completed on consecutive days. All of this was achieved with a single ice axe each and crampons with no front points.

Ten years later, in 1970, Yvon Chouinard made a brief visit which was to trigger a change that would revolutionise winter climbing. Using prototype curved ice hammers he made

Ben Nevis over the Aonach Eagach

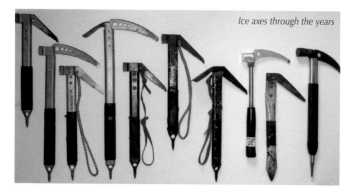

Ice axes through the years

some very fast ascents, demonstrating how to climb ice by direct aid, hanging off the pick itself embedded in the ice. Comparing techniques with John Cunningham, Hamish MacInnes and many others in the Clachaig one night, modern ice climbing was born.

That year Hamish MacInnes developed 'The Terrordactyl', a short, all-metal ice tool with a steeply dropped pick. The 'Terror' and Chouinard's ice hammer dominated the forefront of international ice climbing for several years. Eventually these two designs were combined to create the banana pick, which is still the basis for modern ice-tool design. Today, exactly 50 years on from the Marshall and Smith pinnacle of the step-cutting era, we are still using the same techniques.

Since the last edition of this book some things have changed dramatically. There is now a dedicated car park for climbers in Torlundy, a well-constructed path to the North Face of Ben Nevis and the Mountain Track

from Glen Nevis is much improved, all thanks to The Nevis Partnership. The National Trust for Scotland and the Forestry Commission have continued their excellent work in Glen Coe, maintaining and improving the trails there, with improved car parks as well. The evolution of the internet has made information on new climbs and current conditions far more available, and enabled climbers to share experiences. Some new routes are now fully described online even before the climbers have returned to the valley!

Some things remain constant, though, and today's winter specialists still find more than enough climbing to the highest of modern technical standards to encourage them back, year after year. The hardest traditionally protected winter climb in the world is currently found on Ben Nevis – Anubis, first climbed by local resident Dave MacLeod. The dark art of judging the condition of the snow and ice, and choosing the best route for any given day, is still a skill to be developed over many years and many climbs. Learning how to take care of yourself in full winter conditions is still a requirement for anyone climbing here, and is a skill as important as any climbing technique. Indeed, on some days just surviving the weather is the challenge, whether you manage any climbing or not!

Many of the routes are longer than experienced anywhere else in British hills and are of alpine-like seriousness. It is not a good idea to be lured onto the famous Tower Ridge of Ben Nevis as your first Scottish winter climb. The Lochaber Mountain Rescue Team has escorted dozens of shivering 'all nighters' off this route in the dull grey hours of dawn! Try something shorter to start with as a 'Wee Scottish Apprenticeship'.

A combination of short daylight hours and possible strong winds, poor weather and snow conditions add to the serious nature of Scottish winter climbing. Fitness is of prime importance to sustain climbers through long hours, carrying far more weight in their rucksacks than would be experienced in the summer months. Climbers must be economical with their time and aim to keep moving as fluently as is practical in order to avoid a possibly serious benightment or slip on a dark unknown descent. Records show that novice and experienced climbers alike come to grief on these Scottish mountains, sometimes with fatal consequences. Scottish winter climbing is good sport, but don't treat these routes as 'sports climbs'!

CLIMBING CONDITIONS

Many years are spent learning to judge what climbing conditions will be like, so that the best venue and type of climb can be chosen. Well-experienced climbers will know when the ice is good or when a buttress climb would be better, when the rocks will be rimed up and when they will be verglased. This experience is usually earned from many fruitless trips, when the route chosen is not as expected. Learning how the weather affects the climbs is the first stage – whether the thaw and refreeze is sufficient to produce good ice, whether the turf is well frozen and the rocks rimed up, whether the ice will be hard and brittle or soft and plastic. The best style of climb can then be chosen – a snowed-up rock route, thin-face ice climb, turfy mixed route or classic snow-ice gully.

Winter climbing ethics are strongly held in Scotland, especially when it comes to mixed climbs on buttresses and ridges. To be in acceptable winter condition, buttresses should be generally white with rime and there should be snow on the rocks, and turf should be well frozen. Snow on the ledges and dry rocks is not sufficient, neither is a coating of hoar frost. Dry tooling is the preserve of a few crags in the glens that have been agreed as suitable.

Classic snow-ice on Smith's Route, Gardyloo Buttress

Some buttress climbs are just on rock and will come into condition very quickly, such as North Buttress on Buachaille Etive Mor. Freezing temperatures and a wind blowing clouds onto the crags will freeze the ground and build rime, bringing snowed-up rock climbs into good condition. Other mixed routes rely on turf (such as the buttress climbs on Aonach Mor and Stob Coire an Laoigh), and it is very important to wait for the turf to be properly frozen before it is climbed to minimise the damage done to the ground. It can be a frustratingly long wait for the ground to freeze properly in the autumn, but once frozen it takes a long time to thaw out again.

Early in the winter, with a covering of snow and a good freeze, mixed climbs in Glen Coe can provide the best climbing. Buttress climbs on Stob Coire nan Lochan require a coating of rime and snow, but do not need any build-up of ice. Ben Nevis has seen a steady growth in popularity of mixed climbs, with routes on Number Three Gully Buttress, Creag Coire na Ciste and South Trident Buttress being the best.

In a prolonged cold spell of weather, water courses and low-level streams freeze up, giving great water-ice climbs. The cascade-style ice climbs at Beinn Udlaidh form readily in persistent cold weather, along with the cascades of Sgurr Finnisg-aig and those in Glen Coe such as Blue Riband and climbs on Aonach Dubh.

The January storms bring frequent thaw–freeze cycles that build snow in the gullies and on the faces, transforming them into snow-ice climbs. Point Five Gully, Green Gully and Left Twin form readily given snowfall and some thaw–freeze cycles. However the climbing can be a bit of a lottery early on in the winter, with variable conditions and short daylight hours.

February and March often give the most reliable snow cover and the greatest variety of climbing, with many types of climb in good condition in Glen Coe and on the higher peaks. Late in the season, after all the lower hills have thawed out, Ben Nevis comes into its own, with unique thin-face ice climbs, known the world over as some of the best climbs anywhere!

Ice forms in many different ways, resulting in ice of different types and with different climbing qualities. With a good freeze numerous watercourses form into icefalls of perfect transparent water-ice, often hard and brittle, requiring super-sharp picks. Springs dribbling out of cracks and caves in the crags provide water to freeze onto the rocks, helped by snowfall building on the rocks. Compression Crack, the Carn Dearg Cascades and Vanishing Gully are good examples on Ben Nevis, along with the climbs at Beinn Udlaidh, Blue Riband, Number Six Gully and The Screen on Aonach Dubh in Glen Coe.

Snow patches melt in the thaws, running water down crags below to form hard water-ice. Mega Route X, Gemini and The Shroud on Ben Nevis form in this way, so good snow cover

Ice forms in many different ways – two common examples are delicate rime ice crystals (top) and hoar frost crystals (bottom).

and several thaws with very good refreezes afterwards are required to see these climbs form.

Gullies hold snow that thaws and refreezes successively over the course of the winter and its many storms, forming the celebrated plastic snow-ice that Lochaber is famed for. Point Five Gully, Left Twin, Crowberry Gully and SC Gully are all classic snow-ice climbs that form readily given sufficient snowfall, along with some thaw–freeze cycles. They also survive the thaws the best, as the gullies catch more snow than the faces next to them.

The highest faces catch snow and form rime that builds on the steepest rocks, and this is also transformed by thaw–freeze cycles into a thin layer of ice, often only just thick enough to climb. It is a fine balance between thawing sufficiently to refreeze into good ice and thawing too much, stripping away the snow and ice. Thin-face routes form in this way and include Orion Direct, Hadrian's Wall Direct and Psychedelic Wall. Once you are used to climbing ice only just thick enough to climb you might try Stormy Petrel or Ship of Fools for a truly memorable experience!

The internet is a very good source of up-to-the-minute information on snow cover and climbing conditions. Two good places to start are www.AbacusMountaineering.com and www.WestCoast-MountainGuides.co.uk.

It can take many years to judge correctly the formation of each different type of climb according to the prevailing weather. The best way is to make your best guess and see whether you are right, with the willingness to turn back and learn the lesson if you are wrong!

WEATHER AND AVALANCHES

The area covered by this guidebook is well known for having some of the most severe weather in the British Isles. A combination of strong winds and snowfall, coupled with fluctuating temperatures, provides the climber with a variety of potentially life-threatening hazards.

Knowing the weather forecast before you set out is essential. The best source of accurate weather forecasts is online. The Mountain Weather Information Service (www.mwis.org.uk) and The Met Office (www.metoffice.gov.uk/loutdoor/mountainsafety) both provide free mountain weather forecasts, which can be accessed online and on your mobile phone.

Knowing the avalanche forecast is also essential. The Scottish Avalanche Information Service (www.sais.gov.uk) provides daily snow and avalanche reports in five of the main Scottish winter-climbing areas. These are Glencoe, Lochaber, Creag Meagaidh, Northern Cairngorms and Southern Cairngorms. Specially trained, highly experienced observers monitor snow conditions and the avalanche hazard on a daily basis throughout the winter. They write avalanche-hazard forecasts

which are available to the public through the national media as well as local outlets, on the internet and direct to your mobile phone. This will help the mountain user to make decisions regarding route choice and to plan a safe and enjoyable excursion into the hills.

Avalanche-hazard forecasts predict the magnitude and the location of the hazard. Close attention should be paid to the 'compass rose' as it contains a lot of information, breaking down the hazard areas in terms of altitude and aspect. The scale of the hazard is very clearly defined and should be known to all mountaineers. The forecast also includes the Observed Avalanche Hazard and Mountain Conditions, which include snow distribution, icing and comments further to the forecast, all of which can be used to increase the safety and enjoyment of your day.

It cannot be stated too strongly that even the most sophisticated

Avalanche-hazard forecast
– compass rose and scale of hazard

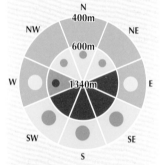

Low	Natural avalanches very unlikely. Human-triggered avalanches not likely.
Moderate	Natural avalanches unlikely. Human-triggered avalanches possible.
Considerable	Natural avalanches possible. Human-triggered avalanches likely.
High	Natural and human-triggered avalanches will occur.
Very High	Widespread natural and human-triggered avalanches will occur.

Fresh snow on Stob Ban and Mullach nan Coirean

forecast is only an adjunct to the range of information available to the mountaineer. The forecast is not a substitute for good judgement. It is an aid to better judgement

Avalanche awareness

Weather

This is the most important factor in determining whether avalanches are likely, and the evolution of the snowpack is entirely dependent on this. Many weather variables affect avalanche release. Temperature, wind speed and direction forecasts enable useful predictions to be made before leaving home. For instance, if a south-west wind of 25mph is indicated, with freezing temperatures and soft snow known to be present, then it may be assumed that some avalanche hazard will be building on north-east-facing slopes. Lee slopes should be avoided after storms or heavy drifting.

Snowpack

When visibility is adequate, snowpack observation can begin from the roadside. Evidence of recent avalanche activity, main snow-accumulation zones, fresh loading by new snow and drifting can often be noted from below. Observations should continue on the approach, noting such details as depth of foot penetration, cornice build-up, ease of release of small slabs and the effect which localised wind patterns may have had on slab formation.

The following features might indicate a dangerous weakness in the snowpack:

- snow blocking or cracking under foot
- whumphing noises caused by collapsing weak layers
- adjacent layers of different hardness, especially very soft layers (fist penetrates easily)
- water drops squeezed out of a snowball made from any layer
- layers of ice

- layers of graupel (rounded, heavily rimed pellets), feathery or faceted crystals, or layers of loose, uncohesive grains
- air space.

Remember that your observations will hold good only for slopes of similar orientation and altitude to your observations. You will need to extrapolate for situations higher up and for instance below cornices, where surface windslab layers may be much thicker. Many avalanches are cornice triggered. In general, climbing below cornices should be avoided during and immediately after (24–48 hours) snow storms or heavy drifting, and during heavy thaw or sudden temperature rise.

Terrain

Most large slab avalanches release on slopes between 25° and 45°. This range includes the average angle of coire backwalls, approach slopes to crags and grade I gullies. Smooth ground such as rock slab is predisposed to large full-depth avalanches, which often occur in the spring. Rough ground such as large boulders will tend to anchor base layers in position, making avalanches less likely. However, the consequences of a small slide can be worse. Once these boulders are covered, surface avalanche activity is unhindered. Convex slopes are generally more hazardous than uniform or concave slopes.

Ridges or buttresses are better choices than open slopes and gullies when avalanche conditions prevail. The crests of main mountain ridges are usually protected from avalanche, while for those in climbing situations rock-belays on ribs and buttresses can often provide security. Gullies funnel avalanches, and even a small slide in a gully can be sufficient to knock you off your feet.

It is rarely essential to negotiate an avalanche-prone slope. It is usually possible to find another way or retreat. Of all avalanches involving human subjects, 90 per cent are triggered by their victims.

Avalanche Danger: Top six warning signs

- Visible avalanche activity – if you see avalanche activity on a slope where you intend to go, go somewhere else.

- New snow build-up – more than 2cm/hr may produce unstable conditions; more than 30cm continuous build-up is regarded as very hazardous. 90% of all avalanches occur during snowstorms.

- Slab lying on ice or névé, with or without aggravating factors such as thaw.

- Discontinuity between layers, usually caused by loose graupel pellets or airspace.

- Sudden temperature rise.

- The 'seat of the pants' feeling of the experienced observer deserves respect.

Avalanche rescue

If you witness an avalanche burial, you are the buried victim's only real chance of live rescue and should take the following steps.

- Observe the victim's progress and, if possible, mark the point of entry and point at which last seen.
- Check for further avalanche danger.
- Make a quick search of the debris surface looking for any signs of the victim.
- Listen for any sounds.
- Probe the most likely burial spots.
- Make a systematic search, probing the debris with axes or poles.
- Send for help.
- Keep searching until help arrives. Although survival chances decline rapidly with the duration of burial, they do not reach zero for a long time.

Recommended reading

www.sais.gov.uk (The Scottish Avalanche Information Service website)
Avalanche! by R Bolognesi, Cicerone Press, 2007
Snow by R Bolognesi, Cicerone Press, 2007
Snow Sense by J Fredston and D Fesler, 4th edition, Cordee, 2001
A Chance in a Million by B Barton and B Wright, 2nd edition, Scottish Mountaineering Trust, 2000

ACCESS RIGHTS

The Land Reform (Scotland) Act 2003 established statutory rights of responsible access to land and inland water for outdoor recreation and crossing land. These are known as Scottish access rights. The Scottish Outdoor Access Code (available from www.snh.gov.uk) gives detailed guidance on the responsibilities of those exercising access rights and of those managing land and water. The Act sets out where and when access rights apply, and how land should be managed with regard to access. The Code defines how access rights should be exercised.

The three principles for responsible access apply to both the public and land managers.

- Respect the interests of other people – be considerate, respect privacy and livelihoods, and the needs of those enjoying the outdoors.
- Care for the environment – look after the places you visit and enjoy, and care for wildlife and historic sites.
- Take responsibility for your own actions – the outdoors cannot be made risk-free for people exercising access rights; land managers should act with care for people's safety.

EQUIPMENT AND SAFETY PRECAUTIONS

Map, compass and GPS

This guidebook will hopefully help climbers to find their route. It must be used in conjunction with a weather-proof map. Most of the areas in this guide are covered by the OS Landranger series, Sheet 41, Ben Nevis, Fort William and Glen Coe, 1:50,000. Also, Harvey Superwalker maps for Ben Nevis and Glen Coe are easy-to-read, detailed maps to a scale of 1:25,000, and the Ben Nevis sheet has a superb inset of the Nevis plateau at a scale of 1:12,500. The ability to use these maps with a compass is of prime importance to all winter mountaineers and climbers.

GPS systems can provide a useful back-up to more traditional map and compass skills, and it is recommended that they are used in this way, rather than as the sole navigational aid. Walking on the bearing obtained from a traditional compass will nearly always be steadier than following that from its satellite-driven GPS cousin. It is recommended that the GPS co-ordinates given in this guide are tested on a clear day and also marked on a map. This is particularly important on Ben Nevis, which is a mountain that will be revisited many times by climbers. At the foot of any steep cliff, treat all GPS readings with a great deal of caution, as cliffs can affect the accuracy and strength of satellite signals.

Ice axes/crampons

Ice axes and crampons are essential for any winter outing, whether walking or climbing. For climbing it is assumed that two ice axes are used. Many good tools are available, and the first-time buyer might consider a modular system which allows new picks to be fitted – this is cheaper than buying a complete axe/hammer. Tools should be 50/55cm in length for climbing. Climbing with leashless tools is becoming more popular at all grades, however they lend themselves particularly to the higher grades, and lanyards connecting your tools to your harness are recommended.

Boots

Stiff (B3) boots with a well-maintained, rigid Vibram sole are best for winter climbing, and when linked to a pair of clip-on crampons they provide a solid and positive base for the necessary footwork involved in climbing snow and ice.

Helmet

A climbing helmet is essential, especially when climbing below other parties who may be dislodging brick-sized lumps of ice from above.

Climbing protection

For protection on steep ground a full rack of wires, hexes and ice screws is required. Camming devices are sometimes useful, but care should be given to their placement in icy and sometimes dubious rock. The current trend is to minimise the use of pegs, although you might consider carrying a few in case of emergency. Be aware, though, that too much gear weighs you down and slows the day. Only take what is required for the route. On Tower Ridge

Iced cracks

Ice screw belay

Big nuts

a set of wires (1–10), two hexes, six extenders and four slings will usually be ample, whilst Point Five Gully will require six ice screws, a set of wires, extenders and possibly a dead-man.

Belay anchors are usually on rock, but big ice routes (such as Orion Direct and Indicator Wall) demand belaying on ice screws. More experienced climbers are obvious by their small but very well-considered rack. 50m or 60m half-ropes are recommended.

Bodily comforts

Food and spare clothing should be carried – light thermal layers are far better than chunky sweaters and duvets. Try and keep the weight to a minimum. A sensible balance between lightness and safety is required. An orange plastic survival bag should be considered, as it will certainly come in handy one day, along with a headtorch. Even the best climbers will not be able to complete their route if they do not learn what to wear, and how to wear it to keep warm and comfortable.

Mobile phones

Coverage is mostly good, but users should be aware of the limitations of mobile phones, especially if tucked away inside any of the coires. When using a mobile phone to raise the alarm, dial 999 or the local police station and ask for Mountain Rescue, give your number to the police and remain switched on until the rescue team arrives or you are given the all clear to switch off. Remember that your phone will make 999 calls on any available network, so it is worth trying even if your phone shows no coverage on your network, whether or not there is credit on your account.

Emergency shelters

On Ben Nevis there is now only one emergency shelter, which is on the summit (GPS NN16684 71256). This should be kept for use only in an emergency. Please remember to close the door of the summit shelter when leaving. In a blizzard it fills with snow very quickly. All the other emergency shelters have been removed from the mountain.

Route cards

As an aid to rescue (if it is required) climbers should leave a note of their intended route and return time with a reliable person in the valley. The police will be happy to take a note for you as long as you 'clock off' on your safe return! This is a very simple and wise precaution to take.

USING THIS GUIDE

Grades

The current two-tier system developed by the Scottish Mountaineering Club (SMC) is used throughout. As with previous systems, the difficulty of a climb increases with a higher number. The grades of I and II can be considered as introductory, whilst only experienced climbers should attempt grades higher than this.

The grades are for average conditions (whatever they may be), and it should be remembered that winter climbs can vary enormously from time to time, depending on snow or ice build-up and the weather. Early in the season, when conditions can be lean, certain routes – particularly on ice – will be harder than later on, when a

Full winter conditions in Left Twin

good plating covers blank stretches and improves the conditions. Mixed routes, by comparison with snow and ice climbs, can benefit from lean, cold conditions, allowing turf which is not blanketed by snow to harden up. Climbers should try to avoid damaging mixed turfy climbs in mild conditions. Also it must be remembered that the arrival of a mild weather system will change the character and difficulty of many climbs overnight. However, it is the passage of many such weather systems that builds the snow required to give us good spring ice-climbing conditions, so they are to be endured with the hope of better things to come!

The two-tier grading system shows a Roman numeral first, indicating the overall seriousness of the climb, and the accompanying Arabic numeral represents the technical difficulty of the hardest sections of climbing. The aim of this system is to grade modern mixed routes to indicate their high levels of technical difficulty, while taking into consideration the frequently greater seriousness of the older style ice routes.

- Climbs of grade IV and above (and some of grade III) have two grades, an overall grade in Roman numerals and a technical grade in Arabic numerals. Point Five Gully (V,5) in average conditions is the benchmark from which other routes are graded.

- The overall grade takes into account all factors affecting the difficulty of reaching the top of the climb, including its technical difficulty, seriousness (frequency of protection and reliability of belays) and how sustained it is (length of hard sections of climbing and number of hard pitches).

- The technical grade reflects the difficulty of the hardest section(s) of climbing, without reference to seriousness. It is not intended to be used as a technical pitch-by-pitch grading. A technical grade of 5 indicates relatively straightforward, steep ice climbing; a technical grade of 6 generally indicates more technical mixed climbing or sustained vertical ice; technical grades of 7 and 8 indicate much more intricate and harder snowed-up rock moves.

- The technical grade normally varies by not more than two below or two above the overall grade. Thus V,5 can be taken as an average grade V route. A higher technical grade than the overall grade would indicate greater technical difficulty, offset by better protection (as frequently found on mixed routes); a lower technical grade would indicate greater seriousness.

- The overall difficulty is reflected in the overall grade, and just as an E1 5a can be a more serious proposition than an E1 5c, a V,4 is not necessarily easier overall than a V,6.

Some degree of variability undoubtedly occurs according to the prevailing conditions. While some climbs will nearly always be possible at close to the given grade, others require special (or even extraordinary) ice build-up, and the grades apply to such favourable situations. At other times these climbs may simply be non-existent. The grades of climbs in this guidebook have been decided after extensive consultation, but further comment is always valuable.

The following is an approximate definition of the overall grades. It is assumed that a rope is always used.

Grade I
Climbs for which only one axe and crampons are normally required, either snow gullies around 45° or easy ridges. Cornices can present problems, and the avalanche hazard is always greatest in grade I gullies.

Grade II
A second tool should be carried because of steep snow, difficult cornices and the occasional short ice pitch. Difficulties are usually short. Ridges at this grade will normally be straightforward scrambles in the summer.

Grade III
More sustained and often steeper than grade II. Sometimes short and technical, particularly for mixed ascents of Moderate rock climbs.

Grade IV
Steep ice from short vertical steps to long sections of 60–70°. The mixed climbs require more advanced techniques such as axe 'torquing' and 'hooking'.

Grade V
Sustained steep ice at 70–80° with short vertical steps. Mixed climbing requires linked hard moves.

Grade VI
Long vertical sections or thin and tenuous ice. Mixed routes include all that has gone before, but more of it.

Grade VII
Multi-pitch routes with long sections linking thin vertical ice and hard mixed moves, requiring strength, skill and stamina of the highest order.

Grade VIII
By the time you tackle this grade and above, you'll know exactly what is involved!

Technical grades on ice
As a rough guideline
3 = 60°
4 = 70°
5 = 80°
6 = vertical

Note A split grade such as II/III indicates the possibility of a wide variation in difficulties depending on condition, usually due to the possibility of great accumulations of snow over the course of the winter.

Length of climb
Length of climbs and, where possible, pitch lengths are given in metres. Route lengths are as accurate as possible and will hopefully give the climber at least a reasonable idea of the scale of the route.

Recommended routes
Where possible a three-star system has been used to indicate quality under good conditions – the more stars the better the route. However, many routes under good conditions would warrant some special mention. The star system will hopefully allow strangers to the area to find some good climbing on their first visit. Difficulty is not a prerequisite for stars, and many simple climbs get a mention on the basis of their character, continuity, structure and adventure at the grade. All very subjective!

Diagrams and route numbers
Nearly all cliffs have a diagram, but for those without, the text is sufficient to locate a route. Not all routes are shown (numbered) on the diagrams in order to avoid overcrowding. A broken line on a diagram indicates that a section of the climb is hidden. The routes numbered offer good reference points for adjacent non-numbered climbs. An index of routes appears at the end of this guide.

RESCUE FACILITIES

The mountain rescue (MR) teams of Lochaber and Glen Coe (civilian volunteers) attend more call-outs than all the other Scottish teams put together. Along with the RAF (helicopter and land-based teams), they provide an excellent service. They are experienced and skilful local mountaineers who undergo regular training in mountaineering and remote-care first-aid skills. Rescues are co-ordinated by the police, who should be contacted by telephone on 999 in case of an accident or possible problem. A direct line to the Fort William or Glencoe police stations will be quicker, and the numbers are as follows:

- **Fort William police**
  (01397) 702361
- **Glencoe police** (01855) 811222.

Do not delay in raising the alarm if you feel someone is in need of help.

Public telephones and MR posts

Ben Nevis	Youth Hostel in Glen Nevis (GR 127717) Distillery (GR 125757)
Glen Coe	Kingshouse Hotel (MR post – GR 259546) Achnambeithach (MR post – GR 140565) Clachaig Hotel (GR 128567)

For climbers on Ben Nevis a direct radio link with the police in Fort William is situated outside the main entrance to the CIC Hut, in the small annexe on the right. Open the door and the flap inside on the wall. This will reveal a simple handset with a sprung switch built into it. Keep the switch depressed whilst asking for the police. The following will be sufficient: 'Fort William police ... Fort William police ... This is CIC Hut ... CIC Hut ... Can you hear me?' Release the handset/switch and wait for the police to reply. Give your message. Do not forget to depress the switch every time you speak and release it every time you want to listen. Should you get no reply, give your message anyway. Be clear and economical with what you say. Give brief details of where the accident has taken place (name the route), the nature of any injuries if known, and how many people are involved. Stay by the radio until the rescue team arrives unless instructed otherwise.

AMENITIES

Fort William and Glencoe are well supplied with all the facilities required by climbers.

Transport

Coaches travel daily to Fort William from Glasgow (passing through Glen Coe en route) and Inverness. Trains arrive at Fort William daily, and it is common for climbers from London to catch the sleeper on a Friday evening, climb on Saturday and Sunday, then head back to work on the Sunday night train! Glasgow and Inverness airports are both approximately two hours' drive from Fort William, with direct coach links.

A lone figure on North Trident Buttress

Shops

Specialist climbing gear can be bought in:

- Ellis Brigham, Fort William
- Nevisport, High Street, Fort William
- Blacks, High Street, Fort William
- The Ice Factor, Kinlochleven

Of particular interest to climbers coming down late are the shops in Claggan (GR 117743) and Ballachulish (GR 083583), where all foodstuffs can be found to fill the hungriest belly. Fort William and the nearby village of Caol have 'chippies'. For the more discerning there are many restaurants and bars that will empty your pocket and fill your stomach. The Clachaig Hotel in Glen Coe provides good bar meals and beer for climbers. A large supermarket in Fort William stays open late most nights and has a cafeteria where the breakfasts are cheap!

Other facilities

Hospital Belford Hospital
(GR 106741),
(01397) 702481

Doctors Fort William (01397) 703773/703136/702947
Glencoe (01855) 811226

Rail and bus station
Fort William (GR 106742) with facilities for left luggage and showers

Ice Factor climbing wall
Kinlochleven
(GR 188619)

Accommodation

Climbers visiting the area covered by this guide should have no problems finding places to rest their weary heads. Everything from five-star hotels to flooded campsites is available. Appendix A lists a selection of what's available, and reflects the price and style of accommodation which climbers generally appreciate! A glance through the back pages of most outdoor magazines will illuminate further possibilities.

A number of climbing huts are available for bookings in the area from Crianlarich to Roy Bridge. A complete list of these is available from the Mountaineering Council of Scotland, www.mcofs.org.uk.

For a complete list of all types of accommodation, from hotels to campsites, contact the Outdoor Capital of the UK office, www.outdoorcapital.co.uk.

Mountain guides

Four locally based members of the Association of British Mountain Guides offer a comprehensive service for anyone wishing to explore the climbs in this book in the company of an expert.

- Mike Pescod, Abacus Mountaineering (01397) 772466, mike@abacusmountaineering.com
- Alan Kimber, West Coast Mountain Guides (01397) 700451, alan@westcoast-mountainguides.co.uk
- Mick Tighe, Nevis Guides (01397) 712356, nevismick@yahoo.co.uk
- Dave 'Cubby' Cuthbertson (01855) 811281, info@cubbyimages.com

BEN NEVIS

North East Buttress (photo: Jamie Hageman)

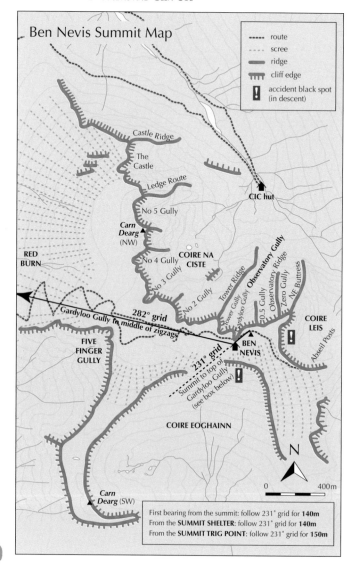

Ben Nevis Summit Map

·····	route
----	scree
▬▬▬	ridge
┬┬┬┬	cliff edge
🚷	accident black spot (in descent)

Castle Ridge

The Castle

Ledge Route

CIC hut

No 5 Gully

Carn Dearg (NW)

No 4 Gully

COIRE NA CISTE

No 3 Gully

Tower Ridge

Gardyloo Gully

Observatory Gully

0.5 Gully

Observatory Ridge

Zero Gully

NE Buttress

RED BURN

No 2 Gully

COIRE LEIS

Gardyloo Gully to middle of zigzags

282° grid

231° grid

Summit to top of Gardyloo Gully (see box below)

BEN NEVIS

Abseil Posts

FIVE FINGER GULLY

COIRE EOGHAINN

N

0   400m

Carn Dearg (SW)

First bearing from the summit: follow 231° grid for **140m**
From the **SUMMIT SHELTER**: follow 231° grid for **140m**
From the **SUMMIT TRIG POINT**: follow 231° grid for **150m**

34

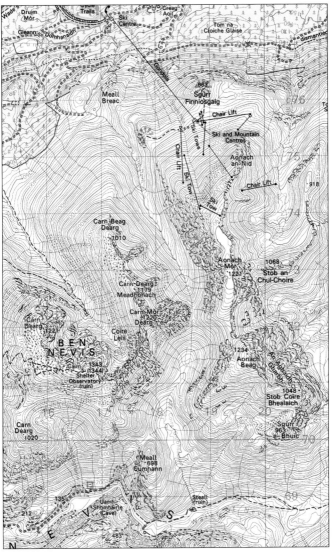

Map taken from a 75% reduction of the OS 1:50,000 sheet.

CENTRAL AREA

APPROACHES FOR BEN NEVIS

Approaches for climbs on the north-east aspect of Ben Nevis all aim initially for the area of the CIC Hut (GR 167722; OS Map sheet 41, Ben Nevis 1:50,000 – GPS NN16739 72218). This hut is private and belongs to the Scottish Mountaineering Club. At the time of writing bookings could be made through Robin Clothier, 35 Broompark Drive, Newton Mearns, Glasgow G77 5DZ. Do not expect to arrive and enter the hut without a booking.

Allt a'Mhuilinn – North Face approach

The North Face Car Park has been developed with help from the Forestry Commission and the Mountaineering Council of Scotland. Turn off the A82 at the sign in Torlundy, GR 143771. Go over a hump-back railway bridge and turn right into the woods, then follow the rough vehicle track to the parking area at GR 145765. Follow the signs which lead to a newly constructed path through the forest to the Allt a'Mhuilinn. Allow 2 hours to the hut.

Glen Nevis approaches

The approach from the west follows the zig-zag Mountain Track to the summit as far as the broad saddle between Meall an t-Suidhe and the main massif of Carn Dearg NW, Ben Nevis. This track can be started from the Ben Nevis Inn at Achintee (GR 125729), the youth hostel in Glen Nevis (GR 127717) or the visitor centre (GR 123731). Above the saddle, which holds the large Lochain Meall an t-Suidhe (or Halfway Lochan, GS 1472), the Mountain Track veers back to the right (south), crosses the Red Burn, and zig-zags up the long slope to the summit plateau. Where the Mountain Track turns south, the route to the North Face briefly follows a large path heading north to the far end of the lochain before following an indefinite path contouring the lower slopes of Carn Dearg for about 1km until it reaches the remains of an old fence on the lip of the Allt a'Mhuilinn glen. From this point it gradually descends for about 30m in a north-easterly direction and continues traversing south-east across the hillside until it reaches the Allt a'Mhuilinn (500m below the CIC Hut). A large boulder, the Lunching Stone, will be seen on the left of the path along this traverse. The route now follows the right bank of the Allt a'Mhuilinn until it is joined by another large stream coming in from the right (out of Coire na Ciste). This is crossed, and the hut, situated on the crest of a blunt spur between the streams, is about 100m above.

The approach starting from the youth hostel is only slightly longer than the route which follows the Allt a'Mhuilinn, but in bad visibility the route-finding is more difficult, and after a big snowfall the saddle and traverse into the glen can be prone to heavy drifting and possible avalanche below the Castle area. Allow 2–2½ hours to the hut.

Other approaches to the North Face include two alternative variations (with little to choose between them) starting from the large car park at the end of the Glen Nevis road, and one approach from the Steall Hut. They are exceptionally steep, but in good visibility give the quickest approach for the fit, valley-based climber to the Little Brenva Face and the normal route on North East Buttress. They are not recommended for use as a means of reaching the majority of climbs on the North Face.

(a) From the car park take a diagonal line up the hillside to reach the saddle between Meall Cumhann and Ben Nevis, then follow the ridge in a north-westerly direction. Finally, when the steep ridge merges into the easier-angled slopes above, veer slightly right to gain the Carn Mor Dearg Arête at the abseil post sign GR 171710 or GPS NN17099 71005 (2–2½ hours). Descend into Coire Leis by the easiest line. If approaching routes on the Little Brenva Face, a traverse left from the col leads in 5 minutes to the foot of Bob Run. Beware of avalanches on this traverse-line.

(b) Climb straight up above the car park and follow the right bank (east) of the waterslide of Allt Coire Eoghainn. Once over the lip of the coire, head up to the right (north-east) to join the previous route on the ridge 200m below the Carn Mor Dearg Arête (2–2½ hours). Care should be exercised on this route, as many fatal accidents have occurred on the slabs at the top of the waterslide.

(c) From the Steall Hut the best way is to join route (a) at the Meall Cumhann saddle. Follow a small indefinite track which leaves upper Glen Nevis immediately above the entrance to the gorge and makes a rising traverse above it, crossing the flank of Meall Cumhann until it is possible to strike up to the saddle. Alternatively, one may follow the Allt Coire Guibhsachan (above the ruin of Old Steall, GR 186687) by the left (west) bank and head directly up the westward branch coire to gain the Carn Mor Dearg Arête. However, there are great areas of slab in this coire which can be very difficult under icy conditions. Also, descent from the Carn Mor Dearg Arête into Coire Leis is difficult and only recommended from the abseil post sign area.

A rare day on the summit of Ben Nevis

DESCENTS FROM BEN NEVIS

The high summit plateau of Ben Nevis is surrounded on nearly all sides by steep and difficult ground (see map at front of guide). Many accidents have occurred in descent. Often this part of the day will call for more concentration and shrewdness of judgement than any other time.

The best descent will be determined not only by your point of arrival on the summit plateau, but also by the weather and snow conditions. The shortest way will not necessarily be the easiest. The best and quickest descent is often by the Red Burn (Mountain Track). Careful use of map, compass, pacing, possibly GPS and the sketch plan of the cliffs given in this guidebook will suffice to get you down, but local knowledge is invaluable. When visibility is good, make a close study of the general topography of the mountain; if possible, visit the summit plateau with a view to memorising its details and recording important compass/GPS bearings. The ruined observatory, topped by a survival shelter, is an unmistakable landmark on the summit itself, even when the neighbouring triangulation point and numerous cairns are covered by snow. It is recommended to start all compass bearings and GPS waypoints from the shelter, even though the observatory ruins can intrude on the initial few metres of the 231° (grid) safety bearing if they are not covered with snow.

The best aids to descending from the summit of Ben Nevis are a map of Ben

Nevis, 1:25,000, and a compass, together with the ability to use both in vile weather conditions. These two items should form essential companions to this guidebook. The insert on the Harvey map (scale 1:12,500) is particularly useful. It shows the sharply indented plateau and the gullies, which must be avoided on compass bearings in poor visibility.

Anyone who visits the mountains in summer or winter without a map and a compass (and the ability to use them in 'white out') is putting their life at risk. Using the map previously mentioned the following descents are recommended.

Red Burn (Mountain Track)

The easiest way down the mountain. Follow a grid bearing of 231° for 140m from the summit shelter or 150m from the summit trig point (use a rope to measure it if you are not sure of your pacing), GPS NN16558 71180. This will avoid the steep drop of Gardyloo Gully close on your right. Then follow a bearing of 282° (grid), GPS NN15721 71384 to the 1200m contour. Don't forget to convert your grid bearings to magnetic (approx. +2° in 2010). On the second bearing you should reach a short steeper section after 300m and continuously steeper ground after 900m of downhill travel. A line of well-built cairns now marks this route at 50m intervals to the point where the Mountain Track route meets the plateau. However, the cairns can not be used alone in poor visibility without following a compass bearing. Continue on down a steep but easy slope for another 1km on the same bearing or GPS NN14756 71865, then turn north towards the Halfway Lochan and follow the burn draining the lochain north towards the Allt a'Mhuilinn.

Note Along this route it is important not to stray left (south) in the first 2km, as this would lead to the steep and serious ground of Five Finger Gully. The steep lip of this gully is 800m (approximately) from the top of Gardyloo Gully. Accurate pacing and compass work is an essential skill for all people climbing on Ben Nevis. If after 800m on the recommended bearing you encounter steep ground and cliffs dead ahead, you are advised to try and avoid them by going right (north) until it is possible to continue on the bearing 282° (grid). This may require that you travel uphill for a short distance to skirt the top of Five Finger Gully.

If you finish up heading south downhill and skirting the top of steep cliffs to your right (west) after 800m from the top of Gardyloo Gully, it is highly likely that you have made a navigation error and are very close to Five Finger Gully. Go back uphill until it is possible to continue on the original bearing 282° (grid).

The Red Burn is well known as a good 'bum slide'. Please be aware that large waterfalls exist at the bottom of the burn before it reaches the track and that many large rocks are present all the way up the burn; these will not only rip your expensive overtrousers, but may put a hole in your head as well! This area has been the scene of fatal avalanche accidents.

GPS towards Mountain Track (Red Burn) descent as follows:

Summit shelter	NN16684 71256	
Gardyloo Gully	NN16558 71180 (140m)	'dog-leg'
Maclean's 'Steep'	NN16262 71232 (310m)	
Red Burn Track	NN14756 71865 (1650m)	

Number Four Gully

For climbers returning to the CIC Hut or Allt a'Mhuilinn area, this descent is straightforward in good visibility. The top of the gully has a metal marker post with the number 4 drilled into it (GR 158717 – GPS NN15837 71708). Sometimes the cornice can be impassable, but an abseil is often made from the marker post. Also it is possible at times to move a few metres to the north along the rim and gain access to the gully down steeper ground. Avalanches often occur in this gully, and the initial entry can be steep, but it soon eases. Take care.

Note A compass bearing due west from the lip of this gully (270° grid) or GPS NN14756 71865 is a descent to Glen Nevis via the Red Burn mentioned previously.

Carn Mor Dearg Arête/abseil post sign

This route can be used with care. It provides a method of descending quickly to a lower altitude, especially if the weather on the plateau is fierce. Many deaths have occurred on this descent over the years. Most of the fatalities have been connected with people straying too far left (north) from the summit on descent.

From the summit shelter a bearing of 134° (grid) GPS NN16897 71017 should be held. Initially the ground will be flat. After 100m the gradient steepens abruptly and some short posts may be seen; keep these to your left (north-east). From the steepening after approximately 200m of descent a slight col will be found to the left (east), 0.5km from the summit. At this point is a metal sign (GR 171710 – GPS NN17099 71005). Only two of the higher posts remain, and with care the person experienced in negotiating grade I ground in descent will be able to move down easily into Coire Leis. Often it is easier to traverse left (west) towards the Little Brenva Face before descending. However, snow build-up will dictate the easiest and most obvious route down. The angle is steep at first, but eases after 150m. As with many snowy descents, be careful after strong winds during periods of heavy drifting to avoid being another avalanche victim on this slope.

Note From the abseil post sign it is possible to descend to the head of Glen Nevis on a bearing of 220° (grid) or GPS NN16459 70018. This leads to the top of the waterslide mentioned elsewhere under 'Approaches'. The original bearing of 134° (grid) from the summit should not be followed for more than 500m as it leads to steep and dangerous ground.

Given sufficient time and strength in the legs a traverse of the Carn Mor Dearg

Arête is a great way to extend the day and gives the opportunity to see the crags of the North Face of Ben Nevis from an excellent vantage point. The crest of the arête is continuously narrow, exposed and rocky all the way to the summit of Carn Mor Dearg, from where a descent is easy to join the Allt a'Mhuilinn a few hundred metres above the forest.

Descents from tops other than the summit
For those climbers 'topping out' on the following routes in poor visibility and not wishing to visit the summit, these bearings will help.

Gardyloo Buttress	214° grid for 75m (GPS NN16501 71181) then 282° grid to Red Burn or GPS NN16262 71232 to GPS NN14678 71590
Tower Gully	214° grid for 50m (GPS NN16426 71198) then 282° grid to Red Burn or GPS NN16262 71232 to GPS NN14678 71590
Tower Ridge	214° grid for 130m (GPS NN16378 71232) then 282° grid to Red Burn or GPS NN16262 71232 to GPS NN14678 71590
Number Two Gully	282° grid to Red Burn or GPS NN14678 71590
Number Three Gully	282° grid to Red Burn or GPS NN14756 71865
Green/Comb Gully	220° grid for 150m (GPS NN16082 71291) then 282° grid to Red Burn or GPS NN14756 71865
Ledge Route	270° grid for 200m (GPS NN15675 72100) then 180° grid for 450m (GPS NN15675 71655) then 270° grid to Red Burn (GPS NN14756 71865)
Castle Ridge	232° grid for 200m then 308° grid. The descent to the Halfway Lochan is over very rough, broken and rocky ground, with one or two small crags in places.

Note The slope north of the Red Burn between the 1125m and 675m contour lines is not very pleasant for descent and contains a number of small crags.

For climbers finishing on routes to the east of the summit (North East Buttress and Little Brenva Face) it is advisable to try and find the summit shelter (GPS NN16684 71256) as a definite reference point before descending, if you are unsure about the descent. To do this, it should be possible to use the north-east edge of the plateau above Zero and Point Five gullies and Good Friday Climb as a 'handrail' to the summit trig point (15m north of the shelter). Cornice collapse has caused a few fatalities in this area so stay roped, with only one member of the party near the edge.

BEN NEVIS – GENERAL TOPOGRAPHY

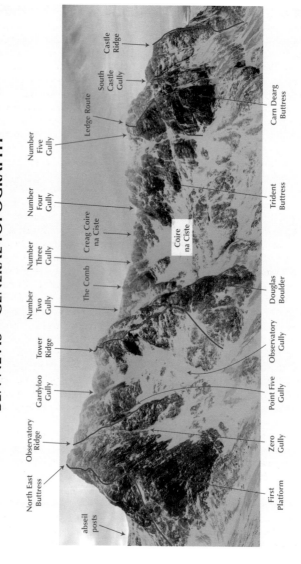

BEN NEVIS – GENERAL TOPOGRAPHY

The northerly faces of Ben Nevis and Carn Dearg NW form one continuous complex of cliffs which attain a maximum height of 500m and extend for 3.5km overlooking the upper part of the Allt a'Mhuilinn glen. It is the most impressive mountain face in the British Isles. The incomparable classic ridges are flanked by formidable walls leading back into deeply recessed coires, which themselves contain numerous large buttresses and gullies. The scale is so vast that it is difficult to appreciate on first acquaintance.

Walking up the glen of the Allt a'Mhuilinn, the first feature the climber will see on the right is Castle Ridge and its flanking North Wall. Beyond this and at a higher level is the recess of Castle Coire, which contains the Castle itself, its two demarcating gullies and, to the left of these, the tapering pillar of Raeburn's Buttress. The cliffs then jut out again. The left-hand side of the Castle Coire is known as the North Wall of Carn Dearg; this cliff connects with a 300m prow of compact rock, a truncated spur, Carn Dearg Buttress. Waterfall Gully is the dividing line between these last two. Round the corner of Carn Dearg Buttress is Number Five Gully, set at a reasonable angle but almost 500m in length. Ledge Route comes out of Number Five Gully to gain the crest of the ridge at the top of Carn Dearg Buttress and follows this to the summit of Carn Dearg. To the left (east) of Carn Dearg Buttress the cliffs fall back to form the great amphitheatre of Coire na Ciste, the floor of which, at over 900m, is a wild and magnificent place to visit. There are three relatively easy exits from the head of the coire: Number Four Gully (hidden) on the right; Number Three Gully, apparently the lowest col, in the centre; and Number Two Gully, which disappears to the left of the prominent triangular buttress of The Comb. Tower Ridge is the next main feature and one of the most important. Narrow and very long, it projects for 0.75km from the summit plateau into the glen to terminate abruptly at the Douglas Boulder above the hut. From the foot of the (215m!) boulder, there is a vertical rise of over 550m before the junction with the plateau.

To the east of Tower Ridge is the long slope of Observatory Gully, which branches in its upper quarter to form Gardyloo and Tower gullies. Observatory Gully, broad in its lower part and tapering as it rises for 500m, is only an approach to other climbs and can be regarded almost as a deep coire. Rising to the left of the gully are some of the most formidable climbs on the mountain: the Minus gullies and buttresses and the Orion Face (all on the flank of North East Buttress); Zero Gully, which lies in the corner between Orion Face and the long spur of Observatory Ridge; and finally, Point Five Gully and Observatory Buttress.

The final great ridge almost at the head of the glen is called the North East Buttress. It is again a massive projection, almost 500m in vertical height, but is steeper and therefore not as long as Tower Ridge. Below the First Platform it terminates in a great rock nose, not unlike the Douglas Boulder. The Allt a'Mhuilinn glen ends in Coire Leis below the col of the Carn Mor Dearg Arête. Overlooking this coire is the east flank of the North East Buttress, now generally referred to as the Little Brenva Face.

North East
Buttress
Approach

Little Brenva Face

1 Final Buttress III
2 Bob-Run II
3 Moonwalk IV,3**
4 Cresta III**
5 Slalom III**
6 SuperG VI,6**
7 Frostbite III
8 Route Major IV,3***

The climbs are described from east to west (left to right) coire by coire.

CLIMBS FROM COIRE LEIS

Coire Leis is the basin at the head of the Allt a'Mhuilinn glen. From the CIC Hut follow either bank of the burn until opposite the lowest rocks below the First Platform of North East Buttress then traverse up the right-hand side of the coire beneath the East Face (about 1 hour from the CIC Hut).

Although all the routes on the Little Brenva Face follow fairly arbitrary lines, they are quite popular. The face is alpine in character and receives the full benefit of any sun, which can cause icefall and cruddy conditions later in the season. Generally the climbs are long (longer than they appear) and give some interesting route-finding; considerable difficulty may be experienced in misty conditions.

Little Brenva Face

Final Buttress   55m III

At the extreme left side of the face is a short buttress. Climb an ice pitch in the centre.

Bob-Run   130m II

I Clough, D Pipes, H Fisher, B Small, J Porter and F Jones, 10 February 1959

Commences almost at the level of the col of the Carn Mor Dearg Arête and follows a couloir in the left extremity of the face. Start to the right of a buttress and climb 30m of ice or iced rocks to gain the couloir. After another 30m the route curls round to the left by either of two variations, both of which generally give at least one further pitch on ice.

Moonwalk   270m IV,3 ★★

K Hughes and J Mothersele, March 1973

Start 10m left of Cresta, below an ice pitch which can vary in difficulty depending on conditions. Climb the ice above and continue over a snow slope to the foot of an ice pitch formed by a rock corner (100m). Climb the ice above to another snow slope (45m). Move up to a steep ice wall (45m). Climb this for 15m and an ice groove to a snow-ice field (35m). Cross rightwards to belay below rock wall (45m). Traverse horizontally right below the wall to a steep rock arête, which is followed to the summit slopes.

Note Many variations are possible in this area, and escapes left (south) can be made with care towards Bob-Run.

Cresta 275m III ★★
TW Patey, LS Lovat and AG Nicol, 16 February 1957
The main feature of this route is a 180m shallow couloir which commences above and to the left of a rocky spur and finishes amongst the small cliffs at the exit from the highest part of the left-hand side of the face. The original start was from the right, but it is now more usual to commence to the left of the rocky spur and about 30m right of Bob-Run. 30m of icy rocks (or ice) are climbed to gain a long broad snow shelf. A small gully leads up from the right-hand side of the shelf to reach the couloir proper, which is followed to its termination in an ice basin. Traverse up to the right to gain an easy snow slope, which leads out to a finish about 50m from the top of North East Buttress. A direct finish has been climbed through the exit cliffs (*IV,4, M Slesser and N Tennant, 18 February 1957*). A direct start from the foot of the rocks to the left of the original start has also been climbed (*IV, K Wilson, N Harper, JR Mackenzie and D Lockie, 1 February 1987*).

Slalom 275m III ★★
D Pipes, I Clough, JM Alexander, R Shaw and A Flegg, 6 January 1959
The upper part of the right-hand side of the face is a steep rock wall, the Central Spur. Both Slalom and Frostbite start in the bay below this wall and to the right of a rocky spur.

Slalom starts up a shallow tongue of snow from the left of the bay and zig-zags up through the rock bluffs towards the middle of the wall of the Central Spur. Below the Spur a long rising leftwards traverse is made to gain an easy snow slope which leads to the foot of a rocky ridge overlooking the couloir of Cresta. The rocks usually give the crux of the climb and lead to the final easy exit slope which is shared with Cresta.

Super G 270m VI,6 ★★
H Burrows-Smith and D McGimpsey, 20 March 2002
Every now and then an impressive icefall forms down the headwall of the face. It is approached in four pitches via the first pitches of Slalom, a rightwards traverse and easy-angled ice below and left of the icefall. Three pitches (40m, 50m and 20m) of very steep ice form the crux of the climb over iced steps and an icicle fringe, finishing slightly leftwards up an icy ramp.

Wall of the Winds 320m VI,5
SM Richardson and I Small, 27 January 2007
Start as for Slalom and climb straight up the vague rib on moderate mixed ground to the foot of the headwall (180m). Climb a ramp 20m right of Super G, traverse right for 10m and climb a steep groove to reach a snow bay (20m). Traverse up and

right for 20m to reach the left-facing corner system that cuts through the wall. Move right to belay in a large niche (40m). Continue up the corner to reach a large vertical square-cut corner (30m). Climb the left wall of the corner and continue up the corner-line to reach the plateau at the same point as Super G (50m).

Frostbite   275m   III

I Clough, D Pipes, JM Alexander, PA Hannon and M Bucke, February 1958

Starts from the above-mentioned bay and follows an icy groove up to the right to gain a 120m snowfield. Follow this rightwards and cross a rocky ridge below the nose of the Central Spur proper to gain further snow slopes slanting rightwards under the spur. These eventually lead out onto the crest of the North East Buttress below the Mantrap (see North East Buttress route).

Isandhlwana   280m   V,5 ★★

R Clothier, G Perroux, J-F Males and P Touvet, 27 March 1999

Described by Perroux as one of his best moments on Ben Nevis! A varied icy mixed route left of Route Major. Starting 25m right of Frostbite, climb icy slabs and mixed ground to join Frostbite. At the top of the snow couloir of Frostbite climb steep mixed ground for 30m to a snow bay. The icefall above and icy ramp lead to a snow funnel that exits on North East Buttress.

Route Major   300m   IV,3 ★★★

H MacInnes and I Clough, 16 February 1969

Not an easy route to find and follow, but for those people who enjoy exploring middle-grade mixed ground, an excellent route when in condition. The route generally follows the line of a summer climb (Eastern Climb). To get a good look at the route, it is advisable to walk up the east side of Coire Leis above the hut until opposite the start of North East Buttress. A hanging ice field high on the face is a key feature towards which climbers should aim. A start from the traverse-line (left end) onto the First Platform of North East Buttress can be made. Follow ice ribs up the wall to gain a snow slope crossed by Frostbite. Cross this and continue up the buttress by a chimney-line going right (difficult route-finding). Where the route goes close to the Mantrap of North East Buttress, break out left on a horizontal traverse then up various small snowfields to the top.

　　Note An alternative start to the climb can be made by walking up directly under North East Buttress and continuing until the ground levels out as it approaches upper Coire Leis. From here turn up right and commence climbing. This start is well right of Frostbite.

North East Buttress   350m   IV,5 ★★★

WW Naismith, W Brunskill, ABW Kennedy, WW King and FC Squance, 3 April 1896

The normal winter route avoids the rocks below the First Platform by going up into Coire Leis until a broad easy shelf leads back up to the right to the First Platform. Getting onto this shelf can involve icy steps if there is little snow, and the shelf can be prone to avalanche. Shortly above the Platform the rocks on the crest become very steep, and the easiest route is to traverse an exposed ledge on the right until a gully leads back up to the left to reach the small Second Platform. Alternatively, the steep step may be turned by grooves on the left or even taken direct. Above the Second Platform the ridge is followed, turning obstacles, until a smooth, blunt 5m nose bars the way. This is the notorious Mantrap, which should be climbed direct, but which can be extremely difficult in icy conditions. Sometimes it can be avoided by a slight descent on the right and a traverse to a scoop which leads to the foot of a steep corner (the Forty Foot Corner). This should be climbed as well, and can also be quite hard, but it might be avoided down to the left, not far above the top of the Mantrap, by a shallow chimney leading up to the left of the ridge crest onto easier ground. This upper part of the route is normally the crux of the climb, but the major difficulties are relatively short and it is not too far to the top; it is probably better to force the route than be faced with the long retreat.

A hard direct start is possible. From the Coire Leis approach traverse, approximately 50m before reaching the First Platform, head up directly via steep icy walls to regain the route below the Second Platform (**Green Gaiters**, *120m, IV,5, R Clothier and P Pibarot, March 1994*).

Spring conditions on Ben Nevis

Observatory Gully Area

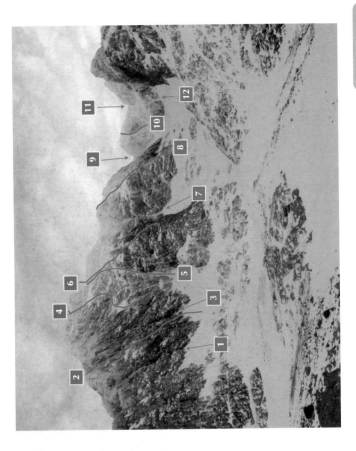

1 Minus Three Gully IV,5**
2 Minus Two Gully V,5***
3 Minus One Gully VI,6***
4 Orion Direct V,5***
5 Zero Gully V,4**
6 Observatory Ridge IV,5***
7 Point Five Gully V,5***
8 Observatory Buttress
  Ordinary Route V,5***
9 Gardyloo Gully II/III**
10 Smith's Route V,5***
11 Tower Gully I
12 Tower Scoop III***

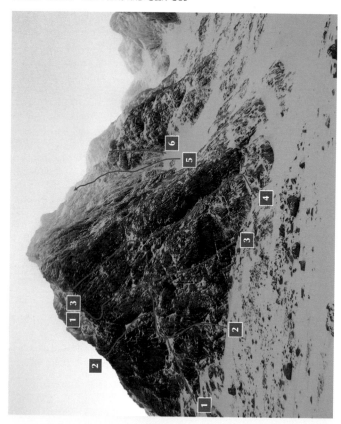

North East Buttress First Platform (right side)

1 Newbigging's 80 Minute Route IV,4
2 Steam Train VI,7
3 Newbigging's Route – Right-Hand Variation V,6
4 Newbigging's Route – Far Right Variation IV,4**
5 Zero Gully V,4**
6 East Face IV,5*

CLIMBS FROM OBSERVATORY GULLY

Due to the nature of the rock, nearly all the climbs on this part of the mountain require good snow-ice, and form only after snowfall and several thaw–freeze cycles. Lower buttresses (below the First Platform and the Minus Face) form snow-ice less often, but the higher buttresses form good conditions every winter. Very large avalanches fall from the upper reaches of this gully, especially after a south-east wind has blown snow into the gullies. It would be wise to avoid the climbs at the top end of this gully during or after heavy snowfall or strong winds, or during a thaw.

Beneath the First Platform of North East Buttress are many good climbs, easily seen on the hut approach up the Allt a'Mhuilinn, and when in condition provide good sport at a lower level. Parties may wish to consider an abseil descent of Slingsby's Chimney from these routes, as the traverse off into Coire Leis can be avalanche prone and is pretty exposed and steep.

Newbigging's 80 Minute Route   230m   IV,4
J Marshall and R Campbell, 25 February 1967
Follow the right-trending rake, starting 60m left of Raeburn's Arête, for 100m. Turn the first step on the left by a groove (20m). The groove and chimney above lead to easier ground (40m), which is followed to the top (70m).

Steam Train   VI,7
D MacLeod and A Hudelson, 20 March 2007
The prominent right-facing corner above the rake of the previous route. Climb grooves and step right into the corner-line (40m). Climb the corner (30m), followed by easier ground and a traverse to finish (30m).

Newbigging's Route – Right-Hand Variation   60m   V,6
DF Lang and AC Stead, 23 March 1996
Starts 30m left of the Far Right Variation and gains a groove which runs parallel to that route by climbing a shallow groove and twin cracks. Ascend on turf in the main groove to belay in a short corner (25m). Go left and continue on loose rock up the groove (two aid pegs) to the foot of a wide corner-crack. Go up on the left side of the crack to a belay (35m). Climb grooves above, left and right, to join the final groove of the Far Right Variation (30m).

Newbigging's Route – Far Right Variation   180m   IV,4 ★★
R Campbell, R Carrington and JR Marshall, February 1972
This route is on the triangular face which falls vertically into Coire Leis as one walks

North East Buttress First Platform (right side)

1   Green Hollow Route IV,4**
1a Bayonet Route III
2   Ruddy Rocks IV,4
3   Slingsby's Chimney II/III
4   Right-Hand Wall Route IV,5
5   Wagroochimsla IV,5
6   Differentiation VI,6
7   Platforms Rib IV,4*
8   Minus Three Gully IV,5**

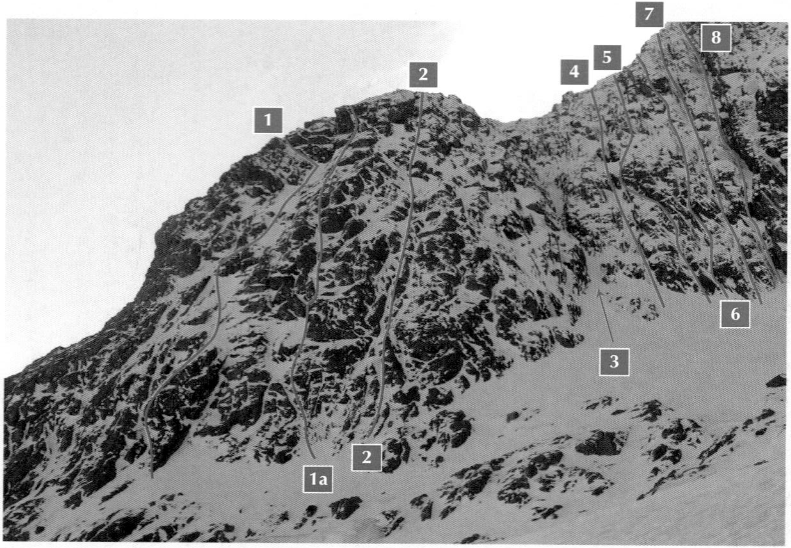

beneath the First Platform of North East Buttress. It starts 10m left of the rocky edge of the face (this edge forms the north and east facets of the buttress) and runs parallel to that edge. The route is a natural winter line and easily seen on approaching the hut. Follow the big corner-groove and slabs, passing an overhang on the left. The main difficulties are in the lower 60m and will require good névé which rarely forms here.

Raeburn's Arête   230m   IV,5 ★★★
DF Lang and C Stead, 25 January 1986
Follows the arête formed by the north and east facets of the First Platform of North East Buttress. A good climb which is not often in condition. Go right below the first overhang to a deep groove, which is climbed to a belay (45m). Follow grooves up slightly right, then go left beneath another overhang to a block-belay on the edge (100m). Follow the arête more easily to the top of the First Platform (90m).

Green Hollow Route   200m   IV,4 ★★
JR Marshall and J Moriarty, February 1965
Start at the lowest rocks on the left (often snow covered) and trend diagonally up rightwards by iced slabs and grooves towards a large snow bay, high up in the middle of the face, the Green Hollow. From the highest point of the bay climb an iced slab left onto the final arête. Follow this easily to the top of the First Platform.

Bayonet Route   185m   III
I Griffiths, E Jackson and C Stead, 7 March 1982
Start midway between Raeburn's Arête and Slingsby's Chimney. Follow a steep icy groove direct towards an overhang. Gain and climb the rib on the left of the overhang, then traverse left onto the arête.

Ruddy Rocks   180m   IV,4
JR Marshall, R Marshall and RN Campbell, March 1967
Start immediately right of Bayonet Route. Climb towards twin chimney-cracks to the right of the large overhang. Follow the cracks and grooves to easier ground and continue to a small overhang, which is turned on the right. Easy ground upwards to the First Platform.

Rain Trip   180m   IV,4
G Hornby and J Fisher, 14 February 1987
Start just right of Ruddy Rocks and follow a series of snow and ice grooves. Turn an overhang on the right and go up to flake-belays on the right (40m). A huge flake is passed at around 80m. A higher roof is passed by flakes on the left and up to a headwall with a flake-belay on the right. Ascend an overlap and finish by a corner and crack.

Green and Napier's Route   130m   III
S Richardson and C Cartwright, 5 April 2006
30m left of Slingsby's Chimney and approached from the right, climb walls and
corners, with much variation possible.

Raeburn's 18 Minute Route   140m   II
EUMC party, March 1952
Start 6m left of Slingsby's Chimney and follow the line of least resistance to the
First Platform.

Slingsby's Chimney   125m   II/III
C Donaldson and J Russell, April 1950
A direct approach to the First Platform of North East Buttress. To the right of the
slabby rocks of the nose leading to the First Platform is an obvious shallow gully
fault. This gives the climb, with a difficult exit up and left.

The Minus Face

Home to some of the finest climbs on the mountain, the celebrated Minus gullies
are much sought-after climbs, and the buttresses in between are a very rare treat
when they form good snow-ice. The Minus Face, between Slingsby's Chimney and
Minus One Gully, often has little avalanche hazard, but the climbs finish on North
East Buttress, which needs to be climbed or descended. The three Minus gullies are
relatively shallow lines running diagonally left up the face, with Minus Three Gully
on the left, and Minus Two and Minus One gullies starting at nearly the same point
further right.

Right-Hand Wall Route   140m   IV,5
R Ferguson and J Higham, March 1972
Just to the right of Slingsby's Chimney is a line of chimneys: follow this line as
closely as possible, the final slabby part below the First Platform giving the crux.

Slab Rib Variation   150m   IV,5 ★
CD Grant and C Stead, 22 March 1982
Climbs the rib immediately right of Slingsby's Chimney.

Wagroochimsla   140m   IV,5
S Docherty and G Adam, January 1972
Start between Right-Hand Wall Route and Platforms Rib, and climb left to the central
bulge; climbed with aid on first ascent. Continue rightwards to the First Platform.

Differentiation   145m   VI,6
S Richardson and R Webb, 13 March 2010
A sustained icy mixed route climbed in three pitches, with an imposing last pitch through the overhanging crest at the top of the face

Platforms Rib   150m   IV,4 ★
H MacInnes, I Clough, T Sullivan and M White, 8 March 1959
Follow the rib to the left of Minus Three Gully until part of the gully is used, before moving back left to the North East Buttress.

Minus Three Gully   160m   IV,5 ★★
R Smith and JR Marshall, 7 February 1960
When in condition, a classic. Climb steep snow to a cave belay, then climb steep ice on the left and continue by a groove to snow. Another steep pitch leads to easier climbing and North East Buttress.

Left-Hand Route   270m   VI,6 ★★
S Docherty and N Muir, 30 January 1972
A delicate climb on thinly iced slabs. Start immediately right of Minus Three Gully and ascend the huge groove/corner for 60m, passing an overhanging section. Steep ice leads to an easier section of slabby rocks and eventually to the Second Platform.

Central Route   270m   VI,7
A Nisbet and B Sprunt, 18 March 1979
The climb follows a line just to the right of the previous route, following the raised crest on the front face to the overhangs. These are gained by a rightward traverse and turned on the right using aid to reach easier ground.
    Note The first ascent took a very long time! Rarely, if ever, repeated.

Right-Hand Route   270m   VI,6 ★
R Carrington and A Rouse, March 1972
To the right of the prominent ridge is a large slabby corner. Climb the large corner (or just to the right), then a short, more difficult corner to gain the easier-angled upper section of the buttress with difficulty. Slabs and grooves lead to the North East Buttress.

Subtraction   270m   VIII,8 ★
V Scott and G Robertson, 15 April 2008
Hard, varied and committing mixed climbing following the summer line into Minus Two Gully. Start 10m right of Right-Hand Route and climb a well-defined groove

The Minus Face

1 Slingsby's Chimney II/III
2 Left-Hand Route VI,6**
3 Right-Hand Route VI,6*
4 Minus Two Gully V,5***
5 Integration VIII,8***
6 Minus One Direct VIII,8***
7 Minus One Buttress VI,6***
8 Minus One Gully VI,6***

to where it steepens and trends left (35m). From the rib on the right climb the overhang (25m). Climb the arête above to a corner (40m), which leads into Minus Two Gully.

Minus Two Buttress   270m   V,5 ★

B Dunn, C Higgins and D McArthur, 5 March 1974

Start 13m to the left of Minus Two Gully and go up an icefall then right to an open book corner. Climb all of the corner to a prominent snow crest. Traverse a snow ramp leftwards and climb an iced gully-line to the North East Buttress.

Minus Two Gully   270m   V,5 ★★★

JR Marshall, J Stenhouse and D Haston, 11 February 1959

The best of the Nevis gullies when in condition. A long pitch of snow and ice leads to a belay below an overhang. Avoid the overhang by a detour to the left and regain the upper chimneys leading to the North East Buttress. The initial chimney can be avoided by thin iced slabs 2m to the left.

Integration   290m   VIII,8 ★★★

I Small and S Richardson, 7 March 2010

Start up the first three long pitches of Minus One Buttress on thin ice before trending left to find and climb the daunting groove (of Subtraction) on the left of the crest of the buttress.

Minus One Direct   290m   VIII,8 ★★★

G Robertson, P Benson and N Bullock, 10 March 2010

A direct and stunning line up the buttress – one of the best climbs in the country. Start up the first three pitches of Minus One Buttress, then continue up and right to find a continuous crack-line leading to the top of the buttress.

Minus One Buttress   290m   VI,6 ★★★

N Muir and A Paul, 5 April 1977

Start at the centre of the buttress, at a corner, and follow the easiest line to the overhangs at 100m. Move across rightwards and follow the buttress, fairly close to Minus One Gully, to the North East Buttress. Fine open buttress climbing.

Minus One Gully   290m   VI,6 ★★★

KV Crocket and C Stead, 23 February 1974

The hardest of the Nevis gullies. Easy climbing leads to an ice wall giving access to a cave below the main overhang. Avoid the overhang on the left before regaining the gully above. Continue past a snow bay to the North East Buttress.

The Minus Face and Orion Face

1 Minus Three Gully IV,5***
2 Left-Hand Route VI,6**
3 Right-Hand Route VI,6*
4 Minus Two Gully V,5***
5 Minus One Gully VI,6***
6 Astronomy VI,5***
7 Astronomy –
   Direct Finish VI,5**
8 Urban Spaceman VII,6***
9 Astral Highway V,5***
10 Orion Direct V,5***
11 Orion Directissima VI,5
12 Slav Route V,5***
13 Observatory Ridge IV,5***

Pitch 3 of Minus Two Gully (photo: Blair Fyffe)

The Orion Face

The biggest face on Ben Nevis forms a narrow fan shape between Minus One Gully and Zero Gully. The toe of the buttress takes the line of Astronomy and projects into the approach slopes leading to Orion Direct, which starts up a steep icefall with the Great Slab Rib to the left. In the centre of the face lies The Basin, a large snow patch, at the top left side of which is a steep icy chimney known as Epsilon Chimney, the easiest escape from The Basin to North East Buttress in the event of poor snow conditions. Up to the right of this basin is the Second Slab Rib, which is often the only feature showing in the middle of the face when snow and ice obliterate all other detail. Higher up is another smaller snow patch, and left of this at a higher level is the exit chimney.

Astronomy   300m   VI,5 ★★★

H MacInnes, A Fyffe and K Spence, March 1971

Start about 16m to the right of Minus One Gully and climb twin cracks to leftward-slanting snow patches. These snow patches lead to a groove. Climb the groove and go right to a large corner. Go up the corner then move right, then back left by walls and grooves. Skirt left below the upper rocks and escape by descending into the top of Minus One Gully (or follow the next route which gives a better finish).

Astronomy – Direct Finish   120m   VI,5 ★★

C Fraser and M Thompson, 16 February 1986

Instead of skirting left below the upper rocks into Minus One Gully, trend slightly right to belay below the right-hand end of the steep upper rocks. Gain the crest of the buttress on the right and climb an iced slab, trending right to gain a fine ice groove near the crest of the buttress. Follow this steeply to easier ground. Less often in condition than other routes on the Orion Face.

(**Author's note** Tim Jepson and Roger Baxter-Jones climbed a similar line in the late 1970s.)

Smith-Holt Route   420m   V,5 ★★

R Smith and R Holt, January 1959

Starts left of Orion Direct and climbs leftward-facing corners immediately left of the Great Slab Rib until it is possible to cut back right into The Basin with difficulty. From The Basin the steep and icy Epsilon Chimney is taken, and the exit made easily via a ledge leading up left to the crest of North East Buttress at a V-notch. A great route which avoids the queues on Orion Direct.

The crucial traverse on Orion Direct

The Black Hole   350m   VI,6 ★★

A Saunders and M Fowler, 5 April 1986

Starts 15m left of Orion Direct. Climb an awkward right-facing corner to gain the left side of the Great Slab Rib (50m). Follow the corner on the left side of the rib for 30m, then move left to an obvious ice-choked overhanging crack, which is climbed to a snow patch (45m). Climb the overhanging fault line above to belay at the top left of another snow patch (35m). Move back right into the fault line, which is climbed to join Astronomy where it traverses left into Minus One Gully (45m). There are another couple of pitches in the same line up thinly iced grooves (60m). Much of this route had been climbed previously.

Urban Spaceman   350m   VII,6 ★★★

D Hawthorn and A Paul, 12 April 1983

Start at the same point as Orion Direct and move up left to below the Great Slab Rib (35m), which is followed on the crest to a stance (30m). Continue on a similar line to a belay (40m). Reach a set of open grooves up right (30m) and follow them to beneath the steep upper section (50m). Move over slabs up right to a stance (30m). Follow a steep ice-filled chimney which overlooks The Basin, then steep mixed ground (45m). A further 90m leads to North East Buttress. An excellent route but not often in good condition.

Orion Direct   420m   V,5 ★★★

R Smith and JR Marshall, 13 February 1960

A classic: the technical difficulty is often low, but in such conditions belays are usually poor. Climb to the left end of a broad ledge stretching out from Zero Gully and take a steep chimney-line above until an upward traverse left leads to the bottom left side of The Basin. It is possible to continue direct to The Basin from the chimney, but harder. Move up rightwards to an obvious rock rib (Second Slab Rib) and take this by the face to the right, or by a longer traverse right below the face. Trend up leftwards in three pitches to finish in the steep icy exit chimneys.

   A direct start in two pitches of steep sustained ice is possible in good conditions to reach the right side of The Basin. Starts just left of Slav Route and stays right of the lower pitches of Orion Direct original route (*V,5***, *S Docherty and N Muir, March 1971*).

Orion Directissima   375m   VI,5

S Richardson and R Webb, 16 April 1994

Much of this route has been climbed in parts before, but it is worth recording as a steeper alternative to Orion Direct. It stays right of the original line all of the time. Climb the Direct Start mentioned above (*Docherty/Muir*). Go up right of a rib on

Donald King climbing Orion Direct exit chimney

the right side of the basin to below the Second Slab Rib. Climb up right of the Second Slab Rib and head up towards the prominent curving corner in the head-wall right of the ordinary finishing chimney. Climb the groove and easy ground above to the top.

The following routes are described from **The Basin**.

Zybernaught 240m VI,5
D Hawthorn and A Paul
Follows a set of zig-zag grooves between Epsilon Chimney and Astral Highway. From the foot of Epsilon Chimney move up right and below a steep bulge (45m). Climb the bulge and ground above to a left-trending groove (45m). Follow the groove to an open corner (45m). Climb the corner and ground above to North East Buttress.

Astral Highway 240m V,5 ★★★
C Higgins and A Kimber, 28 December 1976
A direct finish from The Basin starting at the top of The Basin, left of centre at the groove right of Epsilon Chimney. Gain the groove and climb it and successive grooves to reach North East Buttress above and right of the 40ft corner.

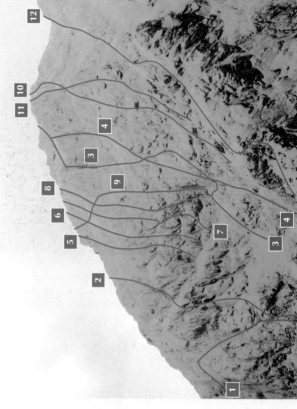

The Orion Face (top section)

1 Astronomy VI,5***
2 Urban Spaceman VII,6***
3 Orion Direct V,5***
4 Orion Directissima VI,5
5 Astral Highway V,5***
6 Space Invaders VI,6
7 Journey into Space VII,6**
8 Space Walk VII,6
9 Long Climb Finish VII,6***
10 Slav Route V,5***
11 Orion Grooves VI,5
12 Observatory Ridge IV,5***

Space Invaders
240m VI,6

J Preston and A Nisbet

Starts 10m right of Astral Highway and follows a steeper line of icy walls and grooves to the right of that route. At one point on the second pitch it would be possible to traverse left onto Astral Highway. Two initial 50m pitches provide the main difficulties.

Journey into Space
240m VII,6 ★★

A Kimber and C Higgins, 8 March 1980

Start midway between Astral Highway and Second Slab Rib. Climb directly to the right of a short corner, where a delicate traverse right leads to a short ice wall, which is climbed to a belay ledge. Climb diagonally leftwards by an obvious iced slab until a break right can be made onto the upper section of the wall. Climb the slab, move right beneath the overhang then go by groove direct, climbing the occasional bulge until the right end of the prominent snowfield is reached. Move diagonally left up the snowfield to the obvious corner finish (possible to finish direct by Space Walk).

Space Walk
200m VII,6

R Clothier and A Forsyth, April 2001

Starts just left of the Second Slab Rib and follows a series of grooves, corners and slabs parallel to Journey into Space before finishing directly, when Journey into Space goes left towards the top of North East Buttress.

Long Climb Finish
240m VII,6 ★★★

A Cain and R Clothier, March 1983

A steep alternative finish to Orion Direct which follows the steep and icy tapering groove that forms the right side of Second Slab Rib. Above the Second Slab Rib climb steeply up left by grooves and a slab, and eventually follow the same snow ledge left as Journey into Space. Finish by the obvious corner of that route.

The following routes are described from the foot of the face.

Slav Route
420m V,5 ★★★

D Lang and N Quinn, 23 March 1974

Takes a line just to the left of Zero Gully, but completely independent. An obvious icefall at 50m is climbed direct, or possibly avoided a long way to the left. Near the top an exit can be made into Zero Gully, but a better line slightly leftwards is taken to an obvious open corner up left of the gully.

Orion Grooves   420m   VI,5

T Stone, I Small and S Richardson, 21 March 2010

Start up the first three pitches of Zero Gully before following grooves on the right of Orion Face and a final steep mixed pitch up a groove on the right side of the steep 50m headwall.

Zero Gully   300m   V,4 ★★

H MacInnes, A Nicol and TW Patey, 18 February 1957

The easiest but most serious of the big three classics: the lack of belays meriting the V grade. Climb the gully to a stance below a left-facing chimney to the left of the main gully. Ascend the chimney, then traverse right to an amphitheatre in the gully. Take the narrow gully above to easy ground by a long pitch.

    Note An alternative start can be made to Zero Gully by climbing the steep ice on the right, thus avoiding the rightward traverse higher up. This option varies with conditions. Also, as with many other steep gully-lines, Zero is not a nice place to be when breezes on the summit deposit vast quantities of powder snow down the climb! Beware of debris from other parties.

Observatory Ridge

The ridge itself is the narrow buttress to the right of Zero Gully, but as an area it is taken to stretch from Zero Gully to Point Five Gully.

East Face   166m   IV,5 ★

B Dunn and C Higgins, 3 March 1974

Below and to the right of Zero Gully, the left side of Observatory Ridge is split by a line of grooves which give the route, until they merge into the ridge itself.

Silverside   115m   IV,4 ★

B Dunn and D Gardner, 17 April 1977

Start 16m below East Face and move up rightwards over snow and iced grooves to the left end of a large ledge. Traverse left and climb a left-slanting line to a snow bay and easier ground.

The above two climbs finish up the following route.

Observatory Ridge   420m   IV,5 ★★★

H Raeburn, FS Goggs and WA Mounsey, April 1920

The finest and most difficult of the classic ridges, the line of the route generally follows the crest of the ridge. Without névé, and especially under powder snow, this will be a long and arduous climb. The first third of the ridge normally gives the most serious problems. About halfway up this section on a good ledge, go right around the crest to find grooves leading up the right side to the first shoulder in the ridge. Above this, difficulties can be turned on the right, and the upper part of Zero Gully is often taken for the final 150m.

The following routes lie on the right (west) wall of **Observatory Ridge**, *overlooking* **Observatory Gully** *and the approach to* **Point Five Gully**.

Observatory Wall   90m   V,6
D Hawthorn and A Paul, November 1985
A crack-line left of Abacus has been climbed. It has a cave at half-height. Climb to the cave by slabs, and exit left and up cracks to the crest of the ridge.

Abacus   106m   IV,4 ★
N Muir and A Paul, 27 November 1977
The route climbs the obvious bow-shaped chimney-groove in the middle of the face between Observatory Ridge and Hadrian's Wall Direct to reach the ridge.

The Frozen Chosin   80m   VI,6
S Richardson and RG Webb, 16 March 2008
Climb the right-facing corner, step left to a second right-facing corner, and climb this to icy slabs and a belay in the shallow cave above (20m). Move up icy slabs on the left and climb the right-trending line cutting through the wall above. Climb up the shallow icy depression overlooking Abacus to below a short wall (40m). Continue easily up the buttress to the crest of Observatory Ridge (20m).

Maelstrom   90m   VI,6 ★★
C Cartwright and S Richardson, 15 March 2002
Not often iced in the upper corner, but a good line when it is. Climb the prominent right-facing corner-gully to the right of Abacus, stepping right around an overhang to a good stance (50m). Climb thin ice on the left wall of the corner to the upper gully. This is climbed past a diagonal break (crux) to snow slopes leading to Observatory Ridge (40m).

Antonine Wall   150m   V,5 ★
N Muir and A Paul, 3 December 1977
Just right of Abacus is a steep ice-filled groove leading to a slab capped by a huge roof. Climb the groove to below the roof and move right over slabs to a snow groove leading to the crest.

Sickle V,5***

Point Five Gully V,5****

Galactic Hitchhiker VI,5***

Hadrian's Wall Direct V,5***

Hadrian's Wall

1 West Face Lower Route IV,5**
2 Nemesis VI,5*
3 Interstellar Overdrive VI,5*
4 Bombing the Pilgrims VI,5*
5 Appointment With Fear VII,6*
6 Matchpoint VI,5*

The last three routes are good bad-weather routes, as it is possible to descend by abseil as did the first ascencionists.

West Face Lower Route   325m   IV,5 ★★

WD Brooker, JR Marshall and TW Patey, 1 February 1959

Start as for Vade Mecum (see below) and climb to twin ice grooves. Follow the left-hand groove to a steep snow bay beneath vertical rock walls. Traverse right beneath the walls to enter a deep icy chimney. This chimney leads to the easier upper section and a variety of plateau exits which include Observatory Ridge or Zero Gully on the left. The route is also known as Hadrian's Wall.

Vade Mecum   320m   V,5 ★★★

D Knowles, D Wilson and party, 1974

Start just left of the ice smear of Hadrian's Wall Direct, and climb over slabby mixed ground to an obvious pointed block. Move left and finish by a steep ice pillar to Observatory Ridge.

Hadrian's Wall Direct   320m   V,5 ★★★

MG Geddes and G Little, April 1971

Between Observatory Ridge and Point Five Gully is a very obvious ice smear. Nowhere steep, this popular climb is rather poorly protected lower down (poor belay stance after the first pitch unless a 60m pitch is taken). Climb the smear in two or three pitches to a chimney with a good belay. Take the chimney to a snow patch and gain Observatory Ridge after two long pitches, or stay right of that route all the way to the plateau.

Sickle   300m   V,5 ★★★

B Hall and MG Geddes, December 1977

Start to the right of Hadrian's Wall Direct and move up leftwards to climb a groove parallel with, and close to, Hadrian's Wall Direct; then go back right to continue by a steep ice corner to join Hadrian's Wall Direct at the snow patch, just above the chimney. It is possible to continue to the plateau by staying right of both Observatory Ridge and Hadrian's Wall Direct.

Galactic Hitchhiker   300m   VI,5 ★★★

MG Geddes and C Higgins, 14 April 1978

One of the first grade VI's climbed on Ben Nevis. Right of Hadrian's Wall Direct the main feature is the rightward-stepped corner system above the great slab left of Point Five. Climb just left of the centre of the slab to a small nose (50m). Move up right into the main groove system beneath the corner. Traverse right above the slab

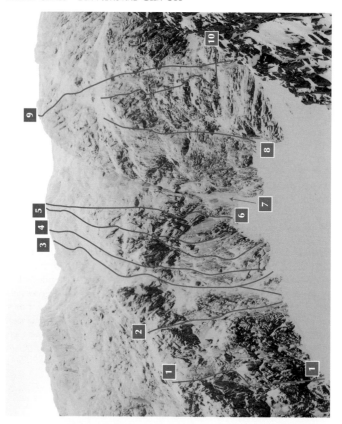

Point Five
Gully Area

1 Antonine Wall V,5*
2 Vade Mecum V,5***
3 Hadrian's Wall Direct V,5***
4 Sickle V,5***
5 Galactic Hitchhiker VI,5***
6 Pointless VII,6*
7 Point Five Gully V,5***
8 Rubicon Wall VI,5**
9 Observatory Buttress
  Ordinary Route V,5***
10 Never-Never Land VI,6

in an exposed position via a pointed block to belay on the right. Continue above by very steep and difficult walls and ledges right of the main corner system to easier ground, which is followed to the top.

Note An easier start (V,5) can be made on the left and nearer to Sickle, followed by a traverse right to a pointed block.

Nemesis   290m   VI,5 ★
M Nunwick and S Ried, 14 March 2002
The Great Slab between Galactic Hitchhiker and Pointless is rarely in condition, but is particularly compelling when it is! Climb a short pitch to the foot of the slab. The slab itself is taken just left of the corner at its top, before a 10m traverse leftwards is made to the pointed block of Galactic Hitchhiker. Two further pitches climb grooves to the right of Galactic Hitchhiker before continuing directly to the plateau.

Pointless   300m   VII,6 ★
N Banks and G Smith, 19 February 1978
A difficult climb, especially on the second pitch. Start on the obvious slab close to the left side of Point Five Gully. Follow the right edge of the slab towards a rock barrier, which is level with the normal first belay of Point Five Gully (bottom of the chimney). Trend up left at the rock barrier to a spike-belay beneath a steep, obvious corner (50m). Climb the corner with difficulty (possible peg on left wall) and trend right at the top. Continue directly for two interesting (III) pitches. Easier climbing leads in three pitches to the plateau rim. A variation start (*50m, VI,5, M Fowler and AV Saunders, 29 March 1986*) can be made by climbing a short corner from the foot of Point Five Gully (8m), followed by a traverse left above the prominent steep slab to the foot of the difficult second pitch.

Note As with many ice climbs, the first pitch of this route may be longer if the build-up at the base of the cliff is lacking.

Interstellar Overdrive   300m   VI,5 ★
I Kennedy and R Anderson, March 1980
Climb the left-hand rib of Point Five to belay below a wall (30m). Go right across the wall until immediately above Point Five. Follow a groove running left to a chimney, which is the right side of an enormous perched block. Climb the chimney to a belay on top of the block (40m). Climb a corner and ice wall (crux) rightwards above to a ledge in a snow bay (40m), followed by a groove on the right, which trends back left to meet Pointless above the difficult section (40m).

Radek Kudibal climbing the chimney of Point Five Gully

Bombing the Pilgrims 330m VI,5 ★

R Clothier and P Thorburn, 30 March 2002

A thin-face climb overlooking Point Five Gully. Start up Interstellar Overdrive and climb the rib to the left of Point Five Gully (50m). The rib is followed more steeply for two pitches (60m). The route then continues directly, crossing the left-hand finish of Point Five Gully, aiming for a prominent V-notch on the skyline.

Point Five Gully 325m V,5 ★★★

IS Clough, D Pipes, R Shaw and JM Alexander, 12–16 January 1959

A justifiably popular route, often in condition and the benchmark grade V,5 from which all other steep snow-ice gully climbs are graded. Approach from high up Observatory Gully by a traverse under Observatory Buttress. The first three pitches give sustained steep climbing, any of which might present the crux. The first is to a belay on the left, the chimney pitch to a belay on the right in a deep recess followed by the Rogue Pitch to easier ground. Above, there is one steeper section (II/III) before trending right to pass the cornice. Beware of spindrift avalanches and falling debris from other parties.

Note For climbers on top form and requiring more excitement, it is recommended that they take to the left wall of the gully after the third hard pitch. Find your own way to the top at about grade IV,4 depending on the line chosen. An escape rightwards is possible (III) onto the Girdle Traverse ledge running towards Good Friday Climb. Move out right from beneath the last hard pitch (pitch 3).

Erik Weihenmayer, the first blind man to climb Point Five Gully

Observatory Buttress

1 Point Five Gully V,5***
2 Pointblank VII,6***
3 Left Edge Route V,5**
4 Matchpoint VI,5*

5 Rubicon Wall VI,5**
6 Direct Route V,4**
7 Ordinary Route V,5***
8 Gardyloo Gully II/III**

Observatory Buttress

The buttress stretching rightwards from Point Five Gully to Good Friday Climb.

Pointblank   325m   VII,6 ★★★
M Duff and J Tinker, 4 March 1984
Direct version second ascent, as described:
M Duff and R Nowack, 24 February 1988
The route climbs the buttress immediately right of Point Five Gully. Start 4m below the foot of Point Five and climb a small steep groove left of Left Edge Route to the snow patch of that route. From the left edge of the snow patch move up right to corner and belay (25m). Climb the right-hand groove/crack above and thin icy slabs to a corner and capping roof. Semi-hanging stance on pegs (22m). 3m below the stance on the right enter a short groove, which is climbed to a narrow chimney-crack. Follow this crack to a roof and go diagonally left till overlooking Point Five Gully. Climb directly via a steep groovy ramp and wall to a snow bay and ledge-system. Belay on rounded spike (43m).

Note It is possible to avoid the hanging stance on the second pitch and thus arrive at the snow bay by using a 70m rope, as did the second ascent party. Right of the belay, climb a sloping groove and more easily above to a series of steps (40m). Follow a series of indistinct corners and steps to the crest on the right of Point Five Gully. The upper section of this climb and small parts of the lower pitches had previously been climbed by Dave Wilkinson on a variant ascent of Left Edge Route.

Left Edge Route   360m   V,5 ★★
D Lang and N Quinn, 9 March 1974
Start at the foot of Point Five Gully and climb a rib to a snow patch. From the right end of the snow patch climb the left-hand groove above, then move up right to the left of two icefalls, which is followed to the terrace. Either move right along the terrace and finish by Ordinary Route (see below) or follow the **Direct Finish**, 200m, V,5 (*D Wilkinson and M Burt, 8 March 1980*). Climb straight up icy grooves right of the crest overlooking Point Five Gully. Quite serious, and 60m ropes are useful.

Appointment With Fear   340m   VII,6 ★
S Richardson and C Cartwright, 25 March 2001
The name says it all! Climb the initial gully and step right at 15m onto a slab to belay at a 30cm block (20m). Continue directly above the block, then trend left to a short chimney-groove and a shallow left-facing groove to join Left Edge Route (50m). Continue up Left Edge Route with its Direct Finish (270m).

Matchpoint 325m VI,5 ★

S Richardson and E Hart, 29 March 1986

Between Left Edge and Rubicon Wall are two left-facing corner systems. Climb the right-hand one (50m). Climb a short steep snow slope to an overhanging inverted triangular wall. Traverse left and climb an icicle fringe to a snowfield. Climb the right-hand icefall above to the terrace (the left-hand one being on Left Edge Route), and continue up the buttress as for Left Edge Route Direct Finish.

Rubicon Wall 340m VI,5 ★★

N Muir and A Paul, 14 April 1977

A prominent icefall forming in a left-facing corner gives the line of this good route, taking three pitches to the Girdle Traverse ledge. Start about 20m right of Left Edge Route, and take a more or less direct line up to the terrace. Finish as for Left Edge Route (Ordinary or Direct).

Direct Route 340m V,4 ★★

D Stewart and W Foster, 23 March 1952

Ascend rightwards on snow patches and short walls, starting not far to the right of Rubicon Wall, to join Ordinary Route above its main difficulties.

Atlantis 340m VI,6 ★★

S Richardson and C Cartwright, 18 March 2001

Start at the foot of the buttress, break through the initial steep wall by a prominent slot and climb the snow slope to the left-facing corner of Observatory Buttress Direct (50m). Climb to the top of the corner and move up and right along a terrace to beneath a right-facing groove, as for Observatory Buttress Direct (50m). Climb the right-facing groove, pulling over a steep wall at its top and continuing up a left-slanting V-groove (40m). The groove continues to the steep headwall, which is taken by a left-trending ramp in a spectacular position to the Girdle Traverse ledge (30m). Easier ground to the top (170m).

Ordinary Route 340m V,5 ★★★

JR Marshall and R Smith, 9 February 1960

In good conditions an obvious narrow icefall forms on the right side of the buttress. Start well to the right of Direct Route, below a chimney some way up the buttress. Climb the buttress by a shallow depression to reach the chimney, which usually gives the crux. From the terrace above the chimney go up leftwards to gain the final easy crest.

Never-Never Land   170m   VI,6

S Richardson and P Takeda, 9 March 1999

Start to the right of Ordinary Route and climb mixed ground to the shallow depression on that route (50m). Go up left from the head of the depression and follow a line of ledges, right to left, until they end below a steep wall. This is the junction with Observatory Buttress Direct (45m). Ascend directly towards the headwall over short steep walls and belay below an obvious groove system, which cuts from right to left through the headwall (40m). Follow the groove with difficulty (35m) to the girdle ledge, and finish up Ordinary Route or traverse off right along the ledge.

North-West Face   100m   IV,4 ★

K Crocket and C Stead, 21 March 1975

Start halfway up the right-hand side of the buttress at a bay and follow a chimney-line leading to Indicator Wall, for which this route provides a good start.

Two more lines can be made to the right of North-West Face climb. The first is 25m right of that route (50m V,6), and the second, easier climb (30m, III) takes a corner-groove at the right end of the buttress.

Indicator Wall

The home of the best thin-face ice climbs in the country is located above the terrace cutting the upper part of Observatory Buttress, bounded on the left by Good Friday Climb and on the right by Gardyloo Gully. Ice climbs here are the highest in the British Isles, starting at 1200m. They are fine routes when in condition, and well worth the long walk. Be prepared for poorly protected leads on steep ground!

Saturday Rib   150m   III

S Richardson and R Clothier, 3 April 1999

Start at the foot of Good Friday Climb and ascend mixed ground to a snow slope on the rib on the left. Climb the arête left of Good Friday Climb, Left-Hand Finish, to the base of a steep buttress (50m). Climb the buttress to the top in two pitches (100m).

Good Friday Climb   150m   III ★★

GG MacPhee, RW Lovel, HR Shepherd and D Edwards, 7 April 1939

Start below Gardyloo Gully and traverse left along the snow shelf until a gully can be followed for 60m, where it is blocked by a wall. Go right, then back left up another gully to the plateau. A possible left-hand finish (90m, III,4) can be made from the top of the initial gully by climbing the rock wall direct and trending left above.

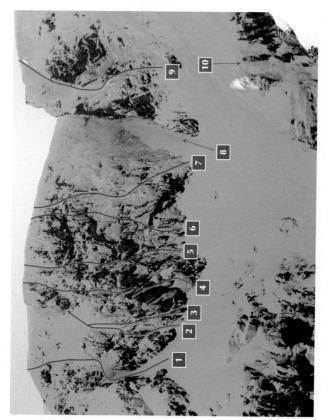

Indicator Wall

1 Good Friday Climb III**
2 Indicator Wall V,4***
3 Indicator Wall –
  Right-Hand Variant V,5**
4 Riders on the Storm VI,5***
5 Albatross VI,5***
6 Stormy Petrel VII,6***
7 Psychedelic Wall VI,5***
8 Gardyloo Gully II/III**
9 Smith's Route V,5***
10 Tower Scoop III***

Soft Ice Shuffle   130m   IV,4

S Richardson and R Clothier, 3 April 1999

Start 20m up Good Friday Climb at a ledge leading right onto the crest. Climb a groove rightwards to a cave, then go left by a short wall and mixed ground to a ledge on the left (30m). Go right into a groove and up to easier ground (50m), followed by the left hand of three gullies to the plateau (50m).

Indicator Wall   180m   V,4 ★★★

G Smith and T King, February 1975

About 50m right of the gully of Good Friday is an obvious icefall on the left side of the buttress. Start at an iced chimney-groove and climb to a ledge beneath a wall (35m). Step right and climb sustained ice to snow slopes topped by a gully (50m). Climb the gully to finish at the indicator post. A **Right-Hand Variant** (*160m, V,5**, DF Lang and NW Quinn, February 1975*) is steeper and more direct. Start 15m right of the original route.

Flight of the Condor   200m   VI,5 ★★

SM Richardson and J Ashbridge, 17 April 1993

Start as for Indicator Wall and climb a ramp to the groove of the Right-Hand Variant (20m), then a short icy wall to gain the buttress crest on the right. Follow a groove to the left of a prominent block, then go up and right to a stance below the slabby groove of Riders on the Storm (45m). Follow grooves until level with the stepped rightward line cutting across the face (25m). Descend and cross Albatross, continuing right. Thinly iced slabs at 25m lead to the upper traverse-line, which is followed to its end (45m). Continue moving right, then up on thin slabs to below an overhanging chimney. Step down right from the base of the chimney to a stance below and left of the final chimney of Stormy Petrel (45m). Ascend the ice wall above (15m), then go on to the top (30m). A steep alternative finish is possible by following the corner that cuts through the headwall between Albatross and Stormy Petrel. Start at the end of the third pitch of the previous climb (**Mickey Mouse Finish**, *50m, VI,6, R Clothier and D McGimpsey, 17 April 1993*).

Le Nid d'Aigle   140m   VI,5 ★★

G Perroux and party, April 1993

The natural line between Riders on the Storm and Indicator Wall, the start of which is rarely iced. If so, start up the right side of Indicator Wall and traverse rightwards to the line. Icy grooves lead to the snow slopes of Indicator Wall, from which the final groove of Riders on the Storm can be reached.

Riders on the Storm   165m   VI,5 ★★★
D Hawthorn and E Todd, April 1986

Climb the obvious buttress to the right of Indicator Wall by a series of corners and stepped icy grooves. Start just to the left of the lowest point of the buttress.

Ship of Fools   150m   VIII,7
S Richardson and I Small, 1 April 2007

A brilliant icy mixed route. Start from the base of the pillar right of Riders on the Storm and climb the discontinuous groove up the broad rib to below the steep pillar (30m). Move up the hanging slab right of Riders on the Storm on thin ice over an overlap and second slab to a small ledge. Continue until a 3m traverse right can be made over the overhang to the foot of the upper pillar (30m). Climb a steep break in the wall above and then go right to overlook Albatross. Move left 2m along a crack before more thinly iced slabs and roofs lead to easier ground below the final icefall (60m). Climb an icy fault left of the icefall for 10m, then step left onto the sharp arête. Sensational climbing up this leads to the top (30m).

Arctic Tern   140m   VII,5
S Richardson and I Small, 25 April 2007

Start as for Albatross and climb straight up icy slabs to a V-corner, 5m left of the twin grooves of Albatross (30m). Step left onto a steep ice runnel, which leads to the slab of Fascist Groove, and continue up an easier groove for 10m. Climb a stepped groove in the left wall (thinly iced and delicate) for 20m, then continue up the crest of the rib (45m) to the traverse-line of Flight of the Condor (45m). A 5m chimney on the right followed by a left-facing groove is climbed for 20m before a step right onto the blunt rib between Nid d'Aigle and Riders on the Storm (45m). Ice on the right of the rib leads to the top (20m).

Albatross   150m   VI,5 ★★★
C Higgins and M Geddes, 21 January 1978

A very open corner descends the face of the buttress about midway between Indicator Wall and Psychedelic Wall. Start slightly right of the main line and climb a groove for a pitch; then move back left to the main corner-line. Follow this.

An alternative start on the left is possible by climbing a groove above the top left-hand corner of the snowy bay at the foot of the route. Climb the groove to a belay at a slab below an overhang (25m). Move up right into a narrow groove above the overlap on the second pitch of Albatross (30m) (**Fascist Groove**, *55m, VI,6*, C Rice and R Webb, 12 February 1983*).

Indicator Wall (right side)

1 Riders on the Storm VI,5***
2 Albatross VI,5***
3 Rhyme of the Ancient Mariner VII,7**
4 Stormy Petrel VII,6***
5 Psychedelic Wall VI,5***
6 Satanic Verses V,5***
7 Shot in the Back IV,4
8 Caledonia V,5**

Rhyme of the Ancient Mariner   160m   VII,7 ★★

B Fyffe, J Edwards and E Tresidder, 8 March 2002 (bottom half)
B Fyffe and E Tresidder, 19 March 2002

This route climbs to the obvious large hanging corner between Albatross and Stormy Petrel, breaking out left onto the arête, and taking a series of icy groves parallel to Albatross. The first two pitches are very similar to the right-hand start of Albatross, but the last two are separate.

Start in icy grooves halfway between Albatross and Stormy Petrel. Climb icy grooves up and left to a good rock-belay below a steep wall (40m). Traverse right from the belay until it is possible to cut back up and left to a hanging slab. Traverse left across this and out along a ledge to a large spike (20m). Climb the icy groove above on the crest onto easier ground. Go straight up to belay at the base of a steep wall (40m). Steep mixed moves off the belay lead to the right end of a diagonal ledge. Step up and left of this ledge and make more steep moves up and right in the depression above (crux) to gain ice again. Climb straight up icy slabs and corners to reach the top, well left of the Mickey Mouse Finish (60m).

Direct Start   90m   VII,7 ★★

I Parnell and V Scott, 24 March 2007

The line originally attempted by B Fyffe, and now the usual line taken. After 30m break out left up an obvious corner-groove (protected by a crack just above). From the top of the groove step left onto a hanging slab and traverse left to belay below a hanging icicle (50m). Steep mixed moves up an overhanging groove gain the icicle lead to the original route.

Stormy Petrel   160m   VII,6 ★★★

D Cuthbertson and R Kane, 1982

A serious route with poor protection. Climb slabs right of the big open corner right of Albatross. Climb rightwards up a shallow ramp, then direct to a rock spike beneath an overlap (30m). Cross the overlap, then go right horizontally over ribs to belay at the roof of an impressive corner (21m). Climb the left wall of the corner to large slab above. Ascend steeply right in two pitches over slabs, corners and grooves (crux), turning a roof on the right. Belay at the foot of another corner (39m and 15m). Climb the corner, then go left, weaving through bulges, and right to a shallow chimney and on to the final slopes, just left of Psychedelic Wall.

Psychedelic Wall   180m   VI,5 ★★★

N Muir and A Paul, January 1978

A direct line starting from the rocks opposite the foot of the left edge of Gardyloo Buttress. Climb iced rocks to a snow bay. Continue up steeply to gain a left-trending snow ramp, and from near its top take a groove leading to the left edge of a large plinth (50m). Continue up slabs and an open corner to beneath thin slabs, which are followed up to a corner, high on the right (40m). Climb the corner and a chimney to a steep wall. Go left and ascend the right hand of three corners to easier ground (45m). Climb up left to pass the cornice (30m).

Note On the second pitch it is possible to climb direct until 5m below an icicle fringe (belay). Climb to the icicle fringe, step left and follow ice to the top.

Satanic Verses   115m V,5 ★★★
C Cartwright and R Clothier, 7 April 1989
Start immediately right of Psychedelic Wall and climb the left hand of four parallel ramps which rise up right across the slabby wall. Climb to a second snow patch at 50m. Ascend grooves directly to a large snow bay (35m), belay. Climb the steep left wall and grooves above to the cornice, which may be overcome to the left if it is too large at the approach point.

Shot in the Dark   120m V,5 ★★★
M Geddes and A Rouse, 11 February 1978
On the left wall of Gardyloo Gully, 30m up from the toe of the buttress and right of Psychedelic Wall route. Aim initially for the oblong roof high on the wall above. Cross several rightward-slanting overlapping grooves to a short corner. Climb this, then traverse right across another groove and steep slab to finish some distance right of the oblong roof.

Caledonia   100m V,5 ★★
D Gardner and A Paul, 18 February 1978
Climbs the steep slab corner about 60m up right of Psychedelic Wall to gain a snow bay. Move up a rightward-trending snow ramp and steep slabs above, turning bulges on the right. This route finishes a little left of Shot in the Dark, left of the oblong roof.

Shot in the Back   70m IV,4
D Wilkinson and B Davison, 20 April 2001
A short route starting 25m below the big chockstone of Gardyloo Gully and climbing a shallow groove right of a rib.

Shot in the Foot   50m V,4
JL Bermudez and N Wilson, 4 April 1993
Climbs an icefall on the left wall of Gardyloo Gully, starting below the chockstone.

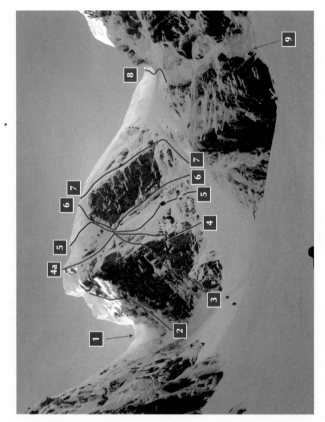

Gardyloo Buttress and Tower Scoop

1 Gardyloo Gully II/III**
2 Shot in the Light IV,5
3 Left Edge VI,5*
4 Kellett's Route VI,6***
4a Augean Alley V,5**
5 Smith's Route V,5***
6 The Great Glen VI,5*
7 Right Edge III*
8 Tower Gully I
9 Tower Scoop III***

Gardyloo Gully   170m   II/III ★★
G Hastings and WP Haskett-Smith, 26 April 1896
The obvious direct continuation to Observatory Gully. Normally a snow slope leads to a great chockstone about 40m below the cornice. Sometimes there is a tunnel beneath the chockstone, which leads to a short steep ice pitch, but in exceptional winters the whole route banks out. The cornice can be difficult.

Gardyloo Buttress

This buttress is an a very exposed position at the top of Observatory Gully, between Gardyloo Gully on the left and Tower Gully on the right. Tower Scoop can be climbed on the way to break the endless climb up Observatory Gully. The cornices can be very considerable above this buttress and may be impossible to breach at times.

Shot in the Light   100m   IV,5
AV Saunders and P Thornhill, 1983
Climb the first break on the right, 50m up Gardyloo Gully, initially up right to a belay (40m) then delicately back up left.

Left Edge   155m   VI,5 ★
R Carrington and A Rouse, March 1976
This route requires a very good plating of ice and snow. A peg for tension was used high up to gain the upper slabs. Start at the left edge of the buttress and climb the arête up rightwards until level with the upper chute of Smith's Route to the right (100m). Move across to the chute and finish up this.

Kellett's Route   120m   VI,6 ★★★
A Paul and K Leinster, 1980
The most obvious line up the buttress is the leftwards-slanting icefall of Smith's Route, leading to a snow chute in the upper part. Kellett's Route starts midway between Left Edge and this icefall, and climbs directly to join Smith's Route (original) just below the chute.

Augean Alley   120m   V,5 (top section) ★★
K Leinster, A Paul and G Reilly, March 1981
This route climbs Kellett's Route (see above) and finishes on the left-hand ridge bounding the finish of Smith's Route.

Gardyloo Buttress

1 Left Edge VI,5*
2 Kellett's Route VI,6***
2a Augean Alley V,5 (top section)**
3 Murphy's Route VI,6
4 Smith's Route V,5***

4a Icicle Variation V,5**
5 The Great Glen VI,5*
6 Right Edge III*
7 Tower Gully I

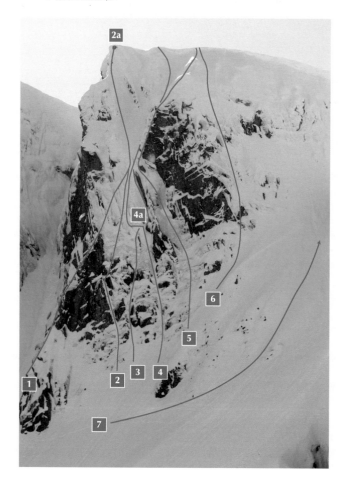

Andy Turner and Dave MacLeod climbing Smith's Route, 50 years after its first ascent

Murphy's Route   130m   VI,6
RG Webb and A Shand, March 1983
Between Kellet's Route and Smith's Route. Climb a short icy groove and mixed ground to a shallow cave beneath Smith's Route (original). Go steeply up to an airy belay on Smith's Route (50m). Climb up towards Augean Alley (30m) and finish up this (50m).

Smith's Route   130m   V,5 ★★★
R Smith and JR Marshall, 8 February 1960
Climb leftwards up the obvious slanting ice grooves and slabs to a belay in an icy bay with an icicle fringe (45m). Move diagonally leftwards to steeper ground, then back up and right to the right-hand groove. Go up this to the snow chute (40m) and an easier finish. A more popular variation is to climb an icicle direct from the icy bay to gain the right-hand groove, which is followed to the snow chute (**Icicle Variation**, *V,5***, KV Crocket and C Gilmore, February 1975*). If the cornice is very large it may be possible to avoid it to the left by a steep wall and narrow ridge finish.

The Great Glen   130m   VI,5 ★
P Braithwaite and P Moores, 12 February 1978
The route follows the steep shallow groove right of Smith's Route to exit left across a gangway to belay right of Smith's Route (51m). Re-enter the groove and follow the steep arête on the right to snow. (Serious – take a long rope.)

Tower Ridge
(upper east side)

1 Tower Gully I
2 Upper Tower Cascade Left III
3 Upper Tower Cascade
  Central VI,5
4 Upper Tower Cascade Right III
5 Tower Ridge IV,3***
6 Eastern Traverse escape
7 Faith Healer VIII,7*

Close to the Edge
100m   IV,4 ★

R Hamilton and S Kennedy, 3 February 2007

A line close to the true right edge of the buttress, requiring a good build-up of ice and starting almost directly below the edge at the lowest rocks. Follow a narrow left-trending groove just right of the edge and move back left at the top onto a slab. Slabs, bulges and overlaps lead fairly directly to the top.

Right Edge
130m   III ★

R Millward and F von Gemert, January 1977

Move up from the start of the Great Glen rightwards to gain the right arête of the buttress. Follow this to the top.

Tower Gully
120m   I

G Hastings, ELW and WP Haskett-Smith, 25 April 1897

Follow a broad snow terrace rightwards from the foot of Gardyloo Gully, below the buttress and above Tower Scoop, to gain the gully proper. This is easy, but the cornice is often large.

To the right of Tower Gully three cascades form, starting at the foot of the gully, the Upper Tower Cascades. **Upper Tower Cascade Left** is III, **Upper Tower Cascade Central** is IV,5 and 100m, and **Upper Tower Cascade Right** is III.

Tower Ridge – East Side

The following climbs lie on the East Side of Tower Ridge starting from Observatory Gully.

Tower Scoop
65m   III ★★★

I Clough and G Grandison, 4 January 1961

Below the snow terrace which runs from the foot of Gardyloo Gully, beneath Gardyloo Buttress to Tower Gully, is a band of icy cliffs which almost block off Observatory Gully at 1150m. The route follows a central ice smear in two or three pitches. Various exits are possible from the top.

Note To the left of this ice smear various short lines are possible, and a little harder than Tower Scoop.

Tower Cleft
75m   III ★

G Pratt and J Francis, 19 February 1949

To the right of Tower Scoop is a deep cave-like cleft formed in the angle with the east flank of Tower Ridge. It can be very entertaining or impossible! (Move out left to escape from the cleft.)

Tower Ridge (lower east side)

1 East Wall Route II/III
2 Faith Healer VIII,7*
3 Echo Traverse III
3a Echo Traverse – Direct Start V,5
4 Going Round the Bend IV,5
5 The Edge of Beyond VI,6**
6 The Brass Monkey VII,8
7 The Great Chimney IV,5***
8 Chimney Groove IV,6
9 Lower East Wall Route III

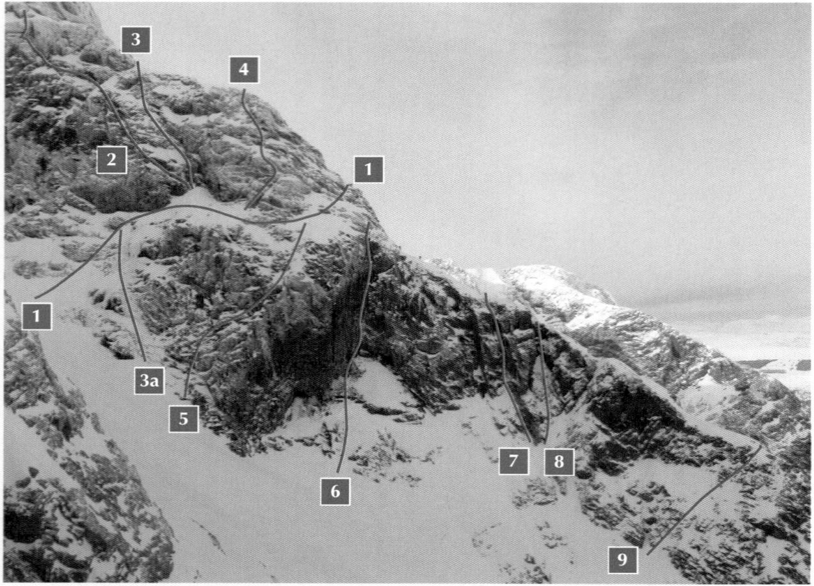

Clefthanger
90m   VI,6 ★★

D Hawthorn and A Paul, January 1985

Start at the foot of Tower Cleft and climb a corner system on the right wall. Climb 20m to a large ledge below a corner. Traverse right round an arête into a clean corner, which is climbed passing a large dubious flake halfway on the left. Move up left by slabs, chimney and grooves.

East Wall Route
110m   II/III

JR Marshall and R Marshall, February 1966

Starts just downhill and to the right of Tower Cleft. Climb one or two pitches to a snow ledge beneath a steep wall. Traverse right on steep snow to join the crest of Tower Ridge.

Faith Healer
170m   VIII,7 ★

I Small and I Parnell, 28 January 2010

An absorbing and delicate icy mixed climb with a superb but savage sting in the tail. Ice on the ledges and slabs was found very useful on the first ascent, but the final corner (avoidable) will always be hard and serious. Climb Echo Traverse for a few metres before a delicate traverse left gains a prominent ramp, which is followed leftwards for 30m. Move up to belay at the base of the big leftwards-slanting corner (50m). Climb the corner to a large snow ledge (50m). Follow the snow ledge diagonally up left until below a steep corner on the left of a rock prow. Climb the first section of the corner for 10m on helpful turf to reach a ledge on the left. Follow this leftwards and step down a short corner to belay on *in situ* threads (50m). Step back right and climb the steep corner to reach the large snow ledge of the Eastern Traverse of Tower Ridge (20m). Follow Tower Ridge to the summit.

Echo Traverse
135m   III

JR Marshall and R Marshall, February 1966

Follow East Wall Route until below a recessed chimney. Take a groove on the left to a spike (6m), and traverse left on thin slabs to a chimney-groove, which is climbed to a snow bay. Continue above in a left-trending fault to the ridge below the Great Tower. A direct icefall start is possible (*50m, V,5, A Paul and P Moores, 22 March 1992*).

Going Round the Bend
120m   IV,5

R Jenkin and A Brett, 31 December 2001

Starting at the recessed chimney of Echo Traverse, climb the right-slanting chimney to its right, then zig-zag right then left to the top of the Little Tower.

Dave MacLeod climbing The Great Chimney, 50 years after its first ascent
(photo: Paul Diffley)

The Edge of Beyond   200m   VI,6 ★★
DF Lang and C Stead, 26 March 1994
Left of The Great Chimney (see below) is the impressively steep Echo Wall. This route starts 15m up left of the projecting left edge of Echo Wall. Gain a ledge-system and go rightwards, passing an obvious flake at 10m. Keep going right until it is possible to move up left to a ledge (40m). Go right for 6m, then up an icy corner and grooves to gain a ledge on the left, then right to an icefall which ascends to easy ground (45m). A further 25m leads to the traverse ledge of East Wall Route, from which Tower Ridge can be gained to the right or by continuing straight up to the top of the Little Tower.

The Brass Monkey   135m   VII,8
T Marsh and P Davies, 5 December 2008
A superb mixed climb following the corner right of Echo Wall. Climb directly up slabs towards the corner (40m). Climb the short wall on the left on thin ice and follow the icy upper slab to base of the main corner (20m). Climb the corner for 3m before strenuous moves right (crux) to reach more cracks leading to a belay (10m). The sustained off-width crack, exiting right, leads to a good ledge (40m). Continue up the corner-crack and back and foot the top chimney in a superb position (25m).

The Great Chimney   65m   IV,5 ★★★
JR Marshall and R Smith, 6 February 1960
Climbs the obvious deep chimney which arrives on the ridge 50m below the Little Tower. Ascend the chimney past a belay under a vertical block, then take the left crack and walls to the ridge.

Chimney Groove   90m   IV,6
C Stead and D Lang, 27 February 1993
Start 60m down from The Great Chimney, go right and up to a flake-belay below a bulge, which is climbed with difficulty to easier ground. The bulge may be avoidable on the right, depending on conditions.

Lower East Wall Route   125m   III
KV Crocket and C Gilmore, 25 March 1974
Start as for the previous route, climb a short overhang and follow ledges rightwards to the ridge above the first steep section.

Tower Ridge   500m ascent, 1000m of climbing   IV,3 ★★★
JN Collie, GA Solly and J Collier, 30 March 1894
This, the most famous of the great Nevis ridges, is a magnificent expedition. It is technically easier than the North East Buttress and Observatory Ridge, but it should

Tower Ridge

1 Tower Ridge IV,3***
2 1934 Route II/III**
3 Vanishing Gully V,5***
4 Garadh Gully II/III or I or IV

not be underrated. The main difficulties are concentrated high up, and the whole route is exceptionally long and arduous, fully justifying its grade of IV.

The normal winter route avoids the face of the Douglas Boulder by entering the foot of Observatory Gully to the left and then cutting back right to climb the East Gully to Douglas Gap (I). An alternative start is via the Douglas Gap West Gully (I). From the gap an awkward 20m groove/chimney leads to the crest of the ridge, which rises gently and becomes quite narrow. It is possible to reach this section and avoid the moves out of the Douglas Gap by traversing in from higher up Observatory Gully over rocky steps and steep snowfields (II). From the narrow section, most teams go out right on a gently rising steep snow ramp until overlooking the west flank above Vanishing Gully. Cut back up left onto the crest and follow it past The Great Chimney on the left to beneath the Little Tower. This usually requires three pitches of climbing, the first over a huge spike with a step right out of a groove above, and the second on the left up a groove leading to a huge flat boulder. Above the flat top of the Little Tower an easier section leads to the foot of the Great Tower, an impossibly steep rock step. On the left side of the tower a very exposed and steeply banked snow ledge (the Eastern Traverse) is followed horizontally left, down slightly and round an edge to beneath a huge fallen-block chimney. Pass the block, steep walls and ledges to the top of the Great Tower with some difficulty. Follow the very narrow and exposed crest towards Tower Gap, descending slightly. Climb down into the gap (tricky and loose) and either ascend the far wall or a slab on the left. The main difficulties are over once

Below the Great Tower of Tower Ridge

Tower Gap has been negotiated. Climb the final section of the ridge to the plateau, moving right beneath a steep wall at the top.

Note It is possible to continue the Eastern Traverse by an exposed delicate step further left from the foot of the chimney. This leads to a very exposed and steeply banked snowfield traversing to Tower Gully and avoids the difficulties higher up. This may be a good ploy for teams who are late and tired and wish to avoid a night out. On reaching Tower Gully it is also possible to descend with care to the hut by a traverse beneath Gardyloo Buttress and on down Observatory Gully.

The first ascencionists overcame the Great Tower by taking the cliff on the west side (**Western Traverse**, *70m, IV,4***). For fast parties on top form and blighted by queues on the Eastern Traverse this more difficult way may offer a chance to get in front (or lose your place in the line). Not for the faint-hearted!

Douglas Boulder

This large area of rock is the lower termination of Tower Ridge and lies immediately above the hut. It is triangular in shape and may provide good mixed climbing when higher routes are out of condition due to strong winds and avalanche potential.

Direct Route   215m   IV,4 ★

JR Marshall and party, 1958

Start at the lowest rocks left of an obvious smooth slab. Follow a shallow groove (45m) to an open chimney. Follow this (60m) to a good ledge. Traverse right and climb steeply to the top of the Boulder.

Note Could be very difficult in lean conditions.

Down to the Wire   220m   V,6

B Goodlad and J Turner, 23 March 1993

Follow Direct Route to the base of the chimney (80m) and then the groove on the right (40m). Move up left, crossing Direct Route to follow the curving corner on the left (30m). Climb the corner to a spike and move to a slab on the right (30m). Overcome a leaning block then icy grooves to the top (40m).

Turf War   250m   V,6

G Hughes and J Edwards, 21 January 2003

Based on the chimney left of Left-Hand Chimney, and starting in the middle of the lower tier directly below the chimney. Climb up into a bay in the middle of the lower tier and head for a short V-groove in the second band. Climb the groove and slant right to overhangs (60m). Avoid the knobbly wall by going right then left, heading for the chimney. Climb this to a thread on a ledge (40m). Climb the

Douglas Boulder

1 Turf War V,6
2 Left-Hand Chimney IV,4
3 North-West Face Route V,5
4 Right-Hand Chimney VI,7

5 Gutless IV,5
6 Cutlass VI,7*
7 South West Ridge III*

chimney (30m). Continue up, then traverse delicately right across slabs to climb a right-facing corner on turf to a large block (50m). Climb easier ground on the left and a short overhanging chimney to a slab. Climb a corner to reach a ledge on the right, then back left to climb the poorly protected arête. Step right to belay (60m). Move up to easy ground to the top (10m).

Left-Hand Chimney   215m   IV,4
R Carrington and JR Marshall, February 1972

This route climbs the left-hand chimney (see next route). Start from the left and traverse over snow from the lowest rocks. Gain the chimney by a short vertical wall and follow it with sustained difficulties to the top. An alternative start in two pitches takes a left-trending line heading for a black overhanging wall, avoided on the right.

North-West Face Route   215m   V,5
A Slater and G Grassam, February 1980

Seen from the CIC Hut, three chimneys form an inverted 'N' on the Douglas Boulder. This route follows the central chimney. Gain the chimney, which is followed until 6m below a chockstone. Traverse slabs to a rib on the right and climb up to regain the top of the chimney. Follow snow ramps and grooves to the South West Ridge. Snow-ice is required in the chimney.

Right-Hand Chimney   215m   VI,7
O Metherell and G Hughes, 19 December 2004

Starting directly under the chimney in a bay, climb to the foot of the chimney (45m). Bridge up the first overhang and belay on the left (15m). Follow the chimney, turning an overhang on the right to a recess. Exit left up slabs to above a second recess (50m). Traverse right to South West Ridge.

Gutless   180m   IV,5
P McKenna and D Sanderson, March 1979

Left of Cutlass is a prominent chimney, which is climbed to a rightward-sloping ledge (90m). Climb the ledge to the edge of the buttress and on to the top of the Boulder.

Western Grooves   195m   IV,5
T Anderson and GE Little, 8 April 1979

Start in the snow bay left of Cutlass and trend up left to the foot of a shallow groove (45m). Climb the corner-groove for two pitches to a flake. Go left round a rib and climb a ramp to belay below a semi-detached flake. Follow the groove above and a right-trending ramp towards the South West Ridge.

Walking Through Fire   130m   VII,7
R Bentley and M Davies, 14 March 2008
The groove system left of Cutlass. Reach the ledge below Cutlass (40m). Traverse left to the end of the ledge and climb the grooves above to below an inverted V-overhang (25m). Climb the overhang directly into a V-groove (25m). Continue up the V-groove and the chimneys to reach the South West Ridge (40m).

Cutlass   145m   VI,7 ★
A Clarke and J Main, 24 March 1989
The clean-cut corner 30m left of the South West Ridge. Climb the corner, a chimney and a cracked wall to reach the South West Ridge.

Jacknife   90m   IV,6
J Baird and A Turner, 26 November 2003
The first groove left of the South West Ridge. Starting to the left, climb slabs to the groove (50m). Climb the groove and the right crack to a ledge (25m). Climb a crack and loose flake then go right to the South West Ridge (15m).

South West Ridge   180m   III ★
JY McDonald and HW Turnbull, March 1934
Follow the crest of the ridge bounding the left side of Douglas Gap West Gully.

Douglas Gap West Gully   180m   I ★★
A straightforward ascent on steep snow with better scenery than the East Gully. A good low-level outing is the combination of Douglas Gap West Gully, followed by the descent of the Douglas Gap East Gully.

CLIMBS FROM COIRE NA CISTE

Generally the climbs in Coire na Ciste are shorter and less committing than those in Observatory Gully. However, it also holds some of the hardest winter climbs in the world. From the CIC Hut there are several approach routes into Coire na Ciste, and the time taken to the higher routes can be as much as an hour. About 200m south-west of the CIC Hut is a steep rocky bluff with deep gorges on its left- and right-hand sides. The most straightforward approach into Coire na Ciste is by the slopes right (north-west) of the right-hand gorge mentioned above, or by the gorge itself, if it has a good banking of snow. This approach can be reached from a crossing of the stream a few hundred metres below the hut. The left-hand gorge has been the

Coire na Ciste

1 Great Tower of Tower Ridge
2 Garadh Gully
3 Number Two Gully
4 The Comb
5 Number Three Gully Buttress
6 Number Three Gully
7 Creag Coire na Ciste
8 Number Four Gully
9 South Trident Buttress
10 North Trident Buttress
11 Moonlight Gully Buttress
12 Number Five Gully
13 The Curtain

scene of some fatal avalanche accidents over the years. When approaching routes on the left (south) side of the coire, it is best to skirt this gorge on the right, where it looks easiest, and traverse in high above the gorge beneath Garadh Buttress. The Vanishing Gully area can be approached by moving in from close beneath the Douglas Boulder, well above the gorge on its left.

The major features of Coire na Ciste when seen from the hut are, from left to right: Tower Ridge and Secondary Tower Ridge, Garadh Gully and Buttress (Garadh na Ciste), the thin gullies of Number Two and The Comb (exits unseen), the triangle of Comb Buttress, the obvious gap of Number Three Gully (lowest point on the skyline), Creag Coire na Ciste, the Trident Buttress area and, low down to the left of Number Five Gully, Moonlight Gully Buttress.

Tower Ridge – West Side

Being clearly visible from the walk in and having a shorter approach than many other areas, these are popular climbs when in condition. The icy mixed climbs on Pinnacle Buttress to the left of Glover's Chimney offer long routes in an excellent position and deserve greater popularity.

Watery Fowls   150m   V,7
S Richardson and I Parnell, 20 November 2004
Starting 20m left of Fawlty Towers, climb a steep cracked wall by a series of corners, then move up easier ground (50m). A vague groove leads over a steep bulge to the top.

Fawlty Towers   155m   II
T McAulay and N Muir, 2 April 1980
Take the first icefall right of Douglas Gap West Gully and follow slightly rightwards to the first narrow crest of Tower Ridge.

1934 Route   185m   II/III ★★
JY MacDonald and HW Turnbull, March 1934
Start 45m right of Douglas Gap West Gully, further right again than Fawlty Towers. Climb via grooves and snow bays until a shallow gully can be gained via icy slabs on the right. This gully leads to the snow shelf above the hard pitches of Vanishing Gully, and leads with one short icy section to Tower Ridge below the Little Tower. An alternative for a short day is to climb direct to Tower Ridge instead of taking the shallow gully up right, followed by a fairly easy descent into Observatory Gully on the east side. A good low-grade, low-level outing.

Tower Ridge (west side)

1 Douglas Gap West Gully I**
2 Fawlty Towers II
3 1934 Route II/III**
4 Vanishing Gully V,5***
5 1931 Route IV,4
6 Italian Climb –
   Right-Hand IV,4***
7 The Chute V,4**
8 Garadh Gully II/III or I or IV
9 Broad Gully II
10 Glover's Chimney III,4**
11 Raeburn's Easy Route II/III
12 Number Two Gully II***

Running Hot   120m   V,5
M Duff, J Tinker and R Nowack, 8 February 1986
Start just left of Vanishing Gully and climb slabs towards a leftwards traverse, which is taken for a short way until it is possible to climb another slab to a recess beneath a roof. Overcome the roof on the right and go diagonally left to a corner and short wall, which gains a stance in a recess. Go right to a groove and descend 3m, then right to another groove, which is climbed to a spike. Exit left and on to the top.

Vanishing Gully   200m   V,5 ★★★
R Marshall and G Tiso, 15 January 1961
Start at an icefall about 100m right of Douglas Gap West Gully and climb to a cave with good belays. Climb out of the cave on very steep ice and continue until easier ground leads right to Tower Ridge. It is quicker to descend the ridge from this point than to carry on up.

Note The cave belay is often blocked out by ice. At the top a shallow gully (1934 Route) can be down-climbed or abseiled leftwards. This is a good alternative if short on time or good weather.

Pirate   150m   IV,4
M Duff and A Nisbet, 3 January 1986
20m right of Vanishing Gully. Move easily up left on a snow ramp, over a wall and into a small left-facing corner (45m). Climb slabs left of the corner to a steep wall bounded on the right by a large corner. Go right beneath the corner and ascend the rib right of the second corner, then slant left into a vertical corner (45m). Follow the corner, then go right into a shallow chimney (30m) and grooves to the crest of Secondary Tower Ridge (45m).

Fish Eye Chimney   150m   V,5
N Holmes and D Lampard, January 1987
Climbs an obvious parallel-sided slot just right of Pirate. Start just left of 1931 Route and traverse on mixed ground awkwardly up left to the base of the chimney. Climb the chimney (50m) and a large groove to the crest of Secondary Tower Ridge.

Fat Boy Slim   120m   VI,6 ★
C Cartwright and S Richardson, 24 February 2002
The overhanging chimney left of 1931 Route. Climb the chimney (30m), then the rib above, before stepping right into the easier upper gully (25m). Follow this (50m), and climb either over or under a prominent chockstone (15m).

1931 Route   125m   IV,4

G Wallace and R Shaw, 21 January 1961

Start in a bay 150m right of Douglas Gap West Gully formed by a steep buttress, from which two chimneys lead to the crest of Secondary Tower Ridge. Climb the right-hand chimney for three short pitches to the large snowfield of 1934 Route, which is followed either up or down.

Rogue's Rib   220m   IV,5

IS Clough and G Grandison, 2 January 1960

Takes the two-tier buttress which projects from Tower Ridge left of Italian Climb. Start up Italian Climb (original line), then go by cracks and grooves to the top of the buttress.

The Italian Climb   180m   III ★

J Marshall, A MacCorquodale and G Ritchie, January 1958

Continuing along beneath the west side of Tower Ridge one comes to a deep gully bounded on the left by a prominent two-tier rib. Climb the gully; after a starting pitch easy snow leads to another pitch giving access to a huge recess. Traverse right and ascend an easy snow slope (frequent avalanche danger) to Tower Ridge.

The Italian Job   200m   VIII,9 ★

D MacLeod and T Emmett, February 2006

The true finish to Italian Climb, including the huge overhang at the top! Climb three pitches into a spooky cave. Work up and left across the overhanging wall on thin hooks to reach the groove, which is climbed to the top. The top groove is bold, but might be a bit easier if iced.

Italian Climb – Right-Hand   65m   IV,4 ★★★

S Belk and I Fulton, February 1973

A popular variation, which takes the obvious icefall above the start of the first pitch and parallel to and right of the main gully. The icefall is followed in one long pitch to a good belay. Many parties abseil from the end of the difficult pitch in order to save a long ascent of Tower Ridge. In this way it is possible to do another route, such as Vanishing Gully, plus another abseil descent.

Bydand   150m   V,5 ★

M Duff, M Aldridge and J Woods, 31 January 1986

Climb two steep icy chimneys and a sharply defined curving groove right of Italian Climb.

Heavy conditions in Garadh Gully

The Chute
230m V,4 ★★

JR Marshall, RN Campbell and R Holt, February 1965

About 40m right of Italian Climb, this route does not often come into condition, but when it does an excellent route is the result. Climb by an extremely steep entry pitch, left then right into a groove, which is followed to a ledge (45m) that leads across a steep wall into a small gully (35m). Traverse up right to beneath a steep ice wall (35m). Climb the ice (25m) and the gully beyond (65m) to the base of a steep buttress. Move easily right into Broad Gully, which can be descended to the coire or ascended to Tower Ridge.

Garadh Gully
95m II/III or I or IV!!

I Clough and M Burke, 16 February 1958

Starts just above and right of Italian Climb and separates the steep little buttress of Garadh na Ciste from Tower Ridge. Can be difficult early in the season, but easy later on (easily seen from CIC Hut).

Garadh Buttress
95m III

N Muir and G Whitten, February 1970

Climb the buttress right of Garadh Gully by a line of snow and ice ramps up its centre.

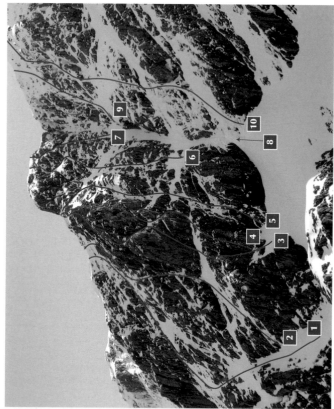

Pinnacle Buttress of The Tower

1 Broad Gully II
2 Fatal Error IV,4**
3 Stringfellow VI,6**
4 Smooth Operator VI,7
5 Pinnacle Buttress Direct V,5**
6 Pinnacle Buttress
7 Right-Hand IV,4
8 Silent Spring V,5
9 Glover's Chimney III,4**
10 The White Line III**

*To the right of the Garadh and above the exit of the gorge approach, a long snow slope tapers up between the flanks of **Tower Ridge** and the prominent conical buttress of **The Comb**, to terminate as **Number Two Gully**. This slope is the approach for climbs from **Pinnacle Buttress of the Tower** to **Pigott's Route**.*

Broad Gully   95m II
IS Clough and M Burke, 16 February 1958
From the top of Garadh Gully follow the line of least resistance up leftwards, skirting the large buttress above (Pinnacle Buttress) to the crest of Tower Ridge.

Pincer   200m IV,4
C Cartwright and S Richardson, 15 December 2002
A good mixed route taking the left crest of Pinnacle Buttress, starting 100m up Broad Gully at the foot of the crest. Climb mixed ground just right of the crest for four pitches to The Pinnacle. The finish is by a 15m V-chimney leading to the summit of The Pinnacle. The easy-angled ridge then leads to the Great Tower.

Pinnacle Buttress of the Tower   175m III,4 ★
DJ Bennett and A Tait, 17 November 1957
Starting from the top of Garadh na Ciste, Broad Gully is followed to the left for about 70m, before traversing right 80m along a ledge above overhanging rocks and beneath the steep crest of the buttress. Beyond the crest the rocks are more broken, and the climb now follows a series of snow grooves in the right flank until it is possible to move leftwards to the top of the buttress. Follow a ridge to the foot of the Great Tower and traverse right until a line of chimneys can be followed to the top of it.

Fatal Error   230m IV,4 ★★
G Dudley and S Richardson, 24 March 1996
Starts 50m up Broad Gully. Climb up over flakes and a short wall to the snow terrace (60m). Climb an icy slab to enter the prominent gully-line on the left flank of the buttress above. Go up the gully to a steepening (35m), then left to the end of a ramp and block-belay (5m). Go right along an upper ramp to regain the gully, which is climbed to its end, followed by an ascending leftward traverse to the left edge of the buttress (45m). Ascend the edge of the buttress to a snowy ledge (35m). Go left onto Tower Ridge 30m below the Great Tower (50m).

Face Dancer   240m VI,6 ★
S Richardson and C Cartwright, 18 February 2001
A good ice route requiring a good build-up of ice on the lower slabs, starting below

Stringfellow. Climb up and left in two pitches to the snow terrace below a prominent gully running up the buttress (60m). A short icy slab gains the gully, then move right into a hanging ramp, which is followed to a good stance below a steep corner (40m). Follow the narrowing ramp to its end, step left and follow a shallow gully over a bulge before trending left to the foot of a right-facing corner (50m). Climb the corner, swing left at a notch at its top and traverse left along an awkward ledge to a small pinnacle on Stringfellow (40m). The easy-angled ridge leads to the Great Tower (50m).

Stringfellow   240m   VI,6 ★★

C Cartwright and S Richardson, 11 March 1996

Start 30m left of Pinnacle Buttress Direct below a shallow gully. Climb the gully to the terrace, which is crossed to below a rake slanting left to right up the lower section of the buttress (50m). Climb the rake to its right end over a steep wall to a cave belay (50m). Climb up left via a shallow gully to a platform just left of the crest (25m). A short icy wall cut by a crack is climbed from the right of the platform, followed by the rightmost of twin grooves above. Climb up to a block, which is climbed by a wide crack on its left, then on up to a belay on the crest of the buttress. A hard pitch (40m). A step down is taken into a short gully on the right, which is climbed to the crest (25m). Carry on up the crest to the foot of the Great Tower on Tower Ridge.

Stringfellow Direct Finish   50m   V,5

J Currie and A Crofton, 2 April 1996

Start from the belay at the top of the hard 40m pitch. Climb the headwall, then go left to a notch. Go up and left, and traverse awkwardly left along a narrow ledge to a wide gap formed by a pinnacle (15m). Go through the gap and up a groove rightwards to the top of the buttress (35m).

Smooth Operator   210m   VI,7

S Richardson and C Cartwright, 26 March 2000

Follows a line close to the crest of the buttress between Stringfellow and Butterfingers. Ascend the initial shallow gully of Stringfellow for 3m, then move right and up onto the crest, which is followed to the terrace (50m) and a belay below the gully of Butterfingers. Follow the right-facing corner on the left, then the left-trending gully to the cave stance (30m). Leave the cave on the right, then go left onto the steep wall. Follow a steep right-facing corner and tight chimney above to a belay on the right of the crest (30m). Climb the difficult wall above to the good stance at the top of pitch 3 of Butterfingers (10m). Follow Butterfingers to the right, then directly by a left-facing corner to broken blocks on the crest. This is a junction with Stringfellow (20m). Climb directly to the top of the buttress via a short left-facing corner and headwall above (20m). Continue to the foot of the Great Tower on Tower Ridge.

Butterfingers
220m   V,6

S Richardson and R Clothier, 13 February 1999

Start below Pinnacle Buttress Direct just right of the small snow bay. Ascend to a small inverted triangular wall and go left of Pinnacle Buttress Direct by mixed ground to the terrace (50m). A gully on the right of a steep corner is climbed to a ramp, which leads left to the cave stance at the top of pitch 2 of Stringfellow (30m). Leave the cave on the right and climb directly on easier ground, followed by a short slot to belay atop a huge block up on the left (35m). Trend up right via a ramp and steep chimney to a large platform on the crest. This is a junction with Stringfellow (30m). Climb the narrow ramp on the right of the buttress and the leftmost of two grooves to the crest (25m). Continue up towards the Great Tower of Tower Ridge along the easy-angled crest.

Pinnacle Buttress Direct
200m   V,5 ★★

R Clothier and G Armstrong, March 1989

Start midway between Glover's Chimney and Broad Gully in a snow bay, below an icefall and an obvious groove in the upper buttress. Follow a break up on the right side. Climb a ramp, then an icy wall, followed by the main groove-line to the Great Tower.

Pinnacle Buttress Right-Hand
150m   IV,4

R Carrington and B Hall, March 1976

Start as for Glover's Chimney, and then climb the icefall to the left of that route to easier ground on the left of the Chimney. Take either of the chimneys above and continue to the top of the Great Tower.

Silent Spring
100m   V,5

C Cartwright and S Richardson, 7 April 2002

On the opposite side of Glover's Chimney to the icefall of The Gutter, this climb takes a groove to a ledge below the Great Tower headwall (50m). A narrow slot then passes a ledge to a corner, then a hidden line of weakness trending left, then goes right to the top of the Great Tower (50m).

Glover's Chimney
200m   III,4 ★★

GG MacPhee, GC Williams and D Henderson, 17 March 1935

Starts above Garadh na Ciste and follows a long couloir leading to a chimney below the Tower Gap. The entry is made by an icefall, often over 35m high and very steep, usually climbed from left to right. The final chimney is the crux. The climb finishes in the Tower Gap. It is possible to descend into Observatory Gully and climb another route if time allows.

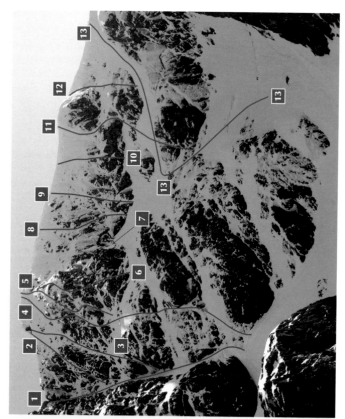

Goodeve's Buttress

1 Glover's Chimney III,4**
2 Mirror, Mirror IV,4
3 The Gutter IV,4***
4 The White Line III**
5 Hale Bopp Groove III,4*
6 Goodytwoshoes V,6*
7 Beam Me Up Scotty III*
8 Upper Cascade Central V,6
9 Upper Cascade Right V,6
10 Le Panthere Rose VI,6*
11 Fin Gourmet IV,4*
12 Expert's Choice III,4*
13 Raeburn's Easy Route II/III*

Note The area from Glover's Chimney to The Upper Cascades is called Goodeve's Buttress. All but the initial icefall of The White Line was originally descended then climbed by TE Goodeve, C Inglis-Clark and JHA McIntyre on 28 December 1907 on an epic escape from Tower Ridge!

Mirror, Mirror   120m IV,4
S Richardson and C Cartwright, 7 April 2002
The icefall to the left of The Gutter over an icy ramp, The Mirror (50m). Mixed ground leads to Tower Ridge.

The Gutter   275m IV,4 ★★★
Climb halfway up Glover's Chimney until an icefall (obvious from below) can be gained by a steep snow ramp on the right. Climb the icefall (50m) to easier ground and finish by the final section of Tower Ridge.

Tales of the Unexpected   200m IV,4
R Clothier, S Richardson and A Forsyth, 11 April 2009
Start by climbing Glover's Chimney for 100m and belay below the prominent icy groove cutting the right wall. Climb the V-groove, then snow, to belay just right of the icefall of The Gutter (60m). Climb ice on the left flank of the buttress for 20m, then pull right onto the buttress itself. Move up this to a good ledge (50m). Cross a gully cutting into the right flank of the buttress, climb a corner, then trend right up an icy groove to reach the top of the buttress (30m). Continue up easy ground to the top (60m).

Close Encounters   140m III,5
S Richardson, 13 April 2009
Start just left of the upper section of The White Line at the foot of the buttress taken by Tales of the Unexpected. Climb a snow ramp leading right, then the gully in the right flank of the buttress, to the buttress crest. Move up to a steep chimney blocked by an overhang, climb out right (crux) and continue easily to the plateau.

The White Line   275m III ★★
M Geddes and H Gillespie, 18 March 1971
Climb the icefall as for Glover's Chimney and continue to the right of the Chimney to a rightward-slanting snow ledge. Climb an icefall to a snowfield. Above the snowfield climb a chimney and gully to finish at the top of Tower Ridge. An alternative start follows the icefall right of the first pitch of Glover's Chimney.

This area is interesting if you wish to lose the crowds and find your own route. If you are confident on grade III/IV ground just follow your nose!

The Upper Cascades

All these cascades require water to run out of the snow above to freeze onto the rocks, so good snow cover followed by several thaw–freeze cycles will be needed to form the routes. Being fairly short, a couple of climbs might be completed in a day with a steep descent of Raeburn's Easy Route getting you back down to the next climb.

Hale Bopp Groove   120m III,4 ★

RG Reid and R Appleyard, 31 March 1996

The prominent groove in the centre of the front face of Goodeve's Buttress. Climb the groove to a fork (20m). Bridge up the main line of the groove and pull left to another groove-line (30m). Follow this groove to a terrace, move right along this and finish up a groove cutting back to the plateau at the top of Tower Ridge (70m).

The Alpine Princess   140m IV,4

S Richardson and Z Hart, 24 February 2009

From the foot of Hale Bopp Groove climb the upper wide snow ramp rightwards to the foot of a steep icy gully with a flat chockstone wedged across its top. Climb the gully, squeeze under the chockstone and exit right onto a good ledge (40m). Finish up Hale Bopp Groove on the left or climb the rib between The White Line and Hale Bopp Groove. Easy ground to the top (60m).

Three Men on a Rope   160m III

A Forsyth, S Richardson and R Clothier, 12 April 2009

A natural diagonal line across the front face of the buttress. Start by climbing the lower of the two diverging ramps at the foot of Hale Bopp Groove and continue all the way to join the ramp section of Beam Me Up Scotty. Follow this to the steep icy bulge and the top.

Goodytwoshoes   140m V,6 ★

S Richardson and C Cartwright, 6 April 2002

Start below a gully in the centre of the face. Climb the gully to an alcove at 40m and pull right over an overhang to a gully leading to a steep wall (50m). Climb the right hand of two cracks in the wall for 10m before stepping to the left-hand crack, which leads to easier ground. Move up and right up a couloir to a huge spike (40m). The icy groove of Hale Bopp Groove leads to the top (50m).

Techno Wall   140m   V,6
S Richardson and A Cave, 20 April 2008
Start as for Goodytwoshoes. Climb up and right through a steep section to gain
the steep blunt rib bounding The Borg Collective. Climb this rib to a large pin-
nacle block beneath the headwall (40m). Steep cracks lead to a steep wide niche.
Climb a steep crack on the right to reach a short hanging chimney-groove (30m).
Continue up easier ground to reach the plateau as for Hale Bopp Groove (70m).

Big Wednesday   140m   VI,6
M Turgeon, S Richardson, I Parnell and Z Hart, 25 February 2009
The left-facing groove in the upper part of the buttress. Start 10m right of the previous routes below a steep wall cut by a fault. Climb the fault and a bulge onto easier
ground. Move up to the foot of a short steep groove with a flake on its left side
(25m). Climb the icy groove to a good ledge that leads right to the foot of a left-
facing groove (15m). Climb the groove, moving left through a bulge at its top (40m).
Continue up easy ground to the top (60m).

The Borg Collective   150m   V,6
C Cartwright and S Richardson, 4 January 2003
Midway between Goodytwoshoes and Beam Me Up Scotty is a prominent chimney cutting through the buttress. Climb mixed ground and follow it to its end at a
steep V-groove (40m). Climb mixed ground on the right to a steep wall. Cracks in
the centre of the wall lead to the foot of a chimney (30m). Climb the chimney and
easier ground to the top as for Hale Bopp Groove (80m).

Beam Me Up Scotty   155m   III ★
RG Reid and I Crofton, March 1987
Start in a narrow snow bay above the beginning of the rightward traverse of
Raeburn's Easy Route and left of Upper Cascade. Follow a ramp-line right before
climbing icy grooves straight up. This route may coincide with an earlier line by R
Harvey and A Meekin, 1986 (see Raeburn's Easy Route).

The Upper Cascade   125m   V,5/6 ★★
G Perroux and J-P Desterke, April 1991
Above The Cascade (see below), go up 100m left to a steep curtain of ice on the top
left of a large snow bay. Climb vertically at first to a belay (40m), then more easily
to the top in two more pitches.

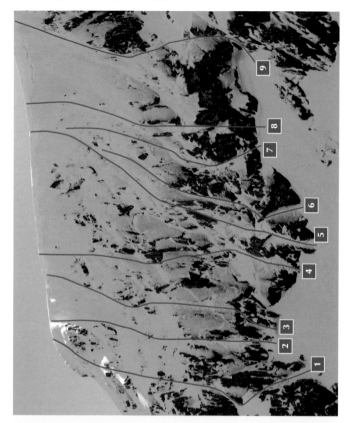

The Upper Cascades

1 Beam Me Up Scotty III*
2 The Upper Cascade V,5/6**
3 Life on Mars VI,6
4 Upper Cascade Central V,6
5 Upper Cascade Right V,6
6 Chiquita VI,5
7 Adieu and Farewell V,5
8 Le Panthere Rose VI,6*
9 Fin Gourmet IV,4*

Life on Mars   100m   VI,6
D MacGimpsey and A Nisbet, 2 April 2007
A large hanging slab reached by climbing steep ice to an alcove underneath the roof (two spike runners) and stepping right to climb a pillar onto the slab (50m). Continue up the groove to the cornice.

Upper Cascade Central   100m   V,6
G Perroux and J-P Desterke, April 1992
The central of the three natural ice lines climbs a short ice wall to a snow patch before taking a line to the left of a rib in the prominent steep icefall above.

Upper Cascade Right   100m   V,6
G Perroux and J-P Desterke, April 1992
Just right of the previous route, straight up steep ice to a terrace, then the steep hidden icy gully to the right of the rib.

Chiquita   100m   VI,5
D MacGimpsey and A Nisbet, 31 March 2007
A thin icefall starting up an inset slab under a left-curving overlap. Cross the overlap, moving left and back right to gain thicker ice leading to a banana groove. Finish direct to the cornice.

The Blue Horizon   100m   IV,4
S Richardson and R Webb, 8 April 1995
Start 25m left of La Panthere Rose. Climb a short steep icefall, then go up and right to an easing (50m). Climb up and right to the cornice, which may be impassable. On the first ascent a 70m traverse left was required to outflank the cornice!

Adieu and Farewell   100m   V,5
S Richardson and C Cartwright, 6 April 2002
Named in memory of Godefroy Perroux. Starting in the cave stance of Le Panthere Rose, this climb starts with steep mixed moves to reach the icefall (rarely formed) to the left of that route. Finish up icy grooves through mixed ground.

Le Panthere Rose   100m   VI,6 ★
R Clothier, B Goodlad, G Perroux and F Bossier, 11 April 1993
Above The Cascade at the top of the snowfield is a large overhung rocky bay. Climb the icefall which forms a vertical column of steep ice on its left side, followed by easier ground in the headwall. The cornice may be a problem.

Fin Gourmet   200m   IV,4 ★

G Perroux and party, 1990s

A logical line left of The Cascade and climbing both tiers to the plateau. Climb iced slabs between The Cascade and Raeburn's Easy Route to reach the cave at the foot of Le Panthere Rose. Traverse right to climb a steep icy corner, then move left around the upper buttress to finish directly.

Expert's Choice   150m   III,4 ★

G Perroux and party, 1990s

The most popular route to the plateau after climbing The Cascade. Go up and slightly right from the top of The Cascade to climb mixed ground and the icefall running down the right side of the steep upper buttress.

Raeburn's Easy Route   250m   II/III ★

SMC party, April 1920

The most obvious feature to the right of Glover's Chimney is the deep slit of Number Two Gully, with The Comb to its right. To the left of Number Two Gully is Number Two Gully Buttress, and to the left again an indefinite wall up which this route winds. Make a long traverse leftwards out of Number Two Gully across a snow slope beneath The Cascade and aiming for a point where the crags peter out. Climb a low-angled ice pitch, then follow a snow shelf back right for a long way until a shallow gully gives access to the plateau 50m left of Number Two Gully Buttress. It is possible to finish direct by going straight up after the initial icefall towards the exit of Tower Ridge (*III*, R Harvey and A Meekin, 1986). This finish is left of Upper Cascade.

Raeburn's not so Easy   285m   III,4

K Bell and D Thompson, 13 March 2000

Most (if not all) of this route has been climbed before, but it would appear never to have been recorded. It is given here to show variations in this area. To gain the snowfield traverse of Raeburn's Easy Route a number of possibilities are available by the original route, depending on snow/ice build-up. Ascend the snowfield steeply rightwards to a large overhung rocky bay, right of centre of the upper cliffs. Go right for 10m and climb an icy chimney-corner as for Fin Gourmet (40m). Go right below a buttress to an icefall (40m). Climb the icefall (Expert's Choice) and snow slopes above to the plateau. It is also possible to head up directly after the icy chimney-corner (III). These last pitches are often used as a finish to The Cascade.

The Cascade   50m   IV,5 ★★

The obvious steep broad icefall below the right traverse of Raeburn's Easy Route. This route gives a good start to the harder climbs on the Upper Cascade area.

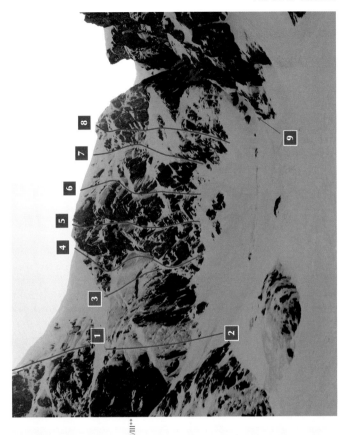

Number Two Gully Buttress

1 Expert's Choice III,4*
2 The Cascade IV,5**
3 Rip Off IV,4*
4 Five Finger Discount IV,4**
5 Burrito's Groove IV,5**
6 JP is Back III,4
7 BD Was Here III
8 Number Two Gully Buttress II/III**
9 Number Two Gully II***

Rip Off   120m   IV,4 ★

P Braithwaite and J Lowe (solo), March 1976

Follow the groove of the next route and traverse left onto a steep slab after 10m. Climb the slab, trending slightly right, with little protection to easy ground.

Five Finger Discount   135m   IV,4 ★★

MG Geddes and C Higgins, 4 February 1978

In the corner between the slabby face of Raeburn's Easy Route and Number Two Gully Buttress there is a deep groove, defining the left edge of the buttress. This groove is followed by Rip Off for 10m. Climb the groove until it bends left and steepens. Move left up an edge to a small gully and the finish.

Burrito's Groove   135m   IV,5 ★★

MG Geddes and C Higgins, 8 April 1978

Between Five Finger Discount and Number Two Gully Buttress route is a distinct groove leading directly up the buttress, well seen from below Comb Buttress. Climb the groove, passing an overhang on the left (45m). Often in condition.

JP is Back   120m   III,4

JP Destercke and G Perroux, 8 April 1995

20m to the right of Burrito's Groove. Start up a steep iced slab, which is bounded on its right by a steep rock wall, to a snow ledge. Follow another similar pitch, then trend right from time to time to avoid overlaps.

BD Was Here   120m   III

B Davison, December 1982

Steep ice at first, leading to the top of Number Two Gully Buttress.

The slopes running up to all routes in this area are prone to serious avalanche risk.

Number Two Gully Buttress   120m   II/III ★★

JR Marshall, LS Lovat and AH Hendry, 23 March 1958

Immediately to the left of Number Two Gully. Steep snow and occasionally iced rocks lead to a shelf below a vertical upper wall. A short but difficult ice pitch on the left leads to easier ground.

The Hard Right Edge   170m   IV,4

S Richardson and C Cartwright, 4 April 2006

Mixed climbing following the right edge of the buttress. Follow the lower arête up snow then mixed ground to a snow crest leading to the right edge of the headwall

(80m). Climb a steep wall left of the crest, avoid a bulge on the left (30m) and follow the crest to the top (60m).

Number Two Gully   120m   II ★★★
J Collier, G Hastings and WC Slingsby, Easter 1896
Hardest, and possibly the most interesting, of the easier gullies found to the left of The Comb, often with a steep ice column at its base on the right. Above the introductory slopes it becomes a deep slit; generally a straightforward but steadily steepening slope, but it can (especially early in the season) offer an ice pitch. The cornice is often quite difficult and usually turned on the left.

The Comb

The obvious triangular buttress is named after the narrow crenellated ridge at its top. The classic snow-ice lines of Comb Gully and Green Gully are reliable and popular. In between, the overhanging buttress is the playground of a very few elite climbers.

Comb Gully Buttress   125m   VI,6 ★
IS Clough and JM Alexander, 8 January 1960
Immediately right of Number Two Gully is Comb Gully Buttress, with Comb Gully on its right side. Climb from just left of the lowest rocks to gain the central snowfield. Entry can also be made from Number Two Gully. Grooves on the left side of the snowfield lead up and right to the foot of a prominent curving chimney, which is followed with a difficult exit to the left.

   Note The curving chimney is not often in condition, and the following variation to the left is a better option and gives good climbing.

Variation   75m   IV,4 ★★
I Fulton and D Gardner, 3 January 1971
After the grooves of Comb Gully Buttress on the left side of the buttress, traverse left to ice columns, which are climbed to ice-filled grooves and easy ground.

Great Circle   160m   VI,7
S Richardson and C Cartwright, 5 January 2003
A natural line slicing diagonally from right to left, to the left of the curving chimney of Comb Gully Buttress. From the foot of the curving chimney, climb the wall on the left via discontinuous cracks to a good ledge (15m). Continue up the corner and fault above to a terrace (25m). Go 5m left and climb the left-slanting flake and offwidth through the wall above. Cross the ice of the above variation and belay in the groove system (40m). Climb the left fork of the groove to the top of the tower (35m).

Tower Face of The Comb

1 Number Two Gully II***
2 Comb Gully Buttress Variation IV,4**
3 Comb Gully Buttress VI,6*
4 Roaring Forties V,5**
5 Big Bad Ben VII,7
6 Comb Gully IV,4**
7 The Comb – Left Flank IV,4*
8 The Good Groove VII,7**
9 Hesperides Ledge III*
10 Quisling Wall VI,6*
11 Tower Face of The Comb VI,6***
12 Bell's Chimney – Variation V,5

Roaring Forties   140m   V,5 ★★

D Lang and C Stead, 28 February 1988

Gain a belay right of the deep curving chimney of Comb Gully Buttress (50m). Follow the deep groove 15m right of the chimney to a ledge on the left (40m) and traverse left to the obvious V-groove, which is climbed to the top (50m).

Big Bad Ben   190m   VII,7

S Richardson and R Clothier, 19 April 1998

Climb the groove as for Roaring Forties to a ledge on the right (20m). Continue with difficulty up the groove on the left to a belay overlooking Comb Gully (30m). Follow the groove until it finishes, and move over into the upper fan of Comb Gully (30m).

Comb Gully   125m   IV,4 ★★

FG Stangle, R Morsley and PA Small, 12 April 1938

The obvious gully running up the left side of The Comb. Easy snow leads to the narrows, from where a long pitch leads to a poor belay. Above is a short steep wall, which often gives the crux. Easy ground then leads to the top.

   Note It is better to climb a short initial pitch in the narrows to good belays on the right wall, followed by a long second pitch to good belays above all major difficulties.

The Comb – Left Flank   100m   IV,4 ★

GE Little and R Richardson, 21 February 1981

Starts 20m above Hesperides Ledge in Comb Gully just above the first narrows. Step steeply out right and climb the steep icefall to a belay in a shallow gully (50m), and then on to the top. The steep ice pitch may be split with a belay on the right wall.

Hesperides Ledge   75m   III ★

JR Marshall, J Stenhouse and D Haston, 12 February 1959

Follows the lower 75m of Comb Gully and then a relatively easy, but highly spectacular, steep curving shelf, which leads rightwards across the wall to the crest of The Comb.

Isami   130m   VIII,8

D MacLeod and K Yokoyama, March 2006

Start up the first pitch of The Good Groove (40m). Instead of going up the right-slanting groove, step left onto The Comb – Left Flank for a move, then back right to a higher right-slanting ramp. Climb a steep corner above (good runners) and belay at the foot of the next right-slanting ramp (40m). Move along this into the right hand of two overhanging corners. Climb the corner to a strenuous and bold finish, with a good belay on the arête above (30m). Climb the deep groove on the right to the knife-edge finish (30m).

The Good Groove   140m   VII,7 ★★
SM Richardson and RD Everett, 27 March 1993
A tiered ramp cuts the wall above Hesperides Ledge. Gain the start of the ramp and move left along the second narrow ramp to a corner, which is followed to a belay at the end of a curving groove, just right of Comb – Left Flank (40m). Climb slabs right of the groove to a small stance below a steep tapering corner (25m). Climb the corner with difficulty, eventually arriving at a platform (25m). Climb the wall above to an arête (50m).

Quisling Wall   200m   VI,6 ★
R Clothier and S Richardson, 29 April 2001
Starting 40m up Comb Gully, where it first narrows, this mixed route follows the left-facing corner high on the face. Climb a break in the wall of Comb Gully and traverse right until in line with the groove above (40m). Climb the left-facing groove, steep at first (50m). Continue in the groove and reach Hesperides Ledge by a short narrow chimney (20m). Move right along Hesperides Ledge and finish up the crest (110m).

Lost Souls   195m   VI,6
J Edwards and E Tressider 24 February 2001
This mixed climb heads rightwards across the face to the forked chimney in the headwall. Start as for Quisling Wall by breaking out of Comb Gully and traversing rightwards for 10m. Climb a steep slab with a wall on its right and traverse right at its top around the wall above (40m). Go up and right to belay at a steep wall below the obvious open corner-line (20m). Bypass the steep wall on the left before getting into the open corner, which leads to the forked chimney (30m). Climb the chimney for a few metres before breaking out left (strenuous) and go up to the crest (15m). Follow this to the top.

Tower Face of The Comb   215m   VI,6 ★★★
R Smith and R Holt, 1 January 1959
A difficult and sustained mixed climb, which is open to much variation/mystery. A large ledge splits the buttress diagonally at one-third height from left to right. From the bottom left end of this ledge, move up to another ledge running parallel to the lower ledge, and go right to the foot of an obvious groove (30m). Traverse a little further right before climbing a steep slabby groove back left to broken blocks and the base of a steep wall (25m). Step left and ascend the groove and cracked wall

above (30m) crux. From this point Bell's Chimney – Variation works up right (see below). Climb the snow patch above to a steep wall, which is passed on the left (30m). Steep broken ground now leads up and right to a snow ledge beneath steep walls (20m). Traverse right to the buttress crest and up to easier ground above.

Tower Face of The Comb – Direct Start   80m   VI,6
A Clarke and J Main, 28 February 1993
Start much lower down, beneath the initial traverse ledge at the start of the original line. Ascend a delicate left-trending crack to below a short wall (30m). Go up the short wall to the groove of the original line and belay on broken blocks (50m).

Tower Face of The Comb – Variation Start   50m   V,5
R Clothier and A Shand, 1987
Follow Comb Gully until it narrows, and take a groove right for 10m. Traverse right below the barrier to a leftward ramp, which joins the original climb on pitch 3.

Bell's Chimney – Variation   65m   V,5
R Everett and S Richardson, 31 March 1996
From the belay after the 30m hard pitch, work up and right via short steep walls and grooves to the base of an obvious chimney (25m). Climb the chimney to exit right onto an awkward rib. Follow the awkward crest to where it eases and joins the original line coming in from the left (45m).

Central Wall Variation   45m   V,5
A Clarke and J Main, 28 February 1993
From the top of the steep wall which is passed on the left with difficulty, go right to enter and climb a chimney to a flake window on the original route.

Don't Die of Ignorance   200m   XI,11
D MacLeod and J French, 16 March 2008
A free ascent based on the 1987 aided route, taking a more direct line at the crux. Climbed ground up, on sight, sixth attempt. Follow the easy snow and ice ramps to a belay before the ledge runs out (30m). Step down into the wide undercut crack and tin opener tenuously to the arête (cams, bulldog). A foot-off tin-opener move gains access to the rib on the right (peg). The aid route continues along the crack. Quit the crack and climb leftwards on the tenuous wall above to gain a ledge. Go right beneath a steep groove and move round its base to gain a thin crack in an open slab. Climb this to below a chimney (30m). Step up and right to gain the huge open groove, and follow this with sustained interest to a hanging belay on the right at a large block (55m). Step left and follow the crest, moving left again across

The Comb and Number Three Gully Buttress

1 Don't Die of Ignorance XI,11
2 Anubis XII
3 Pigott's Route V,6*
4 Mercury IV,4**
5 Green Gully IV,4***
6 Venus V,5*
7 Tramp IV,4*
8 Diana V,5*
9 Aphrodite IV,4**
10 Quickstep V,5**
11 Number Three Gully Buttress
   Original Route III***
12 Two-Step Corner V,5***
13 The Knuckleduster VIII,9***
14 Thompson's Route IV,4***
15 Number Three Gully I***

a fault to a ledge and good belay at a flake (25m). Mantel the flake and step right to regain the crest, which is followed to the snow crest on the apex of the buttress (good spike-belay, 20m). Climb the easy snow crest to a steepening (60m). Climb snow grooves in the buttress crest to a flat knife edge leading to the plateau (55m).

The Flying Groove
220m   VI,6 and A2

C Dale and A Nisbet, 24 April 2001

The next groove right is shallower and accessed the same way, with a longer traverse rightwards on aid. The groove rises from the right end of the snow basin at the end of the first pitch of Don't Die of Ignorance and is climbed to some blocks (15m). Traverse the blocks, move up and right to the top of the groove, then trend left across ice slabs to a wall (30m). Move left and climb grooves to a ledge, which leads right to the crest (45m). Follow the crest to join Pigott's Route and finish up this (100m).

Anubis
200m   XII

D MacLeod, 25 February 2010

Takes a 40m cracked prow in the centre of the face and ice grooves above following the line of the summer E8! The hardest route on the mountain, and one of the hardest naturally protected climbs in the world.

Pigott's Route
245m   V,6 ★

J Marshall and R Smith, 12 February 1960

From the CIC Hut an obvious large ramp/ledge can be seen cutting up from left to right across the bottom section of the triangle of Comb Buttress. Follow this ramp up right until beneath a flake chimney, with a large boulder just down from its base (35m left of Green Gully). Climb the chimney (hard) and traverse left into steep ice-filled grooves, which are followed to the buttress crest.

Naïve Euphoria
180m   V,5

S Yates and P McVey, February 1988

The icy groove between Mercury and Pigott's Route, gained from the chimney flake of Pigott's Route. Move up left from the top of the chimney and follow the groove in two pitches to a snowfield. Move up past another barrier and climb on the left side of the summit tower to finish.

Naïve Euphoria – Direct Start
30m   V,6

S Richardson and J Bickerdike, 14 February 1999

Start just left of Mercury and climb a mixed wall to the right end of the terrace of Pigott's Route, followed by an open corner and an exit left to finish at the top of the flake chimney of Pigott's Route.

The classic Green Gully

Bigot's Route   180m   VI,6

N Gregory and K Pyke, 9 January 1999

Ascend the flake chimney of Pigott's Route and continue to a steep corner just right of Naïve Euphoria (45m). Climb the corner over a bulge and up the steep wall above (40m). Go up to the snowfield and climb an off-width in the barrier wall above, then continue to the left side of the summit tower (45m). Climb a steep groove right of an easy gully and go left over a short wall into a small gully, which is climbed to belay on the summit ridge (30m) and on to the plateau (20m).

Mercury   150m   IV,4 ★★

M Hind and J Christie, 26 January 1985

Ascends the rightmost of four parallel grooves just left of Green Gully. Climb Green Gully for 10m and move left around a rib to belay beneath a chimney with a chockstone (20m, might be possible to climb direct). Climb up and traverse left (loose) past a small overhang to the main groove-line on the left (30m crux). Continue up more easily to the crest of the buttress.

Green Gully   180m   IV,4 ★★★

H Raeburn and E Phildius, April 1906

A classic. The obvious gully running up the right side of Comb Buttress. The first pitch changes in character from steep ice to a grade I/II snow slope depending on build-up. Good peg belays on the left wall after 45m. Above are normally three good ice pitches with belays on the right side of the gully wall. When the gully opens out to a steep snow slope near the top, three exits present themselves – by easy snow to the right, a fine direct ice pitch (**) or a traverse left to the ridge. If the cornice presents a problem, one of these finishes should fix it!

Number Three Gully Buttress

Number Three Gully Buttress is the name given to the steep cliffs extending right from Green Gully to Number Three Gully. The very steep rocks at the left-hand side of the mouth of Number Three Gully are the home of some of the best mixed routes on the mountain. Being high up, this area provides reliable climbing, and the nature of the rock is relatively helpful for mixed climbing.

Venus   190m   V,5 ★

M Duff and A Nisbet, 28 January 1982

Follows the arête which forms the right bank of Green Gully. At half-height it is possible to move into grooves on the right and then back onto the arête higher up. The stances are poor and a long rope (60m!) is recommended to avoid them. Avoiding moves are often possible to the right, making this a fairly artificial line. The top section of this climb is common with Aphrodite, described below.

Tramp   180m   IV,4 ★

R Clothier and C Cartwright, January 1987

A direct approach to Aphrodite, starting diagonally right up the icefall right of Green Gully. Cross the snow ledge above to beneath a left-facing chimney, which is hidden from below. Ascend the chimney and the huge pedestal above, and then a corner-crack which leads to the groove of Aphrodite.

Diana   195m   V,5 ★

M Duff and J Tinker, 16 February 1985

Start further right than Tramp. Climb the icefall direct past a horizontal snow band to belay beneath a steep rock wall (55m). On the left climb a groove/chimney past a roof/chockstone to another snow bank and huge block stance (45m). Follow corners to beneath a huge right-facing corner (30m). Go up to the overlap and pull onto the right wall of the corner, then go straight up on steep thin ice to easier ground (45m). Follow snow to a possible large cornice finish.

Artemis   170m   V,5 ★

E Horne and G Gordon, 16 March 2002

Assuming a good cover of ice, start up the icefall right of Diana to the next rock band (40m). Climb the icefall right of Diana's chimney/groove into a recess (30m). Climb the recess and move onto ice on the right leading to a groove 15m right of Diana (25m). Follow the groove, or its left arête if not fully iced, with awkward moves near the top (45m). Finish direct (30m).

Unleashed   170m   VII,6 ★★★

M Edwards and A Nisbet, 23 March, 2007

A direct version of Vulture with the same first pitch (50m) and continuing up the left side of the ice sheet, through the overhangs and directly to the top.

Vulture   160m   V,5 ★★

M Edwards, D McGimpsey and A Nisbet, 2 April 2002

Another route requiring a good build-up of ice. Start as for Aphrodite to the slabby wall below the line of overhangs at the foot of the big slab left of Quickstep (50m). Go right around the overhangs to find a groove 10m left of Quickstep. This leads to the slab, which is climbed slightly leftwards to a rock outcrop (60m). Climb more easily to another area of rock (30m). Continue to the cornice, which can be big and possibly avoided on the left as for Diana.

Quickstep
130m   V,5 ★★

R Townshend and T Bray, 26 March 1983

The huge leftward-facing corner with steep slabs on its left, directly above the start of the Original Route. Climb the Original Route to the traverse ledge, then continue up to the foot of the corner. Climb steep ice on the left of the corner to belay at 45m. The final pitch leads to a conical basin above, which is often overhung by massive cornices that may be passable to the right by exposed and steep climbing.

Last Tango
140m   VII,8

I Small and S Richardson, 13 April 2008

Climb the first two pitches of Quickstep and belay below the left-facing corner on the right (65m). Climb the corner for 20m and climb right onto the steep wall to reach a small ledge. Climb a small left-facing corner for 10m then traverse back left into the main corner-line. Step left and climb thin ice over a steep bulge to a good stance in Quickstep (40m). Traverse 5m right and climb the fault above to reach the crest of the rib (15m). The rib leads to the cornice (20m).

Aphrodite
200m   IV,4 ★★

MG Geddes and JC Higham, 15 March 1971

Start up the same snow depression as Number Three Gully Buttress Original Route (described below) and aim for the second snow ledge halfway up the face. Move a long way left at the top over snowfields and ledges, then down with difficulty to the foot of an open groove. This groove is beside a rib right of Green Gully and is undercut by a large rock wall. Climb the groove and then the arête beside Green Gully, moving right at the top to a cornice which can be huge.

Number Three Gully Buttress Original Route
125m   III ★★★

LS Lovat and DJ Bennet, 18 February 1957

Climb up into the large snow bay below the prow of the buttress. From the top of the bay traverse delicately right to a platform, then follow grooves rightwards to a steep direct corner finish or traverse up rightwards. The upper part of the route is magnificently exposed. Much variation is possible, with more direct lines to the platform and from here to the top.

Boston Two Step
60m   VI,5 ★★

M Edwards, D McGimpsey and A Nisbet, 2 April 2002

A short but very good line that is sustained and requires a good covering of ice. Start about 15m below and left of the second of the Two-Step Corners at a short corner. Climb the corner and follow the best line of ice to the top (60m).

Number Three Gully Buttress (lower section)

1 The Survivor VII,8
2 Arthur VIII,8
3 The Knuckleduster VIII,9***

4 Sioux Wall VIII,8***
5 The Banshee V,5
6 Thompson's Route IV,4***

(photo: Blair Fyffe)

Two-Step Corner   130m   V,5 ★★★

D Kirtley and D Montgomery, March 1975

Starts 20m to the right of Number Three Gully Buttress Original Route and follows a corner to the traverse ledge of that route. Cross the traverse-line of Original Route and climb directly up the steep corner above to a belay, followed by difficult cornice exit on the right.

Chinook   65m   IV,5

M Edwards, D McGimpsey and A Nisbet, 3 April 2002

Starts from the platform of Number Three Gully Buttress Original Route, 10m right of Two-Step Corner, climbed on ice. Follow the groove trending left at about 25m, then move back right to climb a crack to a large ledge (35m). The left-slanting chimney leads to the top (30m).

The Survivor   90m   VII,8

S Richardson and I Small, 9 March 2008

The prominent triangular corner on the left side of the front face of Number Three Gully Buttress provides a difficult mixed climb. Start directly below the niche and climb snow and ice, trending left across a shallow depression to a short wall. Climb this, and climb a second wall on the right to the niche (40m). Climb the corner to a small triangular ledge and traverse left along a hidden horizontal break to a good stance (20m). Climb a steep bulge and continue up the diagonal fault line to a narrow ledge at 20m. The steep icy groove above leads to the platform on Number Three Gully Buttress (30m).

Arthur   140m   VIII,8

B Poll and T Shepherd, 2 January 2004

Climb up to a ledge below a corner (10m). A steep groove on the right leads to the top of a pinnacle. Step across to a short groove and obvious left traverse behind blocks to a platform (40m). Climb the corner above, then step left to a steep crack in a wall to a small ledge (30m). Go up, then right more easily to follow a groove (40m). Finish up the groove (20m).

The Knuckleduster   120m   VIII,9 ★★★

B Fyffe and S Ashworth, 12 February 2007

A winter ascent based on the summer route, initially following the great groove in the buttress. Climb the groove to belay under an overhang (40m). Turn the overhang by a wall on the right and belay on the outer edge (15m). Climb small grooves in the arête to the right of the main groove to a ledge on the right (35m). The wall on the right leads to the large platform (30m).

The chimney of Babylon on Number Three Gully Buttress

Curly's Arête   175m   VIII,8
S Isaac and I Parnell, 8 March 2007
Committing and sustained climbing, possibly coinciding with The Knuckleduster.
Climb diagonally up and right from the foot of the big groove of The Knuckleduster
to below deep cracks on the slab and arête (15m). Follow the deep cracks to a ledge
below the steepest part of the arête. Avoid this by a traverse up and right into Sioux
Wall and back left to a short crack just before the arête. Committing moves up and
left to the arête itself (35m). Climb the groove above to below a steepening, where a
serious move right gains a right-angled groove. Follow this to the bulges, and traverse
6m right to Sioux Wall (40m). Follow the direct finish to Sioux Wall (30m).

Sioux Wall   90m   VIII,8 ★★★
O Metherell and I Parnell, 1 January 2006
The groove-line just left of centre of the smooth wall to the right of the arête. Start
directly into the groove to an obvious belay niche. It is strenuous but well protected
up the steep wall up into a ledge at the base of the obvious corner-groove. Climb
the groove with surprisingly good protection. A rightward line was chosen to finish
on the first ascent. The first ascent of the complete line up the continuation crack
was by A Turner and D Hodgson on 29 January 2006.

The Banshee   120m   V,5
C Cartwright and S Richardson, 1 January 1999
Start at the base of Number Three Gully Buttress and follow a line of right-trending
grooves and chimneys past an obvious flake to a steep wall. Climb the wall by a
crack on the left (40m). Step right into Thompson's Route and up to a belay on the
right (10m). Go left into a right-angled corner, which is climbed to the easy ledges
on Number Three Gully Buttress (40m). Follow Number Three Gully Buttress to the
plateau (30m).

Thompson's Route   120m   IV,4 ★★★
R Marshall, JR Marshall and J Stenhouse, December 1963
Immediately on the right of the very steep front face of the buttress at the bottom
left of Number Three Gully is an ice-filled chimney. Follow this steeply and with
interest to join the Original Route at the platform. The first pitch is difficult and
poorly protected with little ice.

Direct Finish   140m   VII,7
G Hughes and T Stone, 16 April 2005
The large right-facing corner above the right end of the Number Three Gully
Buttress platform, reached in two pitches up Thompson's Route. Climb the corner

Number Three Gully Buttress (upper section)

1 Sioux Wall VIII,8***
2 The Banshee V,5
3 Thompson's Route IV,4***

4 Gremlins VI,6
5 Gargoyle Wall IV,6*
6 Babylon VII,8**

(sustained) to a block-belay (25m). Step right to finish up cracks (30m). Climbed in snowed-up rock conditions, and may have been climbed before on ice.

Gremlins   130m   VI,6

G Perroux, C Merlin, C Biard and S Hophster, March 1989

Climb the groove to the right and parallel with Thompson's Route to a steep icicle, which is climbed, followed by a steep wall through overhangs. Then follow grooves to a ledge and the crack above direct to the plateau.

Gargoyle Wall   120m   IV,6 ★

R Carrington and I Nicholson, December 1977

From Number Three Gully a prominent head-shaped feature can be seen up on the left wall. Ascend the icy chimneys of Thompson's Route and traverse onto the Gargoyle. Climb the ridge above to a ledge, then traverse right into a corner, which is climbed to a stance below a steep wall (30m). Climb the steep crack above to a platform, then go left to a chimney-crack, which is climbed to a belay (30m). Climb the difficult chimney and then to the top (15m).

Gargoyle Wall – Variant Start   45m   VI,6 ★★★

S Richardson and C Cartwright, 22 February 1998

Climbs the original summer line on Gargoyle Wall, avoiding the chimneys of Thompson's Route, and is now the usual start. 10m up and right of Thompson's Route, climb a steep wall to a ledge and enter a chimney on the left, which is followed to a bay with the Gargoyle visible on the right.

Hobgoblin   110m   VI,7

S Richardson and C Cartwright, 5 December 1998

Start 10m up and right of Thompson's Route and climb a flake, then go up right for 15m, up cracks and a short right-angled corner to a belay level with, and right of, The Gargoyle (30m). Move up and right to reach a stepped ledge, which is climbed to beneath a cracked wall (30m). Climb the wall to a ledge (10m), then go left to a chimney-crack, which is climbed, followed by an off-width to a ledge (30m). Continue to the top (10m).

Babylon   100m   VII,8 ★★

S Richardson and C Cartwright, 8 April 2001

Steep and sustained mixed climbing that gets harder the higher you go, taking the right edge of the buttress and finishing up the hanging chimney overlooking Winter Chimney. Climb the edge of the buttress by a flake-crack and continue up an open groove to a rectangular rib. The groove on the right of the rib leads to the platform

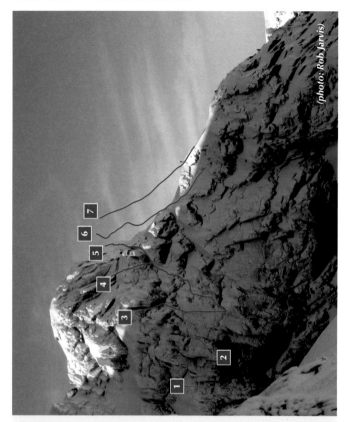

(photo: Rob Jarvis)

Creag Coire na Ciste (left side)

1 Number Three Gully I***
2 Darth Vader VII,7***
3 Stormtrooper VIII,8
4 Archangel VIII,7
5 Avenging Angel VII,8
6 Cold Play VIII,8
7 Salva Mea VIII,8

below the chimney-crack of Gargoyle Wall (40m). Climb this chimney-crack to another platform (15m). Step up and right to make a tenuous traverse right to a small ledge below a roof (15m). Pull over the roof and climb the off-width above to the chimney and follow this to the top (30m).

Snuff Wall   55m   VIII,8
I Parnell, 19 March 2008
Climb 6m up Winter Chimney until it is possible to climb the left side of a wide shallow recess on the left. Traverse right past steep thin cracks to a short ramp. Climb up this, then a delicate traverse right to gain an obvious long curving ice ramp (one of the main features of this wall). Climb this (bold) until a huge chockstone is reached and climbed to another pointed chockstone and a crack-line leading to the top.

Winter Chimney   60m   III,5 ★
D Haston and D Gray, March 1963
Lies in the back of the bay that defines the right side of Gargoyle Wall, well up Number Three Gully, and is rarely climbed. The ice smear which forms on the right wall at the start of the chimney provides two pitches (III,4**). This can be reached by abseiling into Number Three Gully from its south-east rim off rock-belays, if approaching from above and not wishing to confront the large cornices. Two 60m ropes are useful.

El Nino   80m   III,4
C Cartwright and S Richardson, 14 March 1998
The short buttress to the right of Winter Chimney. Start on the right side and climb a wide crack before going left to the top.

Number Three Gully   150m   I ★★★
The lowest point in the skyline looking south-west from the CIC Hut. The first ascent dates back to pre-1870. The angle of the approach slope gradually increases as it rises from the basin of Coire na Ciste, and by the time it narrows to a gully proper it is quite steep. No pitches, but the final section is divided by a pinnacle rib. The exit will be dictated by the cornice.

Creag Coire na Ciste

The left end of this crag has well-featured rock that lends itself to mixed climbing, although it is all very steep. This is the home of The Secret, a climb that was popularised by the internet even before the first ascensionists were back down off the mountain! It also has a selection of very nice mid-grade ice climbs in the gullies.

Trop Belle pour Toi
60m IV,5

P Bresse and G Perroux, March 1996

Early in the season two ramp-lines run across the right wall of Number Three Gully. This takes the lower line, starting in an alcove opposite and a little higher than the start of Winter Chimney. Climb a chimney-crack just left of the alcove and follow snow slopes to belay below a steep crack (20m). Climb the crack and the continuation of the ramp-line on ice, then snow, to the plateau (40m).

Blockhead
70m V,6

C Cartwright and S Richardson, 4 April 1998

Start 10m up and left of Cornucopia in a small alcove. Take the leftmost fault out of the alcove up a short corner (30m). Follow a prominent ramp and steep corner to the top (40m).

The Secret
70m VIII,9 ★★★

A Turner, S Ashworth and V Scott, 10 December 2007

The obvious and much sought-after crack in the right wall of Number Three Gully gives a sustained 35m crack-pitch ranging from fist to finger width. The route was led on sight and in perfect style on the first ascent. News of its ascent was online before the first ascensionists were back down in the valley!

Andy Turner on the first ascent of The Secret (photo: Sam Loveday)

Cornucopia
100m VII,8 ★

C Cartwright and S Richardson, 14 April 1996

The smooth steep corner at the left end of Creag Coire na Ciste overlooking Number Three Gully. Needs a good freeze, otherwise horribly loose. Start opposite Winter Chimney. Ascend left of large blocks, then up a slabby corner to below the corner (20m). Climb a crack-line right of the corner for 5m, then move into the corner (a thread aid/rest point was used on the first ascent). Climb the difficult corner to an alcove. Go right on a narrow ledge, then up to a small stance on the buttress edge (25m). Ascend the booming flake above (3m), then go left into the corner/chimney, which is climbed over two chockstones with difficulty to a large platform (20m). Leave the platform from the top right corner, then go up an overhanging wall left of an arête with a large spike and on to the top (35m).

Darth Vader
100m VII,7 ★★★

S Richardson and C Cartwright, 30 March 1997

Climbs the chimney-crack which cuts through the vertical wall at the left end of Creag Coire na Ciste, just right of Number Three Gully. Start directly below the chimney, and climb up, then right, to a block-belay just right of the chimney-crack (25m). Climb an awkward 3m wall, then up the chimney to a hidden cave (20m). Climb the roof of the cave into a hanging groove (crux) and continue to the large platform of Cornucopia (25m). Climb the chimney at the back of the platform, then go up and right to finish (30m).

Stormtrooper
45m VIII,8

S Ashworth and A Turner, 8 January 2008

The steep groove just right of Darth Vader is climbed (bold) to access a belay niche in the middle of the wall. A hanging and tapering ramp overlooking the steep Darth Vader wall is climbed, with the crux at the narrows, before an easing and arrival at the large ledge.

Archangel
110m VIII,7

S Richardson and C Cartwright, 6 February 2005

The obvious steep corners 15m right of Darth Vader. Climb a steep right-facing corner to a ledge (15m). Climb a steep corner up and right to a good stance (20m). The right hand of two grooves leads to a ledge with a spike on the left. Climb the overhanging wall above to a hard exit onto a narrow ledge. Another steep wall is climbed, trending right to large ledges (20m). Climb a V-slot 5m to the right and continue up the chimney-crack to a sloping ledge on the left (30m). The overhanging chimney-crack and easy snow lead to the cornice (25m).

Avenging Angel
105m   VII,8

N Bullock and O Samuels, 19 March 2006

Start up Archangel. Climb the wall and pull right onto the rib at a large ledge. Good torques and edges up the overhanging open-book corner lead to a hanging belay beneath the overhanging off-width (25m). Climb the corner and fight the off-width. Belay on the right (20m). The striking and obvious corner on the left is climbed by cracks on the left. Steeper than it looks (30m).

Cold Play
110m   VIII,8

I Small and S Richardson, 6 April 2008

Start as for South Gully to the foot of a deep groove that cuts up and left just right of the crest of the obvious rib (20m). Climb the groove past a tower-flake on the left to where it steepens and turns into an off-width. Climb this to a steepening split by a Y-shaped crack and belay on the left at a good block (30m). The Y-shaped crack (crux) is climbed, then move up a shallow slot on the left to a good ledge across the crest of the rib (20m). Climb the left-trending fault line on the right to an exposed position on the left edge of the rib. The overhanging wall on the right leads to the crest again and a finish up the impending crack in the wall above (20m). Continue up easy snow to the cornice (20m).

Salva Mea
90m   VIII,8

V Scott and D Bojko, 1 March 2007

A route based on the groove left of the icicle of South Sea Bubble on blind and brittle rock. Start below and just right of the hanging groove, and climb up and left to a broad easy groove which leads to a steep right-facing corner. Climb this corner on turf into the hanging groove (much of this is shared with South Sea Bubble, 30m). Climb the very steep chimney and up to a slot. Pull through this to a groove, and continue up and left to blocky ground (possible belay). Move right to a snow slope and the cornice (60m).

South Sea Bubble
110m   VII,7

S Richardson and C Cartwright, 8 March 1997

On the steep wall left of South Gully, this route links two right-to-left ice ramps and a hanging icicle. Go up the lower ramp of South Gully to below the hanging icicle (30m). Climb up left to the first ice ramp, which is climbed for 5m, after which a vertical wall is climbed to gain the start of the second ramp. Climb this ramp and traverse right to a hanging stance right of the icicle (40m). Climb the icicle then on to the top (40m).

Wall Street
120m   VII,7

R Webb and S Richardson, 23 March 2007

Low in the grade overall, but pitch 2 is steep and not well protected. Start as for South Sea Bubble below the hanging icicle (30m). Climb mixed ground just right of South Sea Bubble to gain the ramp right of this route. Climb this to a steep corner (20m). Climb the corner with ice at its top to belay by a large block overlooking South Gully (30m). Continue up the crest on thin ice (40m).

South Gully
125m   III ★

GG MacPhee, 10 April 1936

Starts high up on the left-hand side of Creag Coire na Ciste and just below Number Three Gully proper. Use an obvious ramp slanting diagonally to the right. This leads to an ice pitch, which gives entry to a final steep funnel. Cornice is often difficult.

The Sorcerer
140m   VII,8

S Ashworth and N Nielsen, 1 March 2007

Much like White Magic, but longer and harder! Start below a steep corner left of Lost the Place. Climb over ledges to gain the corner, which is climbed with an exit on its right wall. Trend left over ledges to belay directly below the crack splitting the wall above (40m). The magic crack-pitch! Easy ground leads to a belay on Lost the Place (50m). Pull round the corner as for Lost the Place, and immediately take a right-trending ramp-line on a diagonal across the steep upper buttress (50m).

Lost the Place
140m   V,5 ★★

C Cartwright and R Clothier, 17 December 1988

Follow a groove starting just left of Central Gully until it overlooks South Gully, then traverse right to a chossy chimney leading to the cornice. A direct start (60m, V,6) takes the left-facing groove through the lower face of the buttress 30m right of South Gully through a prominent chimney slot.

Cloudwalker
110m   VI,6 ★

S Richardson and R Clothier, 16 April 2000

Mixed climbing in the groove on the right of the Lost the Place buttress. Climb an ice groove as for Une Journée Ordinaire to a small cave. Climb the steep shallow slot on the left, pull over a small roof and continue up the chimney on the right. Climb the short wall on the left to a spike-belay (40m). A short steep corner and groove lead to the top (50m).

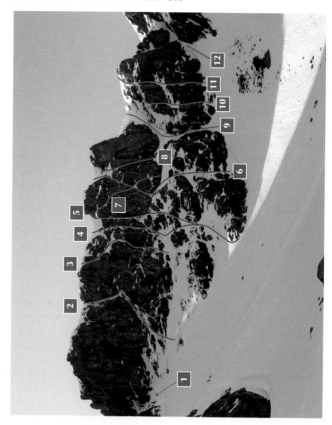

Creag Coire na Ciste

1 Number Three Gully I***
2 South Gully III*
3 Une Journée Ordinaire VI,6**
4 Central Gully III**
5 Central Gully –
   Right-Hand IV,4***
6 Wendigo IV,4**
7 Tinkerbell IV,5
8 Place Your Bets VI,6
9 North Gully II*
10 Forearm IV,4
11 Fore 'n' Daft IV,4
12 Number Four Gully I

Une Journée Ordinaire dans un Enfer Quotidien   105m   VI,6 ★★
G Perroux, F Bossier and J Douay, 15 April 1993
Ascend Central Gully for 10m, then go left to a small cave at the foot of another icefall, which is climbed with an exit left and continuation to belay on the left (45m). Continue up snow and more ice to the cornice, which can be huge and may require a long traverse left with some tunnelling!

Levitation   115m   VI,6 ★★
D Cuthbertson and J George, 20 April 1993
Initially difficult mixed climbing followed by steep ice. Climb Central Gully for 10m and traverse left (crux) beneath an overlap to a steep icicle on the prow, which is climbed (30m), followed by easier snow to belay below the steep upper section (35m). Climb ice then traverse left as in previous route.

Central Gully   125m   III ★★
I Clough and JM Alexander, 27 January 1959
Starting from the lowest part of the crag, snow slopes are followed to the left of a rocky rib to reach the left hand of two parallel ice chimneys which cleave the steep central wall. This is climbed for 40m before crossing to the right-hand gully, which leads into the final corniced funnel.

Central Gully – Right-Hand   125m   IV,4 ★★★
I MacEacheran and J Knight
The right-hand chimney gives a fine long pitch. An independent start can be made by climbing the rightward-slanting icefall to the left of North Gully, then traversing left to the foot of the chimney.
   Note It is possible to abseil from a good anchor after climbing the main pitch of either of the previous two routes and then climb the other route. This gives two excellent pitches. If the cornice is too intimidating, it is also possible to descend by abseil back into the coire (2x50m ropes required).

Central Rib   120m   III,4 ★
RN Campbell and JR Marshall, March 1970
Start at the lowest point of the cliff and climb steeply up the edge overlooking Wendigo to the ledge running round left under the final tower. The rib was climbed direct without deviation into Central Gully Right-Hand and finished directly up the final tower by S Richardson and I Small (*VI,7, 3 April 2002*).

Wendigo
110m   IV,4 ★★

TW Patey and J Brown, 24 February 1963

Start right of Central Rib beneath a steep icefall and go steeply up right to a large ledge. Climb mixed ground above to the cornice.

Tinkerbell
100m   IV,5

C Cartwright and S Richardson, 2 March 1997

Start 10m right of Wendigo below the final tower of Central Rib. Climb up to a narrow left-facing corner and a junction with Wendigo (40m). Ascend a steep icefall and groove directly to beneath the final tower of Central Rib (45m). Go more easily left of the tower to the top (15m).

Tick Tock Croc
90m   IV,5

J Ashbridge, S Richardson and R Clothier, 21 March 1999

Start beneath Place Your Bets and gain a hidden left-trending gully ramp by a steep step, and follow it to Wendigo (30m). Go right for 5m and over a bulge to the left of a rocky fin, followed by a groove above, which crosses Wendigo (40m). Follow the crest above to a cornice finish (10m).

Place Your Bets
100m   VI,6

J Blyth, J Briel, G Perroux and D Colin, 12 April 1994

An overhanging icefall to the right of Wendigo which seldom forms.

North Gully
110m   II ★

JY MacDonald and HW Turnbull, 24 March 1934

The right hand and most obvious of the three gullies on this cliff, which starts to the left of Number Four Gully. The lower section of the gully almost always holds an ice pitch, but its length may vary from 3m to 30m. The narrow lower section leads to a wide easier-angled slope, which is followed obliquely rightwards to the cornice. Beware of avalanche danger on the final slopes. A left-fork finish is possible (*35m, III, D Bathgate, J Knight and A McKeith, February 1964*) up an ice groove at the back of a steep scoop above the upper snow basin.

The Gift
110m   III

A Ferguson and C Sutcliffe, 11 March 2000

The ice smear on the right wall of North Gully. Sometimes banks out completely. Climbed before, but never recorded.

Forearm   125m   IV,4
D Cuthbertson, S Clarke, L Robinson and AN Other, March 1999
The icy groove in the right crest of North Gully, which makes a good route when combined with North Gully left fork. Climb the groove, a section of snow, then an awkward icy chimney to more snow (50m). A choice of directions lead to the top (75m).

Four Play   110m   IV,4
J Raitt and D Gibson, 13 February 1993
A thin V-groove between North Gully and Number Four Gully. Start just left of where Number Four Gully widens, and climb a chimney to a snow bay, followed by an icy groove to easier ground and the plateau. This route can bank out and become easier (III).

Fore 'n' Daft   120m   IV,4
J Lyall, S Frazer and M Twomey, 10 March 2003
The shallow icy chimney right of Four Play leads to a ledge and left-trending fault to belay on Four Play. Go back right onto the edge and up a short wall and crack to easier ground.

Number Four Gully   150m   I
AE Maylard, WW Naismith and FC Squance, April 1895
The easiest winter route on Ben Nevis and the best descent on the North Face. It curls gently round to the right between the cliffs of Creag Coire na Ciste and the South Trident Buttress. Its exit is very wide, so that even given a heavy build-up of cornice, it should be possible to find an easy weakness. This route cannot be seen from the CIC Hut.

The Trident Buttresses

The area which extends from Number Four Gully on the left to Number Five Gully on the right contains the Trident Buttresses (South, Central and North), whose crests can be seen cutting the skyline. The area near Lochan Coire na Ciste (GR 162718) is a useful spot for gearing up ready for the climbs here and elsewhere, with the buttresses above giving an impression of safety from avalanches. However, large avalanches do sweep over Central Gully from the hidden snow slopes above, and the debris has been known to reach the lochan.

Number Four Gully Buttress   100m   II ★
JHB Bell, 1 January 1929
The broken area to the right of the lower reaches of Number Four Gully and left of South Trident Buttress.

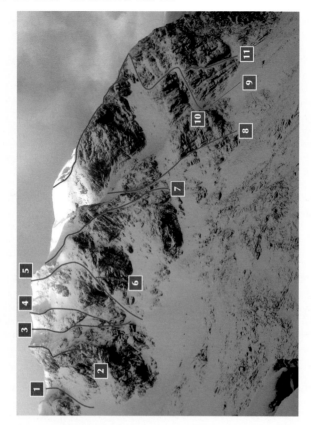

The Trident Buttresses

1 Number Four Gully I
2 Pinnacle Arête IV,4**
3 Central Gully III
4 Nasturtium IV,4*
5 Jubilee Climb II
6 Mega Route X V,6***
7 Neptune Gully III
8 Moonlight Gully I/II
9 Number Five Gully I*
10 Ledge Route II***
11 The Curtain IV,5***

South Trident Buttress *consists of three tiers, with steep easy ground in between. The area between the lower and middle tier is known as Middle Ledge. The mixed climbs on the middle tier can be a good choice early in the season when covered in soft snow, as ice is not required for most of the climbs.*

Poseidon Groove   100m   IV,5

S Richardson and I Small, 3 April 2004

The steep groove splitting the south-facing upper tier. Reach twin grooves in the centre of the wall from the mouth of Number Four Gully. Move into the right-hand groove and climb past two steep sections to a ledge 5m right of a wide vertical crack (35m). Step left and climb the left of two corners leading to easier ground (50m). Further easier ground leads to the top (15m).

Triton Corners   100m   IV,5

C Cartwright and S Richardson, 3 April 2006

Start 25m right of the previous route. Climb a short bulging off-width to a stepped corner system leading right. Continue straight up to a good belay under a steep wall (40m). Step left and climb an icy gully and wide snow chute to the plateau (60m).

South Flank Route   150m   IV,4 ★

A Kimber, N Hicking and C Collin, 29 March 1994

To the left of the steep rocks above Middle Ledge of South Trident Buttress on the middle tier, overlooking the approach to Number Four Gully, are some steep ice smears. Follow the steepest of these, and snow slopes and chimneys above, to the flat section below the upper tier on the crest of South Trident Buttress, whose fine shattered arête is followed to the plateau rim.

Rattled   100m   V,5

A Nisbet and J Preston, 28 January 2005

Start at the big corner left of The Groove Climb. Enter the corner by a turf groove right of the corner, then climb the chimney to a ledge (35m). Go left 10m. Climb a ramp to a long narrow ledge and traverse right until above the chimney of The Groove Climb (30m). Cross this and go up turf to a shallow groove leading right through a steep wall into Sidewinder (15m). The prominent narrow chimney and its continuation lead to the crest of the buttress (25m).

The Groove Climb   80m   V,6 ★

J Main and A Clarke, 22 December 1992

On the left end of the middle tier, above Middle Ledge, is a deep chimney-groove which is climbed to a deep cave (30m). From the cave an awkward exit is made

South Trident Buttress – Middle Tier

1 South Flank Route IV,4*
2 The Groove Climb V,6*
3 Sidewinder VII,8
4 Strident Edge VI,7**
5 Devastation VII,8
6 The Slab Climb VI,7*
7 The Clanger IV,5**

to a belay (10m). Go left by an icy ramp to the top, from where it is possible to descend left.

Sidewinder   100m   VII,8
I Small and S Richardson, 8 April 2005

The triple-tiered corner starting 15m right of The Groove Climb. Avoid the first chimney by easy ground on the left. Continue up the corner (20m) and the crack and large flake to the top (30m).

Strident Edge   100m   VI,7 ★★
E Brunskill and G Hughes, 13 January 2005

Sensational but amenable climbing up the arête to the right of Sidewinder. Start as for Sidewinder by easy ground on the left to belay in the corner. Move out right and climb the steep crack just left of the crest, with a possible belay at 15m (35m). Turn the overhang above by a spike and cracks in the left wall to regain the groove above to the top of the middle tier.

Spartacus   100m   VI,7
A Nisbet and J Preston, 11 November 2002

Climb the corner 20m left of The Clanger over an overhang, then traverse right to a belay (30m). Traverse right across a wall to the arête and follow Slab Route for 10m (15m). Continue directly, then left, above an overhang to a flake-crack. Follow this, then traverse left to a belay on the arête (25m). Climb the groove above (30m).

Devastation   80m   VII,8
A Benson and I Parnell, 30 November 2008

The corner right of Spartacus is climbed to a flake, then continued into a niche and up the steep crack above (40m). The steep crack is followed to the top (40m).

The Slab Climb   90m   VI,7 ★
A Nisbet and J Preston, 9 November 2001

Between The Groove Climb and The Clanger is a cracked wall leading to a conspicuous chimney. Gain the cracked wall by steep moves up and right from Middle Ledge (25m). Climb the cracked wall to the chimney (25m). Climb up the chimney, which is difficult to start, and its continuation (40m).

The Clanger   90m   IV,5 ★★
JR Marshall, R Marshall and RN Campbell, March 1967

Access from Middle Ledge. Climb the chimney-groove at the back of the corner near the right end of the middle tier to a steep cave pitch (35m). Exit the cave by a

Heavy spindrift on Slab Climb

through-route on the right wall leading behind a large flake onto the buttress crest. Easier to the top. A route for people of slight stature!? The chimney-groove has been followed all the way, avoiding the tight squeeze, over good steep bulges at VI,7 (*I Small and D Hawthorn*).

Pinnacle Arête   150m   IV,4 ★★
RH Sellars and J Smith, 1 February 1959
Start from the right end of the snow ledge (Middle Ledge) and climb a series of grooves just right of the crest.

Rien ne va Plus   50m   V,5
G Perroux and J Blyth, 10 April 1994
An icefall which sometimes forms on the left side of the lower tier of South Trident Buttress. Descend easily leftwards by Middle Ledge.

Eastern Block   125m   VI,6
G Livingston and M Charlton, January 1987
A hard mixed climb which starts about 30m right of the lowest rocks of South Trident Buttress at a steep wall (30m). Go left of the steep chimney, then trend left to a belay ledge (25m). Traverse the ledge to some stacked blocks and climb the bulging wall above to another ledge (15m). Continue more easily to the right end of Middle Ledge, from where it is possible to descend leftwards.

Under Fire   85m   VII,7 ★
D MacLeod and M Tweedley, 6 February 2008
Start below a roofed chimney in the centre of the face. Climb the chimney through the roof (hard) and the corner above. Exit left onto a ledge underneath an over-hanging wall and traverse left for 5m, round to the base of a large slanting corner. Climb the corner and crawl right along a thin ledge to another corner, which leads to the top.

The Minge   105m   VII,8
E Edwards and P Macpherson, 6 February 2009
Start just below the obvious black wide crack at the foot of a right-trending icy ramp. Climb the icy ramp on thin ice and turf and belay below a crack-groove. Climb the tenuous crack-groove, then a shallow left-facing corner and the bulging crack above, to belay halfway up a slab (20m). Traverse delicately right across the slab to a crack. Climb this to an easing in angle and follow the groove/chimney system above to a turfy ramp (40m). Follow a choice of grooves to the right of the ridge to reach the crest (70m).

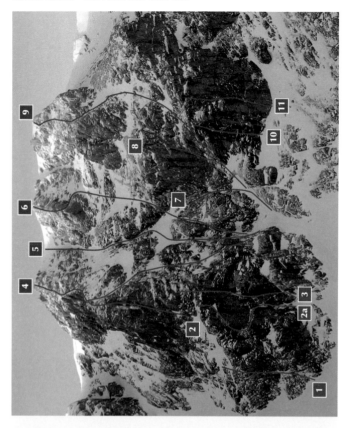

South and Central Trident Buttresses

1 Rien ne va Plus V,5
2 The Clanger IV,5**
2a Under Fire VII,7*
3 The Minge VII,8
4 Joyful Chimneys IV,5
5 Central Gully III
6 Nasturtium IV,4*
7 Jubilation IV,4*
8 Mega Rêve V,5
9 Jubilee Climb II
10 Mega Route X V,6***
11 Heidbanger Direct VIII,8

Joyful Chimneys
180m IV,5

R Campbell and JR Marshall, February 1971

A discontinuous line of chimneys can be seen on the north-east flank of South Trident Buttress facing the CIC Hut. Starts 50m left and downhill of Central Gully (described next). These chimneys are either climbed or avoided on their flanks, depending on conditions. The crest of South Trident Buttress is gained by a series of grooves above the chimneys.

Central Gully
240m III

H Raeburn and Mr & Mrs C Inglis-Clark, April 1904

Immediately above (west) of the small lochans (Lochan Coire na Ciste) and right of the steep rocks of South Trident Buttress. This gully can fill up almost completely. Often a steep ice column is found barring the way. Either pass it by mixed ground up to the left (as on the first ascent) or climb direct (30m, III,4, LS Lovat and K Bryan, 11 March 1956). Above, a variety of routes leads to the top, avoiding difficulties as necessary.

Raeburn's Rib
90m III,4

C Cartwright and S Richardson, 16 February 2003

The well-defined rib splitting the upper reaches of Central Gully. Start above the toe of the rib on the left at an alcove. Climb the icy chimney-corner past a tiny pine tree and continue up the fault to the crest (40m). Follow the crest to the top (50m).

Nasturtium
250m IV,4 ★

D Cuthbertson and Notts-Trent University party, 26 March 2002

Start by following Central Gully to the foot of a curling groove on the right (20m). Climb the groove and belay under a right-facing corner (40m). Climb the corner and belay on a plinth at its top (50m). Climb snow and a 15m icefall to reach another snowfield (40m). Reach the crest of South Trident Buttress up and left, and follow it to the top.

Morton's Neuroma
170m V,5

N Gregory and C Foubister, 10 February 2000

Climbs on the small buttress between Central Gully and Jubilation. Ascend a steep icefall for 6m at the toe of the buttress, then go up left and climb a second icefall to a shallow gully (50m). Go up right to the snow slope above by short icy steps (60m). Continue to join Central Gully, which comes in from the left, and finish up this.

Jubilation   240m   IV,4 ★
R Marshall, JR Marshall and J Stenhouse, December 1963
Follow Jubilee Climb for about 75m. Traverse left into a chimney and climb it on
steep ice to a snow bay. Move left into a second chimney and follow this until it
eases. A choice of routes leads over easier ground to the top.

Mega Rêve   60m   V,5
G Perroux, JP Destercke, C Deu, P Gratadour and F Domanget, 4 April 1994
Climb a narrow chimney on the left of the rightward ramp of Jubilee Climb and
well up right of Jubilation. A short steep icefall is followed by the central of three
vertical icefalls.

Jubilee Climb   240m   II
GG MacPhee, GC Williams and D Henderson, May 1935
In the lower part of Central Gully is a rightward-leading branch, which is followed
on snow and small ice pitches to easy ground and a choice of routes to the top.

Feeding Frenzy   70m   VI,7 ★
N Gresham and C Smith, 24 January 1999
At the left end of the buttress containing Mega Route X a free-hanging icicle sometimes forms. This presents a fierce climb, accessed by mixed climbing up a left-
slanting ramp and powerful moves to reach the icicle.

Mega Route X   70m   V,6 ★★★
J Murphy and A Cain, 18 December 1982
One of the steeper ice climbs on Ben Nevis, which takes the lowest section of
Central Trident Buttress, 50m right of Jubilee Climb. There is a good belay at 40m
on the left, below an overhang.

Heidbanger Direct   75m   VIII,8
R Cross and A Benson, 23 November 2008
Follow the deep lightning crack of Cranium Start in the arête to belay in the cave
(25m). Follow the off-width crack out of the cave and trend up and left to the arête
(20m). The corner-lines past a flake lead to the top (30m).

Metamorphosis   105m   VIII,9
I Small and G Hughes, 23 March 2009
Follow the deep lightning crack of Cranium Start in the arête to belay in the cave
(25m). Tenuously cross the wall on the right by twin diagonal seams to reach the
corner, and follow this to a long ledge on the right wall (25m). Make bold thin moves

up and right to gain the flake-line. Difficult climbing up this, then climb the blank-looking wall above, leading to easier ground (30m). Climb to easier ground (15m).

Nereid Gully   90m   III
DF Lang and C Stead, 13 February 1994

Between Central Trident Buttress and Left Hand Ridge of North Trident Buttress is a wide, open gully. This route climbs the gully in three pitches, starting by traversing round the base of Central Trident Buttress. Most of the difficulties can be avoided on the right.

Left Hand Ridge   150m   IV,4
DF Lang and C Stead, 12 February 1994

The ridge left of Neptune Gully. Climb an icefall corner just left of Neptune Gully and follow the crest above, taking the rock tower by a central groove and finishing on a level crest.

Neptune Gully   160m   III
AJ Bennet and J Clarkson, February 1956

This S-shaped gully splits the crest of the North Trident (right-hand) Buttress. It has an indefinite entry pitch 10m to the left of the upper section of Moonlight Gully (described below) from the large flat ledge. Climb first on the right and enter the gully higher up, which is followed, turning ice pitches on the left to a large platform overlooking Number Five Gully. Ascend an easy ridge and slopes above to the plateau. In certain conditions all pitches can be taken direct.

North Trident Buttress   200m   III
J Maclay, H Raeburn, CW Walker and H Walker, 1904

Climbs the buttress on the left of Moonlight Gully. The line is variable depending on conditions, and the final tower is not climbed.

Central Rib Direct   150m   IV
P Macdonald and A McKeith, 18 February 1967

Gained from the upper section of Moonlight Gully, this climb ascends the middle of three distinct narrow ribs on the right side of North Trident Buttress. A lot of aid was used on the right arête of the final tower.

Moonlight Gully Buttress *is at the bottom of Number Five Gully on the left, and is split at two-thirds height by a very large (almost flat) ledge. At such a low altitude the climbs will not be in good condition so often, but they offer alternatives when the weather high up is bad. With no snow-ice, some of the routes will be quite hard.*

Moonlight Gully   150m   I/II
W Inglis-Clark and T Gibson, 3 January 1908
This gully is on the immediate left of Moonlight Gully Buttress and provides a steep and narrow snow climb which ends in the upper area of Number Five Gully.

Diagonal Route   150m   II/III ★
D Hawthorn, C MacLean and A Paul, 17 December 1983
Start at the foot of Moonlight Gully. Traverse up right to a broad ledge and continue by the left-hand chimney above to the big ledge. Climb the upper tier by the continuation of the chimney.

Fifties Revival   100m   IV,5
DF Lang and C Stead, 30 January 1994
Start 10m right of the entrance to Moonlight Gully. Climb a steep icy groove to a ledge crossed by Diagonal Route (25m). Ascend 2m left of a bulging crack to gain an ice smear and the groove-line, then a belay beneath a chimney (40m). Ascend the chimney past a pedestal at 10m, then a crack to easier ground (35m).

Right-Hand Chimney   135m   III,4 ★★
D Hawthorn, C MacLean and A Paul, 17 December 1983
Two chimneys split the front face of the buttress. The right-hand one is better defined. It is climbed direct, and its continuation followed on the second tier above the big ledge, sustained.

Gaslight   90m   IV,4
M Duff and R Parsley, 8 February 1989
Climb to the right of Right-Hand Chimney to a large roof, then enter Right-Hand Chimney. Above the roof gain the right edge of the buttress, which is followed to the top.

Phosphorescent Grooves   175m   III,4 ★
KV Crocket, A Walker and RT Richardson, 22 December 1985
A traverse-line up the face overlooking Numbr Five Gully. Start just left of the gully entrance and climb easily to a large ledge. Go up a steep wall and right to belay on a large ledge by a slab corner. Climb the corner to a belay and go right into an awkward 5m chimney, which is climbed to another belay. Descend a little, then go up to the large ledge above.

Number Five Gully
460m I ★

Collie and party, April 1895

Obvious from the CIC Hut. Prone to very large avalanches. Lies between the Trident Buttresses and the Great Buttress of Carn Dearg, and commences below and well to the right of the main basin of Coire na Ciste. It is a straightforward snow climb. Above a small pitch the gully narrows, and then opens into a huge funnel. The normal route keeps to the right, to exit near the top of Carn Dearg NW, depending on the cornice.

Number Five Gully Buttress *lies halfway up Number Five Gully on the right-hand side. The rock is sound, and there are several summer rock climbs, but only one winter route so far …*

Slanting Slit
140m VI,6

M Duff and S Greenhaugh, 26 February 1994

Climb out of Number Five Gully at the foot of the buttress to a diagonal gangway and follow this to a cracked slab (30m). Climb the cracked slab on thin ice and continue up corners to a bollard belay below a slit in a roof (25m). Descend to a ledge (5m). Go along a snow ledge, past one corner to a second corner, to a large detached block (30m). Climb this corner slightly leftwards to an icefall and easier ground (50m).

Ledge Route
450m II ★★★

SMC party, Easter 1897

The best on the mountain at this grade. A very interesting excursion. Start up Number Five Gully, but leave it by a rightwards-rising ramp shortly after it becomes a gully proper. The ramp leads out above the top of The Curtain onto a broad, almost horizontal ledge, which fades out to the right. Before the ledge narrows, leave it by a leftward-slanting gully, which comes out onto a broad sloping snow shelf. This shelf gives an easier but less interesting start; it comes out of Number Five Gully and slants easily up to the right to a large platform at the summit of the Great Buttress of Carn Dearg. A large top-heavy pinnacle, a useful landmark, is passed just before rounding the corner to reach the platform. The route now follows the ridge and is in places very narrow. A further connecting ridge leads on up to the summit of Carn Dearg NW. In good weather this route gives a more interesting, if slower, descent than the gullies.

In Descent

The ridge should be followed down to the top of Carn Dearg Buttress, and then the broad highest shelf (marked by the top-heavy pinnacle at the start) can be

Fresh snow on Ledge Route

followed easily into Number Five Gully. Instead of descending the gully (which may have a small pitch in it), continue to the far side, where a similar broad shelf leads gradually down from the large ledge at the top of Moonlight Gully Buttress towards Lochan Coire na Ciste. This descent passage also provides a good approach if avalanches are possible in Number Five Gully.

CARN DEARG BUTTRESS

The Great Buttress of Carn Dearg lies to the right of Number Five Gully. On the steep tier of rocks 100m below the buttress a number of icefalls may form called the Carn Dearg Cascades, providing good practice at a variety of grades. The big left-hand cascade often gives sustained vertical climbing, and the next right is the best at III, or IV if you finish up and left. These first two cascades have good boulders for anchors at the top, and an abseil descent is easy. Many lines form further right, and all the cascades are around 55m. (See diagram on page 164.)

The Curtain Rail   80m   IV,4 ★
DF Land, RT Richardson and C Stead, 31 January 1988 (first recorded ascent)
Follows the grooves left of, and parallel to, The Curtain (see next) and can provide an interesting alternative to that overcrowded climb.

The Curtain   110m   IV,5 ★★★
J Knight and D Bathgate, February 1965
The prominent ice climb on the left of the buttress has formed far less often in the last decade than in the decade before. When fully iced it is a popular climb due to its short approach. Climb the long slab to a belay on the right (45m). Zig-zag up the next pitch to belay on the left wall. Traverse right and climb the final steep ice wall and slab. If you are using 60m ropes it should be possible to climb the second and third pitches in one exposed run-out.

    Note If the belayer lets the ropes hang down the second pitch, they can easily get caught under the icicle fringe. Descent is made into Number Five Gully by a steep snow slope on the left after the final difficulties.

PM   110m   V,6
B Hall and A Rouse, 10 February 1986
From the foot of The Curtain, an obvious ledge runs right above very steep ground to a large deep chimney (Route I, see next) after approximately 60m. This line follows a corner (turf) to the left of the chimney for two pitches, then crosses the chimney for an exciting finish on the right.

    Note Climbed in good conditions on the first ascent, this route may vary in difficulty considerably. Also it appears that this route was climbed in 1985 by Mal Duff and J Tinker using the direct start of Route II, following the turf line mentioned on PM, and finishing up Route I instead of crossing that climb, as did Hall/Rouse. They called their climb Sod's Law (*300m, V,6*).

Moonlight Gully Buttress and Carn Dearg Buttress

1 Neptune Gully III
2 Moonlight Gully I/II
3 Diagonal Route II/III*
4 Right-Hand Chimney III,4**
5 Number Five Gully I*
6 The Curtain Rail IV,4*
7 The Curtain IV,5***
8 Route I Direct VI,6***
9 Route II Direct VI,7***
10 The Shadow VII,6**
10a Right-Hand Start Shadow VI,6*
11 Ring The Alarm VI,5***
12 French Connection VII,6**
13 Waterfall Gully IV,4*

Route I   175m   VI,6 ★★
D Knowles and D Wilson, 1972

An obvious ledge runs right from the foot of The Curtain. After about 60m it arrives at the bottom of a large obvious chimney. This chimney gives the top half of the climb, and can be very hard. It is possible to take a more direct start by climbing the minor buttress below and to the right of The Curtain and traversing the ledge mentioned above to the foot of the chimney section.

Route I Direct   80m   VI,6 ★★★ (grade for the combined route)
D Cuthbertson and J Sylvester, March 1984

Start as for Route II Direct, but transfer into the left-hand crack after approximately 10m. Climb the corner and then move left across the wall to gain the rib, which leads more easily to the ledge beneath the chimney.

Route II   150m   VI,6 ★★
M Geddes and A Rouse, 12 February 1978

Climb the first pitch of the chimney of Route I (20m). Then follow an upward diagonal line across the slabs, beneath the overhangs, rightwards to a groove-line at the far edge of the buttress. Follow this groove-line up the crest to easy ground. A superb climb in an exciting situation, not often in condition. Three pegs were used for tension on the first ascent.

Route II Direct   275m   VI,7 ★★★
G Smith and I Sykes, 15 February 1978

Starts in a deep corner at the lowest point of rocks right of Route I Direct start. Climb the corner and traverse left beneath an overhang. Climb up to a large block and climb a groove above it. Traverse right round an arête to a ledge, and climb the bulge above to the traverse ledge. Follow the Geddes/Rouse route to the top. Combined with the original Route II climb (Geddes/Rouse), the Direct provides a high-quality route of considerable difficulty when in condition.

Ring The Alarm   270m   VI,5 ★★★
M Duff and J Tinker, 1 February 1986

Start just right of the direct start to Route II and climb the crack (45m). Follow Route II for 10m and traverse across The Shadow to a stance on the slab edge (30m). Stay calm whilst traversing the lip of the slab to a groove, which is climbed over an overlap to a stance (45m). Climb ice (The Weep) above to reach Route II (30m), which is followed to the top (120m).

Carn Dearg Buttress

1 Centurion VIII,8
2 Sassenach IX,9
3 Shield Direct VII,7***
4 Gemini VI,6***

Overload Finish   155m   VI,6
R Clothier and D Heselden, 27 February 1988
From the top of the previous route climb the icefall and slab, then go right to
Centurion (45m). Overcome the step above and go horizontally right above the over-
lap to the edge of the buttress (30m). Go up the groove to Route II, (20m) which is
followed to the top (60m).

The Shadow   245m   VII,6 ★★
P Braithwaite and D Pearce, March 1979
Starts 10m right of Route II Direct. Follow a crack-line and groove to belay (20m).
Traverse right, continuing to an obvious line of overhangs beneath the traverse-line
of Route II. Continue this traverse right to the junction with Centurion, which is
gained with difficulty (40m). Continue across Centurion and up right to below a
large overhang (20m). Climb the exposed broken crack-line through the right side
of overhangs to a snowy recess on the arête (15m). Climb the overhanging groove
until a difficult move left can be made onto an icy rib. Climb the rib with difficulty,
then move slightly left to join Sassenach and follow the grooves above to finish.

Right-Hand Start Shadow   40m   VI,6 ★
R Clothier and D Heselden, February 1989
Climb a groove just right of the original route, then overcome a block and make a
difficult move left to gain the original climb.

French Connection   270m   VII,6 ★★
F Damilano and D Lewale, February 1995
A sensational route above the traverse of Route II, accessed by climbing the Right-
Hand Start Shadow, followed by Ring The Alarm to the traverse-line of The Shadow.
Follow this to its junction with Route II. Move up and right around a small buttress,
then descend slightly to reach a hanging slab leading to an icefall. Climb the steep
and delicate icefall and finish up its continuation gully.

Centurion   190m   VIII,8
Originally climbed solo using considerable aid over two days (*R Milward, 1975*).
Another ascent (*J McKenzie and K Spence, 9 February 1986*) over two days used a
bivouac and a rest point at the top of pitch two. The upper section has been avoided
by finishing up Route II.
    Start at the foot of the obvious corner in the centre of the face, climb the left
wall to a belay (15m), then go right into the corner, which is climbed to a belay in
an overhung bay (35m). Go left to the edge and follow grooves until level with an
overhang, then step right and up to a stance (25m). Go back into the corner, then

Carn Dearg Cascades

1 Waterfall Gully IV,4*
2 Raeburn's Buttress –
   Intermediate Gully IV,4**
3 South Castle Gully I/II*
4 The Castle Direct IV,4
5 North Castle Gully I/II*
6 Castle Ridge III**
7 Carn Dearg Cascades

left across the wall to beneath an overhung crack. Ascend the arête to a stance (20m), then on up slabby grooves past a block to join Route II (40m).

Sassenach   270m   IX,9
A Turner and T Stone, 9 March 2009

The summer route, the prominent chimney on the right of the buttress, was followed throughout. Start to the right of the chimney and climb it with the crux on the overhanging groove and flake of the second pitch. Only a perfect storm will ensure it is snowy and iced in the crux groove.

Shield Direct   290m   VII,7   ★★★
M Fowler and A Saunders, 15 March 1979

Originally the first recorded grade VI on the mountain, a soaring line of great difficulty. A long way right of the previous climbs, the front face of Carn Dearg Buttress turns to form a vertical line of cliffs facing north. Waterfall Gully (described later) is an obvious feature to the right. On the vertical wall is a series of steep chimneys, which give the line of the route. Start in a steep icy groove (often blank), directly below the chimney-line. Follow the groove to a stance at 24m. Climb steeply to a large ledge on the right at the foot of the chimney. Climb the difficult chimney to a cave (30m). Steep ice grooves lead to easier climbing at the top of the chimney flake (75m). Move left past a flake and bulges to trend right by the easiest line to ledges (45m). Climb up right then left to easier ground, followed by an arête, to the junction with Ledge Route.

Gemini   300m   VI,6   ★★★
A Paul and D Sanderson, 23 March 1979

Climb the first two pitches of Waterfall Gully (described below). Above on the left wall a series of rightward-sloping ice ramps and steep ice smears sometimes forms. These are followed to an enormous detached flake. Climb very steep ice on the wall left of the flake to a ledge and rightward-sloping grooves. Move up and right to obvious twin grooves, either of which can be climbed to a broad ledge, which is followed right. Climb up via iced slabs to easier ground.

A very steep direct start to the left of the first pitch of Waterfall Gully can be climbed, thus avoiding that route entirely. Combined with this start, Gemini becomes one of the finest routes on Ben Nevis (A McIntyre and A Kimber, V,6***, 1 April 1979). **Note** The direct start had been climbed previously by at least two parties as a more difficult start to Waterfall Gully. One of them reported it to be in grade IV condition at the time!

Gemini Left-Hand Finish   130m   V,5 ★★

A Fanshawe, A Orgler, GE Little and R Sailer, 16 February 1988

From the ledge below the right-sloping grooves climb the groove on the left to a ledge. Then go blindly left and continue directly up steep mixed ground (45m). Go right by an ice scoop then left along a narrow ledge to a shallow cave (50m). Go left up into an open slabby corner, then on to the top (35m).

Bewildabeast   130m   VI,6

M Garthwaite and A Wainwright, 21 March 1995

Starts just above and right of the enormous detached flake on Gemini at the base of a corner. Climb an ice smear on the left of the corner to a steep wall. Go right on thin holds to a small ledge in the corner, then up a chimney to a belay (30m). Go up the thin corner, over a small roof, and right to the foot of another corner, which is climbed over a second roof to a small belay on the right (35m). Ascend a very thin groove in the arête on the right of the corner, then go right to another short corner. Belay on the terrace. Go up a thin tongue of ice on the final wall, then move left onto the icefall and direct to finish (45m).

Waterfall Gully   215m   IV,4 ★

D Pipes, I Clough, J Alexander, R Shaw and A Flegg, 8 January 1959

The obvious gully immediately right of Carn Dearg Buttress. After the first steep 45m the angle eases and leads with a rightwards traverse after 150m to the large basin below the summit buttresses. Keep to the left of this area and climb towards Ledge Route. The first pitch of this route offers a good ice pitch, followed by abseil if time is short.

Waterfall Gully Direct Finish   100m   VI,6 ★★

D Cuthbertson and C Fraser, 1984

A direct finish to Waterfall Gully is possible by continuing straight up where the gully swings right onto the ridge. Two pitches – the first on ice up the big corner; the second (crux) a short stiff pull over the overhang. The crux is escapable.

Wray's Wrib   120m   III

S Powell and J Wray, February 1994

Go right from the top of the first pitch of Waterfall Gully and gain a snowy rib from an icy groove. Follow the rib, then a small buttress above by a crack-line on the right to a snowy col. Climb a groove and regain Waterfall Gully after it exits right into the snow basin.

Staircase Climb   215m   IV,5 ★
D Haston and J Stenhouse, February 1987
Starts 15m to the right of Waterfall Gully and climbs the higher of two shelves sloping up rightwards. Around the corner a stepped slab is climbed up right to beneath a clean-cut crack in a corner. Climb the crack and a short wall to a platform. The chimney above is climbed to easier ground, and the buttress crest followed towards a pinnacle, which is turned on the left. Descend a little into Waterfall Gully, then move up to a steep slab leading to the col beyond the pinnacle. Take the left hand of two chimneys and continue up towards the top of Carn Dearg Buttress.

Staircase Climb Direct   190m   VI,7
S Richardson and C Cartwright, 24 January 1999
Climb the initial ramp of Staircase Climb and go up to the foot of a deep-cut chimney (15m). Desperate body jamming up the chimney to a ledge on the right (15m). Follow the chimney to where it eases (40m). Two more easier pitches on the left side of the buttress lead to a prominent pinnacle (80m). Follow a turfy ramp on the right of the pinnacle to a col, then follow a broad chimney above to easier ground (40m).

The Cone Gatherers   310m   VIII,7
I Small and S Richardson, 14 December 2008
A good varied mixed route up the wall left of MacPhee's Route. Start up a ramp and move right past a tiny pine tree to join a second ramp (taken by MacPhee's Route) trending back right. Belay below a steep crack cutting through the wall above (70m). Climb the crack to the terrace above (30m). Cross the right-to-left break, steep and bold, to enter the V-groove and climb this to the top of the wall (30m). Easier ground up and right leads to a belay below the deep chimney cutting the left side of the triangular wall right of Waterfall Gully (60m). Climb the chimney over a couple of overhanging chockstones (40m). Continue up the upper section of Waterfall Gully for two pitches to join the ridge section of Ledge Route (80m).

MacPhee's Route   165m   V,6
C Cartwright and S Richardson, 12 February 2000
Start 50m right of Staircase Climb and follow a shelf to a vegetated groove on the left of the North Wall. Follow the groove and a chimney to a terrace (40m). Ascend a narrow vegetated groove from the left end of the terrace, then go right by a slab to the left end of another terrace (25m). Go right along the terrace to the top of a downward step (40m). Descend a chimney and go down into a crevasse and along its base to a large block at the end (20m). Go down a chimney, then right to an obvious block, from which it is possible to abseil in 25m to easier ground (40m).

Kellett's North Wall

1 Shield Direct VII,7***
2 Gemini VI,6***
3 Kellett's North Wall Route VII,7
4 The Shroud VI,6**
5 Harrison's Climb Direct IV,4***
6 Boomer's Requiem V,5***
7 Castle Ridge III**
8 Lobby Dancer VI,6***
9 The Moat II**

Kellett's North Wall Route
200m VII,7

M Charlton and M Burrows-Smith, 1 February 1991

Starts left of The Shroud below a large flake with a deep chimney to the right. Climb the chimney and exit by a window to continue to a terrace (25m). Climb the corner to the left of an obvious crack to reach another terrace (20m). Go 6m right then move up to a recess, then go right to a steep groove which is climbed to a ledge (30m). Move up left along the ledge and on up a steep turfy groove-line (30m). Exit left into Waterfall Gully, which is followed to the top (95m).

The Past is Close Behind
200m VIII,8

B Fyffe and I Small, 18 February 2010

A line up the steep wall just left of The Shroud starting up Harrison's Climb. Climb the easy snow ramp of Harrison's Climb, then turn left and climb one short wall to a good ledge (40m). Thin climbing up the wall leads into a technical groove. Belay on a ledge on the left (35m). Back right into the groove, then the wall and rising rightwards traverse (15m). There is quality climbing up the big corner, locking-off on solid chockstones (35m). Bold slabby climbing leads into an inverted V, and there is bold slabby thin ice climbing out of the inverted V (30m). Follow more thinly iced slabs and easier ground to Ledge Route (45m).

*High up above and to the right of **Waterfall Gully** is a large hanging snow coire. At its bottom lip an overhung icefall (**The Shroud**) can sometimes be seen from the approach to the CIC Hut. To the right of this icefall is an obvious snow/ice gully which gives*

Blair Fyffe finding The Past is Close Behind

the start to some of the following routes. Access to these climbs can be made from below the hut over the steep and rocky ground beneath The Castle. Please be aware that many avalanche fatalities have occurred in this area over the years. This approach is exposed to these dangers for most of its length. A far safer approach is to ascend from the hut to beneath the **Carn Dearg Buttress** *and traverse below it towards the climbs. Descent from the large hanging snow coire is easiest by* **Ledge Route***, which is gained by ascending the steep slopes on the left side of the coire to the ridge above. Alternatively, one of the Carn Dearg Summit Gullies can be climbed to the top.*

The Shroud   200m VI,6 ★★
A Clarke and J Main, 2 February 1993
In exceptional conditions an icy drape extends over the cliffs below the hanging coire left of Harrison's Climb Direct. Climb up to belay on the right side of the ice-fall (50m). Continue to another belay on a narrow ice ledge right of the free-hanging fang (25m). Follow the fang to the upper ice wall and a semi-hanging belay on ice screws (25m). Continue more easily above (100m) to the hanging snow coire.

Harrison's Climb   275m III ★★
CGM Slesser and N Tennent, 1962
Down to the right of The Shroud is a deep chimney which separates the main wall from an isolated buttress (Cousin's). Start 10m left of the chimney, climb up then right to enter the chimney and follow the ice corner above to the col. Go left to a 30m icefall, which is climbed by its right edge and followed by easier ground into the upper coire, from which a variety of exits can be made.

Harrison's Climb Direct   300m IV,4 ★★★
KV Crocket and C Gilmore, 7 February 1976
This climb ascends the steep icy chimney direct then follows the original climb to the col. From the col traverse left to the icefall, and from its right end climb a line up right on Cousin's Buttress to gain the edge overlooking Raeburn's Buttress. Continue for several pitches to the upper coire and a variety of exits. A fine route.

> **Note** The hanging snow coire often releases large avalanches, so be wary after strong winds and/or heavy snowfalls.

North East Face Route (Cousin's Buttress Ordinary Route)   275m III ★
GG McPhee and GF Todd, April 1935
Down to the right of The Shroud, this buttress has deep chimneys on either side. Climb the hidden chimney on the right side with one short ice pitch to a saddle. Follow a ledge left and climb the right side of a large exposed icefall to the coire above, as for Harrison's Climb. A variety of exits are possible.

The Great Corner VIII,8

Raeburn's Buttress and The Castle

1 Boomer's Requiem V,5***
2 Raeburn's Buttress –
  Intermediate Gully IV,4**
3 The Crack VIII,8
4 Compression Crack V,5*
5 South Castle Gully I/II*
6 Godspell VI,8
7 The Castle II/III*
8 The Castle Direct IV,4
9 The Keep IV,5

Boomer's Requiem
170m   V,5 ★★★

C Higgins and D MacArthur, February 1973

Above the approach gully on Raeburn's Buttress is an obvious icefall leading to a snow patch. This is easily seen from the path up the Allt a'Mhuilinn. Climb the ice-fall and up another ice pitch above the snow patch to beneath the summit gullies.

Continuation Wall
180m   IV,4

B Dunn and D Gardner, February 1977

Head up towards Boomer's Requiem and the bifurcation in the gully. Continue up the continuation chimney, overcoming an ice step and heading up right to a steep snow gully which finishes on the Girdle Traverse ledge. Either traverse easily left and finish up one of the summit gullies (described below) or take the next route.

Baird's Buttress
90m   IV,4

B Dunn and D Gardner, February 1977

This route lies on the right edge of the upper coire just left of Raeburn's Buttress, and starts from a large ledge below a crack which splits the front of the buttress. Climb the crack and a steep wall above, then easier climbing to the top.

Raeburn's Buttress – Intermediate Gully
230m   IV,4 ★★

WD Brooker and JM Taylor (by the buttress finish), 31 January 1959

Raeburn's is the tall thin buttress above the left-hand corner of the Castle Coire, up left of the foot of South Castle Gully. It finishes as a slender tapering arête, to the left of which is the prominent narrow Intermediate Gully. The start is the same as for the approach to North East Face Route and Boomer's Requiem. After about 65m an obvious chimney-line, which is hidden from below, leads up right to a cave (the impressive icefall of the left branch is Boomer's Requiem, described above), and then the route takes the right wall to reach the foot of Intermediate Gully. There is a cave exit at the top of the gully, which is otherwise straightforward. The crest of Raeburn's Buttress proper is immediately to the right of the foot of the gully. It narrows to a sharp blade at the top, but this may be turned by a corner on the right.

The Crack
360m   VIII,8

C Cartwright and S Richardson, 13 February 2000

This very steep route lies on the front face of Raeburn's Buttress to the right of the entrance gully to Boomer's Requiem and follows an obvious crack. Mixed ground is climbed to a block-belay beneath slabs guarding the entrance to the crack. Go left and up a short wall to a vegetated slab. Move up right and climb overhanging steps to a block just right of the crack (25m). Go up the chimney-crack to a ledge on the right (15m). Go back into the crack and up it to a ledge on the left, with possible rests en route (25m). Climb down right to a ledge and along it for 3m, then up a number of overhanging walls to easier ground (20m). Climb the crest of Raeburn's Buttress for 125m, passing the last rocky blade on the left. A variety of exits towards the plateau exist, depending on the avalanche potential (150m).

Carn Dearg Summit Gullies

These form a logical continuation to some of the previous climbs. They may also be reached by descending into the basin from high up on Ledge Route.

Colando Gully   105m I

I Clough, PS Nicholson and D Pipes, 8 April 1958
The left-hand gully. Straightforward.

Arch Buttress   185m II/III

D Pipes and A Flegg, 3 January 1959
Between Arch and Colando gullies. After 45m on the crest, the route follows a groove on the right then easier climbing to some difficult chimneys.

Arch Gully   105m I

I Clough, PS Nicholson and D Pipes, 8 April 1958
The central gully marked by a huge block which forms the Arch at about half-height. Straightforward but steep.

Surprise Buttress   190m III

I Clough and B Halpin, 3 January 1959
On the buttress to the right of Arch Gully, following the crest as closely as possible to a steep wall above the Arch block. A 33m rightwards traverse below this wall is followed by short awkward walls leading back slightly left to a small ledge about 10m above the traverse. A move downwards and to the right gives entry to a steep 35m corner, which gives a strenuous final crux pitch.

Surprise Gully   185m I/II

I Clough, PS Nicholson and D Pipes, 12 April 1958
The shallow right-hand gully leads by broken rocks to a shoulder and to the top by an ice groove on the left.

CLIMBS FROM CASTLE COIRE

On the approach up the Allt a'Mhuilinn, the first main feature is the North Face of Castle Ridge up on the right, and to its left is Castle Ridge. The area to the left of Castle Ridge is known as Castle Coire, and is only seen fully from a point approximately 0.5km downhill of the hut. The main features are the North and South Castle gullies, which are separated by The Castle at their top, and join at their foot into a steep rocky icefall/gully descending towards the Halfway Lochan approach path. An approach can be made through the band of rocks at the foot of the coire by a right-slanting snow ramp. Please be aware that many avalanche fatalities have occurred in this area over the years. This approach is exposed to these dangers for most of its length. A far safer approach is to ascend from the hut to beneath the Carn Dearg Buttress and traverse below it towards the climbs.

The Great Corner   340m   VIII,8
I Small and S Richardson, 24 January 2010
The awe-inspiring clean-cut corner on the right flank of Raeburn's Buttress. Start on the Girdle Traverse terrace, reached by climbing the first two pitches of the Compression Crack icefall. Move left along the terrace to belay below the chimney cutting up into the corner (50m). Climb the chimney to a small exposed ledge at its top (40m). Continue up the imposing corner above and exit into the upper groove. Follow this (sustained) to the top of Raeburn's Buttress (50m). Continue up easier ground to the summit of Carn Dearg NW (150m).

Compression Crack   130m   V,5 ★
M Hind and C Rice, 9 February 1985
On the steep wall left of South Castle Gully and below Raeburn's Arête, a series of imposing ice smears can often be seen. Climb this ice and traverse a long way right to reach iced cracks. Follow the corner above vertically for 15m and a further 20m to easy ground.

Winter Chimneys   145m   IV,4
IS Clough and R Sefton, 28 January 1960
After climbing the icefall of Compression Crack and traversing right, continuing traversing for about 30m to a deep chimney topped by a huge capstone. The capstone was avoided by pegging on the right wall on the first ascent.

Plum Line   230m   V,6 ★
C Bailey and P Downthwaite, 6 March 1999
Start up South Castle Gully to its last narrow section and an icefall running down

the arête on the left. Climb the icefall with a bulge at 30m and continue steeply above to snow (50m). Climb the next icefall direct, trending right at the top to rock anchors (50m). Easier ground leads to the top.

The Castle

The two Castle gullies can be anything from straightforward snow ascents to awkward chockstone-filled trenches, depending on the amount of snow. They are also very prone to avalanches after strong winds and/or snowfall. Between them lies The Castle, which is not often visited but which gives good climbing.

South Castle Gully   230m   I/II ★

W Brunskill, WW King and WW Naismith, 1 April 1896

The long gully between Raeburn's Buttress and The Castle. Normally an easy snow climb. One small pitch may be particularly difficult early in the season; climbed by a gangway on the left wall. Near the top of the left wall of the gully is an obvious icefall, **Plum Duff** (*60m, V,5, D Hawthorn and J Murphy, February 1984*).

Godspell   215m   VII,8

S Richardson and K Cordes, 6 March 2005

The obvious line of chimneys on the left side of The Castle. Start 50m up The Castle and move left up easy mixed ground to a terrace (50m). Climb the short steep icy gully on the right side of the wall above. Follow the corner above to another terrace (50m). Climb the chimney past a chokestone (15m). Climb the right side of the square-cut recess to a small ledge and the wall above to a terrace. Another chimney leads past a chokestone to the top of the headwall (45m).

The Castle   330m   II/III ★

W Brown, J MacLay, WW Naismith and G Thomson, April 1896

In summer an awkward bulging little wall guards the base. This may be hard in winter, but more probably it will be entirely obliterated by an avalanche cone. The route then goes straight up. The upper rocks are climbed by means of a gully, slabs, a chimney and a further shallow gully, all in the centre of the buttress, to beneath the final very steep wall. The route now goes up to the right over snow-covered slabs to the top. Great care should be taken on the slabby sections, which are prone to avalanche.

The Castle Direct   90m   IV,4

S Powell and J Wray, February 1994

Follows a steep line 25m right of the gully in the upper reaches of The Castle and finishes directly at the normal finish of The Castle.

The Keep   80m   IV,5

M Duff and I Oates, 13 February 1994

Follow The Castle to the exit from the shallow gully, then go down right on a ledge to a block-belay beneath a corner. Ascend above the belay, then right at a ledge, then a groove to another ledge. Go up past a projecting block to belay (30m). Go up a groove and over a bulge to easier ground and a flake-belay (20m). Follow either the groove or slab edge above to finish (30m).

North Castle Gully   230m   I/II ★

JH Bell and RG Napier, 4 April 1896

The gully bounding The Castle on the right. Steeper than South Castle Gully, it contains several easy chockstone pitches, often completely covered, giving a straightforward snow climb.

Castle Ridge   275m   III ★★

JN Collie, WW Naismith, G Thomson and MW Traverse, 12 April 1895

A fine outing. The easiest of the Nevis ridges (after Ledge Route) and possible in most conditions. If avalanche conditions prevail, it is very difficult (if not impossible) to avoid them on the approaches from beneath or the traverse from below Carn Dearg Buttress. Start 150m below the point where the Castle gullies meet and traverse right onto the blunt crest of the ridge by the easiest line. Ascend via ledges, walls and slabs using the easiest line until the crest is blocked by a band of steep walls. Traverse up and right with difficulty via a flaky chimney in a very exposed position overlooking the North Face (crux) to a good ledge and belay. Another difficult pitch leads to an easing in the ridge. Follow more easily to the top of the ridge.

Note Teams who are considering descending to the Halfway Lochan (GS 1472) should follow 232° grid for 200m from the top of the ridge, then 308° grid. The descent to the Halfway Lochan is over very rough, broken and rocky ground, with one or two small crags in places. A number of accidents have occurred in this area with people falling down the North Face, which is immediately on your right at the top of the ridge. In good weather and with enough time, a fine way to round off this ascent is to go up to the north summit of Carn Dearg NW (1214m, GR 159721) and descend Ledge Route. Alternatively, a bearing heading south-west from that summit will lead into the easy Red Burn descent.

North Face of Castle Ridge

This very extensive, steep, broken area of rock is the first significant part of the climbing areas as seen across the Allt a'Mhuilinn approach on the right. The left edge is Castle Ridge, and to its right is an overhanging section of rock with an

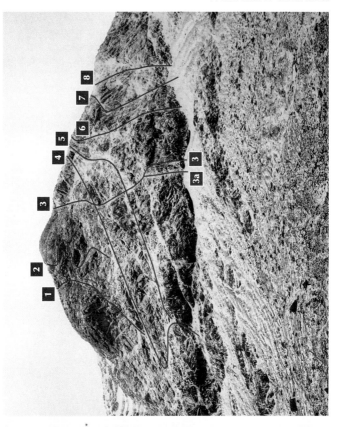

North Face of Castle Ridge

1 Lobby Dancer VI,6***
2 Last Day in Purgatory V,5**
3 Nordwand IV,3*
3a Nordwand – Direct Start IV,4**
4 The Moat II**
5 The Serpent II
6 Casino Royale V,5
7 La Petite III
8 Le Mechant IV,4

obvious groove on its right (Lobby Dancer). Large snow terraces traverse the face from bottom left towards the shoulder of Carn Dearg NW.

Cherry Pickers   380m   IV,4
M Duff, D Horrox and D Potter, 21 February 1994
Climbs the icefall 40m left of American Pie (see next). A slanting right-to-left shelf halfway is a feature of this route. Ascend the icefall on its right side to belay in a corner, then up to the shelf and climb a steep icicle on its left (75m). Go up the snowfield in two pitches and belay beneath a small roof (90m). Move right then left to beneath a hidden (from below) icefall (45m). Ascend the icefall (45m). Head up left over mixed ground in two pitches towards a small tower on the slight ridge on the left (80m). Finish up behind the tower by a crack and shallow chimney (50m).

American Pie   770m   V,4 ★★
DF Lang and NW Quinn, 18 February 1978
Start to the left of The Serpent and climb to the foot of a steep, narrow and hidden right-slanting chimney (30m). Ascend the chimney past a snow bay (30m) and its twisting icy (10m) continuation. Gain the buttress edge and ascend to a snow bay (60m). Climb the short icy groove above to beneath a ramp (15m). Follow the ramp rightwards to the upper amphitheatre (420m). Continue left to a rock band (100m). Go through the rock band on the left (30m). Traverse up right to finish below the top of Castle Ridge (75m).

The Serpent   300m   II
I Clough, D Pipes and J Porter, 12 February 1959
The easiest of the routes on the North Face of Castle Ridge. No technical difficulty, but serious, with route-finding problems. Above and to the left of the Lunching Stone (Glen Nevis approach), a small right-slanting gully gives access to a wide shelf which curves up to the right. After 165m this leads into a couloir which slants rightwards, steeply up the face, to come out on the shoulder of Carn Dearg NW.

The Moat   500m   II ★★
I Sykes, I Rae and I Dewar, 8 February 1972
A great highly banked snow ledge runs across the face above The Serpent and gives the line of the climb. Follow The Serpent for 70m, then move left to gain the ledge. At the end of the ledge finish by a steep gully. A fine outing across this huge face.

Lobby Dancer   280m   VI,6 ★★★
C Higgins and A Kimber, 28 February 1977
The left-hand section of the face is dominated by a clean overhanging wall split by a groove. Come in to the foot of the groove from the left by a diagonal ledge, or

more directly by ice pitches. Climb the groove for three pitches to a barrier, from where an escape left is made (possibly on aid) to another groove. Up this groove and on up to Castle Ridge.

Alchemist   270m   VI,5 ★★

A Paul and D Sanderson, 26 March 1979

Start as for The Serpent then follow an icefall to the foot of the groove system, just right of the main groove of Lobby Dancer. Climb the groove system to the barrier, which is crossed by the right wall of a huge flake, on aid, to a narrow ice chimney. Climb the chimney, and move left then right to a cave. Go right around the arête and follow the groove to Castle Ridge.

Mist Dancer   50m   VI

R Clothier and C Cartwright, 1988

This provides a free finish to Alchemist. To the right of the huge flake, climb a chimney-groove, exit left and go left to join the final groove of Alchemist.

Last Day in Purgatory   330m   V,5 ★★

C Higgins and M Geddes, 8 April 1979

Takes an impressive zig-zag line up ledge-systems to the clean face right of Lobby Dancer.

Nordwand   425m   IV,3 ★

I Clough, D Pipes, B Sarll, F Jones and J Porter, 11 February 1959

A fine mixed route. Technical and route-finding problems similar to those on the Little Brenva Face, but no sunshine; a genuine, grim nordwand atmosphere. Starts fairly well to the right of the centre of the face at a slight bay. A long, vertical snow-filled trench on the screes below the face often shows the way. Nordwand follows a short gully up the face for 30m, and climbs an ice pitch before moving left (or works diagonally left below the ice pitch). It continues to follow the icefalls direct up the centre of the wall, crossing the couloir of The Serpent and continuing by snowfields to the steep summit rocks. An awkward left rising traverse leads to the top. **Direct Start** (*100m, IV,4**, G Suzca and party, 1989*). Two pitches just left of the original start (poorly protected).

Casino Royale   190m   V,5

M Duff, R Nowack and A Bond, 29 February 1988

Starts at an obvious thin gully just left of La Petite. Climb the walls, snow bays and an icefall to below a roof. Move left with difficulty to a thin ice smear in a corner, which is followed to the top. Go rightwards at the top to finish.

Le Chat Noir   225m   IV,4

M Duff, D Horrox, J Robson and H Ousby, 17 February 1994

Easily up the buttress between Casino Royale and La Petite (80m). Go up a square turfy recess in the middle of the buttress and over a small overlap to a snow patch (45m). Climb a very steep iceflow above by a runnel on the right (50m). Easy to the top (50m).

La Petite   200m   III

D Pipes and I Clough, 11 February 1959

The climb starts about 30m right of Nordwand and goes up steeply for 40m to gain entry to a couloir. This entry will generally give a 25m ice pitch and then ice-glazed rock. The couloir, which leads obliquely right (not obvious from below), should give two more good ice pitches before finishing on the Carn Dearg shoulder.

Le Mechant   140m   IV,4

A Perkins and M Duff, 9 February 1991

50m right of La Petite, climb a small buttress to belay below a thin gully (35m). Overcome a slab and enter the gully, which is followed over an icy bulge (45m). Carry on up icy slabs and grooves to the crest of the buttress and easy ground (80m).

   A small buttress well to the right of the face is split by an obvious gully (**Red Gully**, *120m, II, D Pipes, IS Clough, J Porter, B Sarll and F Jones, 1959*).

The Girdle Traverse   4000m   V,4

SM Richardson and B Davison, 21 April 2006

A right-to-left girdle traverse from Castle Ridge to North East Buttress. From the top of Castle Ridge go over The Castle, then descend mixed ground into upper Castle Coire. Cross Ledge Route and the Trident Buttresses, descend Number Four Gully, climb North Gully and traverse across Creag Coire na Ciste into Number Three Gully. Climb Thompson's Route, descend Number Three Gully Buttress, climb Green Gully and descend Hesperides Ledge. Traverse across Comb Gully Buttress, move along the first part of Raeburn's Easy Route and continue left into Glover's Chimney. Drop down from Tower Gap into Observatory Gully and head off under Indicator Wall and across Observatory Buttress and enter Point Five Gully above the Rogue Pitch. Exit Point Five via the Left-Hand Finish, continue across Hadrian's Wall, Observatory Ridge and Zero Gully to finish up Slav Route and reach the crest of North East Buttress.

A BIG RIDE by Dave Macleod

Standing in the dark on the Great Tower, having climbed a grade V on Pinnacle Buttress, we felt panicky as ill-equipped teenagers on the Ben for the first time, tackling unknown territory in Tower Gap with our one torch. In the gloom I spotted a straightforward snow-ramp leading down into Tower Gully, and we quickly decided that would be a good alternative to get to the plateau before the rising storm got any worse.

After a swim, we arrived under the cornice rim. Peter got there first and began to dig. I traversed left looking for a way around the overhangs, busy listening to the roar of wind just overhead and worrying about navigation.

I think Peter made a sound, I probably heard the first syllable of 'WATCH!' as Peter's sterling dig had made the whole cornice rim suddenly release and crash on our heads. Peter, now well inside his own tunnel was simply pummelled down into his own pit by the weight of it. No such luck for me, as I was leaning back to look over the cornice and was catapulted off backwards into a snowy somersault.

I made a quick assessment of things in the following second. Sound? Roar. The gully has avalanched. Orientation? Up has changed many times in the last second. I'm tumbling. Sensation? The snow on top of me feels like a river of concrete, it's squashing my chest. Speed? Definitely getting faster quickly. Can't bear to linger on that thought. Options for stopping? Bloody hell – where have my ice axes and rucksack gone? What next then?

I thought about the gully below – the 200 foot rocky, icy cliff of Tower Scoop that forms a barrier across the gully. If I couldn't stop by the time I went tumbling off that in a few seconds, I was finished for sure.

Desperate punching and clawing into the soft snowpack below followed. But I seemed to be suspended in the moving train of debris and I could never have matched its momentum. So I curled up and cringed, ready for the drop and smash.

I bounced once and the floor disappeared from under me. Falling, I was struck by the sensation of the huge weight of snow lifting gently away from me as we dropped. With each passing second I cringed more, but tried to take comfort in the thought that the long fall would at least make for an instant conclusion.

The snow behind me made a splatting noise for a split second before I smashed into some off-vertical cliff, cushioned from bone breaking

Dave MacLeod nears the top of Point Five Gully on the 50th anniversary of its first free ascent (photo: Paul Diffley)

deceleration by the vast quantities of aerated snow all around. Acrobatics followed, before being thrown hard into the bed of sliding avalanche once more.

As I was sinking into acceptance, or probably hypoxia, the roar became a gentle hiss and everything stopped, like quietly pulling up to the lights in a car. The feeling of cold air on my face and going into my lungs was most vivid and invigorating. As well as half my face, I could feel one (gloveless) hand sticking out of the debris. I dug out and sat, wide eyed for a minute figuring out what had happened. I'd survived a big ride. Quite a welcome for a career of Ben Nevis climbing.

SOUTH AND EAST OF BEN NEVIS

STOB BAN, 999M GR 147654 – MAMORES

The North East Face of this steep-sided and rocky peak provides good climbing on ridges, buttresses and gullies when in condition. The shapely summit cone is best seen from Glen Nevis Youth Hostel. An easy approach on a good path is made from the Lower Falls (GR 145684) up the east bank of the Allt Coire a'Mhusgain. Ascend this path to a point opposite the cliffs (GR 155660, 1½–2 hours), then descend for a short distance to cross the main stream below the cliffs. Approaching the cliffs from this point allows for a good reconnaissance before choosing the correct line of ascent, as the cliffs are more complicated than they may at first appear.

From this point on the path the features are as follows, left to right: East Wing, South Gully, South (summit) Buttress, North Gully, Central Buttress (this appears as a triangular mass of rock set forward and at a lower level than South Buttress), and a long flat col has North Buttress to its right.

Early morning light on Stob Ban (photo: Jamie Hageman)

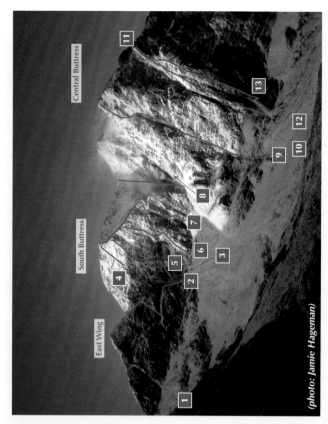

(photo: Jamie Hageman)

Stob Ban

1 Eag Blanc II
2 East Wing V,5
3 South Gully I*
4 Summit Groove IV,4*
5 Groove Rider IV,4*
6 Banjo IV,4
7 North Ridge Route IV,4
8 North Gully I
9 No Toddy III,4
10 Central Gully IV
11 Gendarme Ridge IV,4
12 Triad III*
13 Skyline Rib IV,4*

Ollie   45m IV,4
D McGimpsey and V Chelton, 25 February 2005
The hanging turfy ramp left of Eag Blanc gives poorly protected climbing with an awkward chimney at the top.

Eag Blanc   100m II
V Chelton and D McGimpsey, 25 February 2005
The big groove on the left side of the East Wing is mostly grade I, with a couple of grade II steps.

East Wing   180m V,5
D McGimpsey and A Nisbet, 26 February 2006
Starting about 15m up South Gully at the highest ramp leading out left, this is a devious but spectacular line near the crest of the very steep East Wing. Reach the crest out to the left, always keeping above steep lower walls (35m). Gain the highest ledge up thick moss, then traverse it leftwards to a vertical column of wedged blocks, which is very unstable if not well frozen (25m). Climb the column then a ramp leading up right (40m). The crest leads easily to the top of the buttress (80m).

South Gully   150m I ★

Summit Groove   140m IV,4 ★
A Nisbet and C Wells, 18 March 2008
Halfway up South Gully climb a shallow gully leading to close to the summit. Would be grade III if well iced.

Groove Rider   160m IV,4 ★
A Nisbet and C Wells, 18 March 2008
Start as for North Groove by traversing out right, but climb a smaller well-defined groove straight up in two pitches. Gain and climb the ridge to the summit (75m).

North Groove   160m III,4
S Kennedy and A Paul, 30 December 1996
Starts 30m up South Gully at a prominent rocky recess on the right. Go right below a steep wall, then up and left into a deep groove (45m). Follow the groove and broken ground to the North Ridge Route and the summit.

Banjo   200m IV,4
V Chelton, D McGimpsey, A Nisbet and J Preston, 20 November 2004
Start up the fault at the foot of the buttress and soon move right onto steeper

ground. Go right, then back left up a V-groove in a steep wall about 6m right of the original fault (30m). Climb mixed ground on the right of a long smooth V-groove on the right to reach North Ridge (45m) and finish up this easily.

North Ridge Route
150m IV,4

S Kennedy and A Nelson, 29 January 1995

At the foot of South Buttress, near the bottom of South Gully, are two corner-lines. Follow the left-hand line (35m) then go right to a belay just before the ridge (15m). Climb the ridge easily to finish close to the summit.

North Gully
150m I

There are three gully-lines on the left (north-east) flank of Central Buttress. The right-hand two are close together, and all three are the same grade.

No Toddy
150m III,4

D Hawthorn, R Lee and DN Williams, April 1986

Climbs the left-hand gully. Start at a small snowfield some distance up the left flank of the buttress. Climb a steep ice pitch to easier ground and a stance on the right. Move back left and ascend the gully easily until it slants right. The right slant has been climbed on an earlier ascent by Malcolm Creasey and party, and on that ascent the whole climb was graded IV. Traverse left and bridge up a continuation of the lower line. Follow mixed ground to the top of buttress.

Banter
200m III

M Edwards, D McGimpsey and A Nisbet, 24 February 2006

The buttress right of North Gully, starting right at the toe and closely following the crest.

Stertor
200m IV,4

B Davison and D McGimpsey, 19 February 2005

The line of twisting grooves up the buttress starting at the bottom left. Climb turf up and right to a short right-facing groove near the right edge (60m). Climb the groove to a ledge, cross slabs to the groove above and climb this for 10m (40m). Continue up the groove to a terrace, then up another groove reached by a corner on the left (30m). Traverse right to an arête (30m), then follow the buttress above (40m).

Central Gully
150m IV

J Grieve and C MacNaughton, 1969

Follow the gully and go back left along an easy ramp to gain the crest of the ridge, which leads easily to the top of the buttress.

Gendarme Ridge 150m IV,4

J Maclay and Parr, 4 January 1904

On the slender buttress right of Central Gully. Climb up to and past a gendarme 'look-alike', then steeply to where the angle eases (60m). Finish easily on Central Gully and the ridge above.

Triad 150m III ★

D Hawthorn, R Lee and DN Williams, April 1986

Climbs the right-hand gully. Start between two narrow rock buttresses. Ascend the gully, which gradually steepens and narrows to a chimney. Reach a stance where the right-hand buttress finishes and a ledge runs across the left-hand buttress. Follow a snow ramp on the right and traverse left along a narrow ledge to the buttress crest. Join the easy leftward-slanting ramp above as for the previous route.

South of Ben Nevis

Skyline Rib 120m IV,4 ★

RG Webb and BA Mattock, 13 February 1987

Climbs the narrow buttress crest right of Triad (loose). Finish up the ramp of Triad.

Rampant 250m IV,4

D Hanna and S Kennedy, January 1995

Climbs the large triangular face between Skyline Rib and Bodice Ripper. Ascend to the leftward-slanting ramp of Bodice Ripper, which is followed until it fades, then up to another ramp, which is followed to within 20m of the edge of the buttress. Climb steeply rightwards onto a narrow ramp below the buttress crest and follow it for two pitches. Traverse leftwards steeply across a small buttress and finish just below the top of Triad, then finish up the ramp of that route.

Bodice Ripper 150m IV,4 ★

J Murphy and DN Williams, March 1984

Climbs the large triangular face on the front of Central Buttress. Start right of centre at the foot of an obvious rightward-slanting gully. Ascend easily to a prominent leftward-slanting ramp. Follow this until it fades, and take a poor stance at the foot of a steep and narrow rightward-slanting slab. Climb the slab with difficulty to its end, and zig-zag up the snow slope above (crux). Continue to the top of the snow-field and ascend the obvious gully. At the top, squeeze up the narrow chimney (Bodice Ripper) leading rightwards. A broad ramp leads left and then by a narrow crest towards the summit.

    Note A short section of arête at the end of all of the routes on Central Buttress links to the main ridge 200m north of the summit.

Flake Chimney

150m III

RN Campbell and M Naftalin, March 1985

Climb to a bay on the first pitch of Bodice Ripper. Go via a chimney on the right to a notch behind a large flake, then right over a slab and two leftward grooves to another chimney, slanting up right. Climb the chimney to easy ground.

North Buttress – East Ridge

200m II/III

Brown, Hinxman, Tough and Douglas, Easter 1895

This ridge is best approached from the same direction as all the other routes on Stob Ban, with a traverse across the coire floor, hard right (north-west) beneath Central Buttress. Head up towards the route from a flat spot (GR 151660). An excellent exercise in route-finding, with tremendous views down Glen Nevis and a fine arête near the top.

Overlooked Gully

150m I

J Lyall, S Fraser and M Twomey, 8 February 2004

The gully to the right of the previous route can be descended after the fine arête to reach Foxtrot.

Fresh snow on North Buttress East Ridge on Stob Ban

Foxtrot   150m   III,4

M Cooper and C Bailey, 5 December 1996

The broad north-facing ridge dropping from the upper part of the East Ridge, just right of an obvious easy gully. Start on the right of the base of the ridge below a narrow chimney. Ascend up to, then left of, the chimney to a belay on the crest of the ridge (20m). Follow the crest to easier ground.

Descent

From the summit two fine airy ridges can be used to descend. The North Ridge is the shortest and descends steeply over two subsidiary summits. After approximately 2km bear north-west to avoid steep grass and rocky outcrops before arriving back at the start point. Alternatively, it is possible to descend the steep East Ridge, taking care to avoid the sharply incut gullies to your left (north-west). After approximately 1km, good paths lead back in a northerly direction towards the original ascent path.

Note *These two descent ridges can also be used as an interesting method of ascent, and should really be graded in their final 100m (I). Continuing around the Devil's Ridge to the summit of Sgurr a'Mhaim makes a fantastic circuit with very narrow ridge sections also at grade I.*

MULLACH NAN COIREAN, 850M   GR 135656

Between Mullach nan Coirean and Stob Ban, facing north, the base of this granite crag is at 850m and rises to 80m high, with a very steep bottom 25m. The routes are purely snowed-up rock climbing. There are several fine moderate ridges left of the crag as well, up to 200m long and about grade II or III. The best approach is from Achriabhach (GR 142684) on a path through the forest on the west side of Allt a'Choire Dheirg.

Captain Caveman   70m   III,4

M Brownlow, D King and M Pescod, 17 January 2006

The obvious line on the left end of the crag, passing several caves.

Not Bad for a Dad   80m   VI,7

D King and A Turner, 27 November 2005

An undercut chimney at the left end of the main section of cliff. Climb into the steep chimney with bold initial moves to an alcove (30m). Continue with tricky moves, exiting the alcove to the top (50m).

Donald King making the first ascent of Kindergarten Corner

Himalayan Shuffle 80m VII,8

D King and A Turner, 27 November 2005

The central left-slanting crack-line on the front face of the crag. Bouldery starting moves involving a can-opener mantelshelf move, no protection for 8m and sustained tenuous climbing with difficult protection lead to the right side of the same alcove as on the previous route. Move right from a big block to stand on a small pinnacle and go straight up to the top.

Yo Bro
70m   VIII,9

D MacLeod and M Kent, 14 December 2008

The next groove to the right. The first 20m are sustained, and the first 10m very poorly protected. Climb the overhanging groove with little respite until the angle relents, and continue on easier ground to large ledges (35m). The same line leads more easily to the ridge (35m).

Kid Gloves
70m   IV,4

M Brownlow, D King and M Pescod, 17 January 2006

The right arête of the crag.

Kindergarten Corner
50m   VII,8

D King, M Brownlow and M Pescod, 17 January 2006

A right-facing corner on the right face of the crag, finishing with a steep move left at the top. Easy finish up the arête of Kid Gloves. This route gives fantastic sustained climbing with good protection, apart from the last 6m. The crux moves are getting off the ground and the move left at the top.

GLEN NEVIS

The following routes are outlined as alternatives for a short day if the weather and conditions (deep freeze for two weeks or more) allow.

Achintee Gully
200m   II/III

Burns, Newbigging and Raeburn, 1904

The obvious deep slit in the hillside above the car park (GR 126730). Requires a fall of snow low down, followed by prolonged freezing.

Five Finger Gully Area

This quite infamous feature on the south-west side of Ben Nevis has been the scene of many (often fatal) accidents involving climbers descending the Mountain Track after a climb on the north side. The upper section is in fact a fairly large coire (Coire Ghaimhnean), and it is only much lower down that the climbing starts, at The Junction (GR 146708), around 440m. At this point the main gully cuts into the mountain, and another less deep gully climbs north-east for 100m, then splits into two narrow defiles known as The Digits. In good icy conditions or on old, firm snow The Digits give good climbs of grade II. They can be quite sheltered, and it is possible to climb up one and down the other. Access to the foot of the gully is by going over the bridge at the Glen Nevis Youth Hostel (SYHA) and walking along the floor of the glen, aiming for the old graveyard (GR 137702), which lies within a stand of mature beech trees. It may also be possible to wade over the River Nevis if is very low. Take a pair of wellies and dry socks! The gully issues from the mountain above and is marked by a waterfall at its foot at approximately 360m. Entry to the gully is on the north side of this waterfall.

The Tendon   100m   II
M Tighe, L Peters, J Henderson, M Johnston, J Ashby and J Cox, 7 March 1996
A short, interesting mixed climb up the ribs between The Digits.

Five Finger Gully   200m   IV,4
M Tighe, S McNeish, P McKellar, G Hunter and J McDonald, 31 January 1996
The main branch provides a magnificent ice climb, although rarely in condition. Climb the deep gully over a series of short pitches to the final 35m waterfall. This was climbed on the left by a steep icy groove. It is possible to traverse right below the upper waterfall to a broad rib, which leads in a fine position to the summit of Carn Dearg south-west. If Coire Ghaimhnean is gained, an easy gully (I) leads north-east to the Nevis plateau.

Antler Gully   120m   II
This lies 200m to the right (south-east) of Five Finger Gully and can be followed towards Carn Dearg (south-west).

Surgeon's Gully   400m   V
M Tighe, P Coates, A Finch, M Jackson and T Littler, 4 February 1996
A considerable undertaking. A drystone wall leads into the foot of this gully, which is a further 550m right of Five Finger Gully. It was climbed as far as the horizontal deer track at 600m in very icy conditions with little snow. Pitch 13, a 35m ice cascade, was the main feature, along with a difficult overhanging chockstone on the pitch above, which proved to be the crux. Three pitches in the untrodden central branch above the deer track were also climbed before an abseil descent.

Christmas Gully   500m   II/III
M Tighe, C Bezant, R Sutherwood, A Nuttall and P Bent, 14 February 1991
Further right again than Surgeon's Gully, this route is recognisable by a waterfall low down. The first section was avoided before entering the gully higher up. Ascend a series of steps to a narrow section. Climb the narrow section before exiting left, then rejoin the gully higher up and continue via a snow gully to the summit of Carn Dearg south-west.

Winter Wall – Polldubh Crags   30m   II/III

As with a number of water weeps on these cliffs, a good freeze will bring this climb into condition, offering a bit of fun in the valley. Use the Glen Nevis rock climbing guidebook!

Steall Waterfall   120m   II/III ★★

IG Rowe, 1 January 1963

The large waterfall above Steall Hut (GR 177683) can provide good sport, if it freezes enough. Abseil descent using the trees on the left side, followed by a steep walk down through the wood.

AONACH MOR, 1221M	GR 193730
AND AONACH BEAG, 1234M	GR 196715

With the development of the Nevis Range ski area on Aonach Mor, these peaks have become increasingly popular for climbers wanting some help with the approach. Being very high, the climbs are reliable, and it has been the case that the only winter climbs on offer are found on Aonach Mor East Face and Ben Nevis. Check with Nevis Range for times of the early morning climbers' gondola lift (tel: 01397 705825/6).

Climbing on the flanks of these peaks is varied and interesting. The main areas are the East and West Faces of Aonach Mor and the North and West Faces of Aonach Beag.

APPROACHES

On foot from the valley!

Aonach Mor West Face

From the north a start should be made at the Nevis Range ski car park. Forestry tracks are then followed to emerge at a dam (GR 162759). The Allt Daim is followed until directly under your chosen climb, which is then reached by steep snow slopes (2 hours).

From the south the approach begins at the head of Glen Nevis (GR 167691). Walk to Old Steall Ruin bridge (GR 186687) and follow the west bank of the Allt Coire Guibhsachan to the watershed (GR 187722). Traverse high above the right (east) side of the Allt Daim glen to reach the routes (2½–3 hours). This approach can be used for routes on the West and North Faces of Aonach Beag. It is also a fine way to approach Carn Mor Dearg if you intend traversing the spectacular arête which links that mountain with Ben Nevis.

Note Care should be taken when approaching the Aonach Mor/Beag col (GR 194720) from either of the previous directions. Many accidents have occurred on this slope, especially in descent.

Aonach Mor East Face

A rough path exists beneath the line of the gondola on Aonach Mor, which may be of use, especially in descent if the last gondola has been missed. This is the shortest and quickest approach on foot from the valley.

Aonach Beag

An approach to the eastern facet of Aonach Beag (Stob Coire Bealach, GR 206708) and the long North East Ridge descending from the main summit of Aonach Beag can be made by continuing past Old Steall Ruin to GR 215690. Then strike up the hill to the north, aiming for the col, 731m (1:25,000 map, GR 211705). From here a long and tiring traverse of the coire must be made to the foot of the North East Ridge, 3–3½ hours.

Gondola approach

Having studied the detail and digested the time involved in the previous methods of approaching these climbs, it may become clear that shelling out on the gondola fare is a small price to pay for a day's climbing! The uplift facilities can be found by turning right (GR 143771) after driving three miles north out of Fort William. It is worth phoning before you leave to find out if the gondola is running, as it is frequently affected by the strong winds blowing in this area (tel: 01397 705825/6).

The gondola reaches 650m (GR 186756 approximately). From here it is possible to traverse south-west into the Allt Daim (descend 100m through steep ground) for climbs on the **West Face** of Aonach Mor, 1–1½ hours. Many climbers new to the West Face have difficulty locating the start of the routes. If you own a GPS the following co-ordinates might help:

- NN18446 73103 West Face – attack point by Allt Daim
- NN18962 72971 West Face – bottom of gully between Golden Oldie and Western Rib.

For those without GPS, go to GR 186729 (stream junction) and up hill (east). The climb between these gullies is Golden Oldie.

Three approaches for climbs on the **East Face** present themselves.
- Traverse east beneath Aonach an Nid then south into Coire an Lochain, 1–1½ hours.

- Ascend the ski slopes to the south aiming for the ridge above Aonach an Nid on your left (east). The north-bounding ridge of Coire an Lochain is then used as a short steep descent to the Climber's Col on Lemming Ridge (GR 193742). Beware of large cornices in this area, 1–1½ hours.

- Find the top of Easy Gully (grade I), and either climb or abseil down from its northern rim.

Note Due to the large cornices which can form in this area, the first approach is recommended if parties are unsure of the cornice formations on the second and third approaches. All the approaches involve traversing steep ground. The coire is best avoided if avalanche warnings are in force. It may be necessary to abseil back down the cliff if the exit to your chosen route is blocked by a large cornice! Lemming Ridge is a name given by Nevis Range Ski Development. The definition of a lemming (*Collins Concise Dictionary*, 1988) is 'A member of any group following an unthinking course towards destruction'. ... You have been warned!

Aonach Beag approaches using the gondola

Go over the top of Aonach Mor, 2.5km (1½–2 hours), and descend to the Aonach Mor/Beag col previously mentioned (15 mins). The North Face routes and North East Ridge are accessible by descending to the north-east from this col (beware of large cornices and windslab). Routes on the West Face are reached by descending steeply to the south-west from the col, or by approaching on foot from Glen Nevis via the Old Steall ruin and the glen of Allt Guibhsachan (2–2½ hours).

Aonach Mor East Face – Coire an Lochain

These routes come into condition quickly and early in the season due to their altitude. The gullies form snow-ice readily, and the turfy buttresses offer good mixed routes, with the rough granite usually offering good protection. It should be possible to climb a number of routes in a day, as they are short and access is fairly easy. Many parties catch the chairlift from the top of the gondola (check before arrival, tel: 01397 705825/6), which leaves 315m of ascent to the top of the climbs. It is then possible to either abseil in or descend Easy Gully to the foot of a route. Check the avalanche conditions before trying this, and if late in the day beware of parties ascending from below. Later in the winter or after heavy snowfall the routes will bank out, and huge cornices form over some of the climbs and access routes, making them either unclimbable or very serious undertakings. Due to its sheltered easterly orientation this coire can often be a serious location for avalanches. Some of the climbs may have been climbed by RAF parties in the 1960s and never recorded. The climbs are described from left to right as the climber faces

AONACH MOR EAST FACE

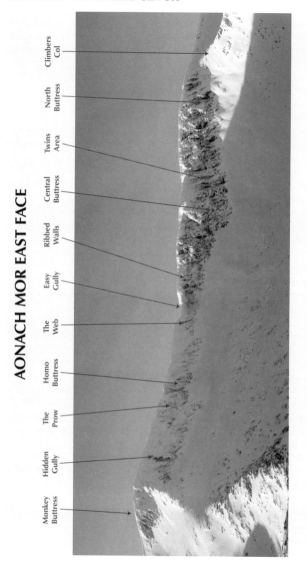

Climbers Col
North Buttress
Twins Area
Central Buttress
Ribbed Walls
Easy Gully
The Web
Homo Buttress
The Prow
Hidden Gully
Monkey Buttress

the coire. For parties new to the coire and unsure of the start of routes, it is advised that a first visit is made on a clear day from the lochain beneath the cliffs in order to sort out the main features.

The first climbs are found on **Monkey Buttress** *on the left side of the south-defining ridge of Coire an Lochain.*

Chimpanzee   60m   III

S Richardson, 1 January 2009
The prominent ice line to the left of Monkey Business is climbed with a step right at a bulge.

Monkey Business   70m   V,6

S Richardson and R Webb, 30 December 2007
The prominent slim right-facing groove in the upper half of the buttress. Climb easily towards the upper groove (20m). Continue up ice, then climb the groove, with a steep exit and short snow slope to the cornice (50m).

Drunken Monkey   70m   III

R Webb and S Richardson, 30 December 2007
The right branch of the central gully leads to the main gully. Climb this over a steepening to exit left onto the upper snow slope.

Monkey Puzzle   70m   III

R Webb and S Richardson, 30 December 2007
The fault in the right-hand buttress. Easy snow leads to a steepening in the fault, which can be avoided on the right or taken direct (III,4).

Muggle-Wump   70m   II

S Richardson, 1 January 2009
The gully defining the right edge of the buttress containing Monkey Puzzle. Climb over a short bulge to reach a snow slope and follow this to the top.

South Pole   60m   IV,5

D McGimpsey and A Nisbet, 16 January 2007
An icefall in the centre of the leftmost buttress, left of Sprint Gully, climbing the right side of an inverted-V recess. Either continue to the plateau (often no cornice here) or descend to the south for another route.

Esat of Ben Nevis

Outer Limits
90m III

R Hamilton and S Kennedy, 6 March 2004

The buttress to the left of Sprint Gully is climbed from its lowest point.

Sprint Gully
120m III

S Richardson and C Cartwright, 8 January 1995

Climbs the wide gully left of President's Buttress, with difficulties at half-height.

President's Buttress
120m III

S Richardson and J Ashbridge, 4 December 1994

Climbs the slabby buttress left of Hidden Gully via the central grooves.

Hidden Gully
120m II ★

R Webb and C Rice, 21 January 1989

At the south end of the coire, some way left of the open descent gully (Easy Gully), is an attractive narrow twisting couloir.

Ribbon on Edge
120m IV,6

S Richardson and C Cartwright, 8 January 1995

The fine arête right of Hidden Gully. Start at the base of Hidden Gully and follow a rightward break to a platform on the buttress front, then follow a groove on the right with difficulty to a belay (30m). Ascend the turfy wall above and then by the arête, passing two towers on their right side (45m). It is a further 45m to the top.

Ribbing Corner
100m IV,4

D McGimpsey and A Nisbet, 16 January 2007

A steep ice-filled corner which leads direct to the top of the gully right of Ribbon on Edge. Climb the corner and continue to below a chimney (40m). Move right and climb steep snow to the top.

Downstairs
100m III

S Drummond and A Nisbet, 22 February 2009

Climb the groove right of Ribbing Corner to below a steeper buttress (45m). Climb the icy buttress to below a final wall (35m). Turn this on the right to reach the cornice (20m).

Lord's Groove
120m IV,4

S Drummond and A Nisbet, 22 February 2009

The icy line left of Two Queens, starting at a prominent rib in the lower tier. The icy groove on the right of the rib leads to an icy right-facing corner to the left in the steep wall above the terrace (50m). Climb the steep corner and trend slightly left to an upper buttress (40m), which is climbed to the cornice (30m).

Two Queens   70m   IV,5 ★
D King and M Pescod, 29 January 2006
Start 5m left of Three Kings. Climb a steep groove, then an easier corner leading into a shallow gully. Climb the gully (50m). Climb a short wall and the upper slope (20m).

Three Kings   70m   IV,5 ★
R Hamilton, S Kennedy and A MacDonald, 6 March 2004
The obvious right-leading ramps linked by a steep wall. Reach the corner (20m) and climb it (crux) on the left to a ledge where an exposed move leads back right to the upper ramp. Follow this to a thread-belay (50m). Easy ground to the top (20m).

Streamline   90m   III ★
R Hamilton and S Kennedy, 16 February 2004
A wide fault-line left of The Prow almost forms a gully in its upper reaches. This route takes a rightward-leading ramp at the left side of the fault to below a steep wall (40m). Climb the corner directly under the wall to finish on the left in a spectacular vertical cornice.

Sideline   90m   III
S Kennedy, A Nelson and D Hood, 25 January 1998
Take a narrow groove to reach the upper gully (45m). Follow a groove on the right to a large cornice, which may have to be outflanked by a long traverse left.

*The following climbs are located on **The Prow**, a buttress which lies approximately 100m left of Easy Gully and just left of a distinctive deep gully.*

Whitecap Gully   80m   IV,5
M 'Ed' Edwards, A Nisbet and C Plant, 18 February 2007
The gully left of Back Street Boogie, often topped by huge cornice.

Back Street Boogie   70m   VI,6
M Pescod and F MacCallum, 20 December 1999
A short way to the left of The Prow and slightly higher is a small buttress, 5m wide. This climb is on the front of that buttress. Go slightly left via a bulge and icy slabs to a right-facing corner, which is climbed to the top of a pillar (30m). Climb turfy cracks above, followed by a snow crest (40m).

Esat of Ben Nevis

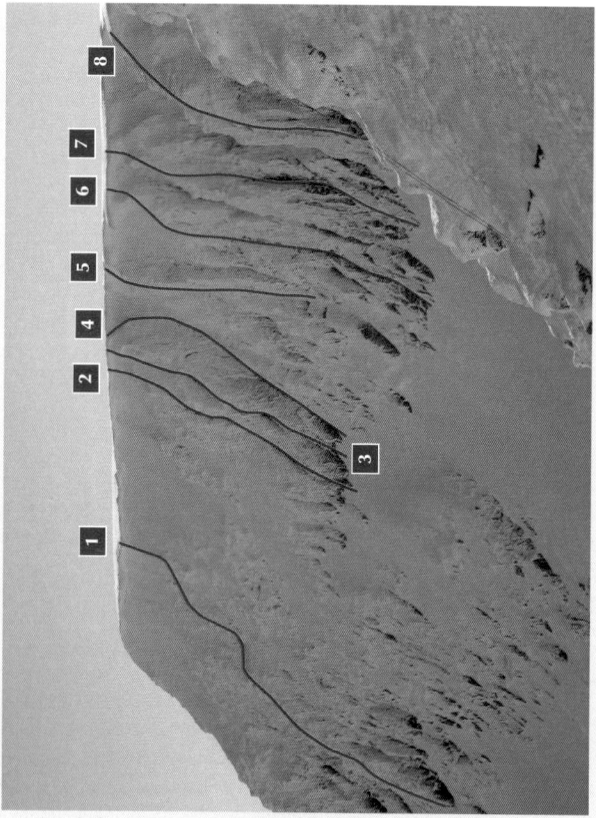

Coire an Lochain (south side)

1 Ribbon on Edge IV,6
2 Two Queens IV,5*
3 Three Kings IV,5*
4 Streamline III*
5 Back Street Boogie VI,6
6 The Wave V,5
7 Stirling Bridge V,7**
8 Homo Robusticus VI,7**

Riptide
60m   IV,4

T Gilchrist, E McGlashan and S McLean, 28 March 1990

Takes the corner immediately left of the two parallel grooves on the front face of the buttress.

The Betrayal
90m   IV,4

S Kennedy and D Ritchie, 28 March 1990

The left hand of the two parallel grooves on the front of the buttress. Follow the groove over bulges to a small snow bay immediately beneath the prow. Move steeply and awkwardly left to reach easier ground and a cornice finish.

The Wave
70m   V,5

A Clarke and M Thompson, 11 January 1995

Follows the prow between The Betrayal and The Guardian, first by grooves, up and then left to a bay (40m). Keep going left to reach the small snow bay on The Betrayal, followed by a wide V-groove above, then a rock wall right of the large cornice (30m).

The Guardian
90m   IV,5 ★

S Kennedy and D Ritchie, 28 March 1990

Climb the right hand of the two parallel grooves and a prominent flake chimney to steep but easier ground.

Pro Libertate
90m   V,6 ★★

S Kennedy and R Hamilton, 6 March 2004

Sustained mixed climbing taking the prominent corners in the upper part of the buttress. Climb the buttress just right of The Guardian into a corner leading up and right to another big corner. Climb the left wall to a ledge and back to the next corner on the right. Exposed moves left lead to a belay near The Guardian (45m). Climb the right wall of the prominent chimney on the right and the corner above to belay overlooking Stirling Bridge (20m). Finish easily as for Stirling Bridge (25m).

Stirling Bridge
70m   V,7 ★★

S Kennedy and D Ritchie, 4 April 1990

An excellent route with a memorable first pitch (steep and strenuous). Follow the prominent right-angled corner near the right edge of the buttress, going right near the top. A short groove above and a block-belay on the left lead to easier ground below the cornice.

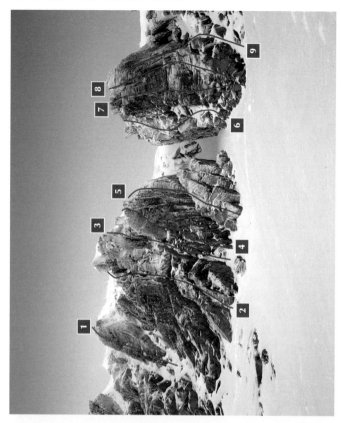

The Prow and Homo Buttress

1 Back Street Boogie VI,6
2 The Wave V,5
3 The Guardian IV,5*
4 Pro Libertate V,6**
5 Stirling Bridge V,7**
6 Ribbon Groove IV,4
7 Gowan Hill V,6
8 Homo Robusticus VI,7**
9 Piranha VII,8**

Heavy rime on Stirling Bridge (photo: Blair Fyffe)

Ribbon Groove
60m   IV,4

A Forsyth and J Turner, January 1995

Climbs the left side of the barrel-shaped buttress 20m right of Stirling Bridge via a large recess and groove above on the left. Start from the toe of the buttress.

Ribbon Development
60m   IV,4 ★★

A MacDonald and K Grant, 13 February 2003

A variation on Ribbon Groove starting up the same line into the groove on the left, but then moving up and right into a narrowing chimney. Climb the well-protected chimney over a chockstone to easier ground, and belay on the left as for Ribbon Groove.

Gowan Hill
60m   V,6

M Robson, D Jarvis and T Ward, 25 January 1998

High on the front face of the barrel-shaped buttress is a prominent hanging off-width crack. This route starts at the foot of the buttress and goes up left to a belay. Gain the foot of the crack and follow it over an overhang and continue, using either the crack or the right wall, to easier ground above.

Homo Robusticus
60m   VI,7 ★★

M Garthwaite and A Clarke, 31 December 1994

The barrel-shaped buttress crest 20m right of Stirling Bridge. Climb up to a wide crack, climb it and exit steeply at the top.

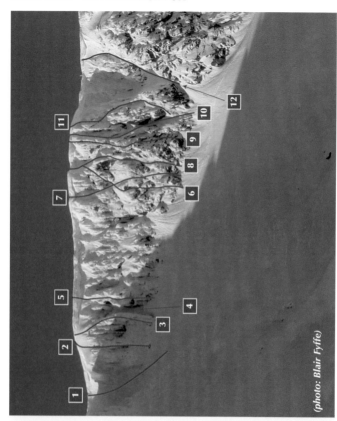

(photo: Blair Fyffe)

Ribbed Walls

1 Easy Gully I
2 Barrel Buttress IV,4
3 Nid Arête IV,5*
4 Temperance Union Blues III
5 Pernille III
6 Twisted Blood V,6
7 Aquafresh IV,4*
8 White Shark IV,4***
9 Tinsel Town V,4**
10 Maneater V,5**
11 Hammerhead Pillar VI,6
12 Tunnel Vision III

Piranha · 70m · VII,8 ★★

M Pescod, T Riley and J Baird, 19 December 2001

Climbs the right-facing corner right of Homo Robusticus. Climb the icy groove right from the base of the buttress to below the corner. A steep wall leads into the corner, which is climbed with many adze torques until an exit left at the top of the corner can be made onto the front of the buttress to join Homo Robusticus. Finish as for this route.

Nausea · 90m · II/III

J Naismith and C Watkins, 25 November 1989

An icefall 50m left of Easy Gully which banks out after heavy snow.

The Web · 100m · II/III

C Grindley and S Kennedy, 25 November 1989

An icy chimney 30m left of Easy Gully is climbed. It banks out after heavy snow.

Spider Rib · 90m · II

S Richardson and C Cartwright, 16 November 1996

Climbs the buttress between Easy Gully and The Web. Start just left of Easy Gully and aim up and left towards a short wide crack, which is climbed, exiting left at the top.

History Won't Mind · 90m · IV,5

M Dowsett and C Randall, 23 March 2008

The steep chimney/groove immediately left of Easy Gully. Follow a snow ramp up into the foot of the groove and climb it onto the upper snowfield directly overlooking Easy Gully.

Easy Gully · 100m · I

The broad snow gully which cuts deep into the plateau and can provide a useful descent route. A large cornice can often be avoided on the right in ascent. Beware of off-piste skiers!

The area between Easy Gully and Tunnel Vision is known as **Ribbed Walls**. *There are many routes all at around grade III which can bank out and be topped by a large impassable cornice, in which case an exit can usually be made just to the left of the final tower of Gondola With the Wind.*

Barbie Boy · 80m · IV,5

C Cartwright and R Webb, 18 December 2002

A widening chimney in the crest of the buttress between Easy Gully and Muddy Waters. From the toe of the buttress, immediately right of Easy Gully, climb the crest on the right, then on the left, to a leftward-trending ramp. Move right and climb a left-facing corner to a ledge below the chimney (35m). Climb the chimney and snow slopes to the top (45m).

Muddy Waters   90m   III

C Jones, S Kennedy and D Ritchie, 17 November 1990

About 10m right of Easy Gully is an obvious chimney high on the buttress, which is climbed trending right towards the cornice. The lower section is often banked out.

Groove Armada   90m   IV,4

D Gunn and P Farr, March 2002

Right of Muddy Waters, but before Barrel Buttress, is an icy groove. Climb this to join Muddy Waters below the ridge.

Barrel Buttress   60m   IV,4

S Kennedy and S Thirgood, 7 February 1993

Between Muddy Waters and Temperance Union Blues is a small recess with a sharp narrow arête on its right and a broad buttress on the left. Climb the buttress directly, starting just to its right and avoiding the steep wall at the top on the left.

Nid Arête   90m   IV,5 ★

S Kennedy and S Thirgood, 7 February 1993

A well-protected mixed route which climbs the groove-line on the left side of the narrow arête to the right of Barrel Buttress. The groove is climbed direct, taking the furthest corner on the right overlooking the final section of Temperance Union Blues.

Temperance Union Blues   90m   III

S Richards, G Armstrong, C Millar and J Owens, 18 February 1989

50m to the right of Easy Gully the cliff is split by a deep cleft at half-height. Climb either of two converging lines to the bottom of the cleft (45m). Ascend the cleft, exiting where it steepens onto a ramp, which is followed to the cornice (45m). Difficult if not sufficiently iced.

Pernille   70m   III

C Jones and A Taylor, 27 March 1990

The buttress immediately right of the deep cleft of Temperance Union Blues. Gain an obvious scoop just right of the cleft. Continue up right to a steep left-trending ramp, which is followed to a snowy bay and exit rightwards to reach the cornice.

Immediately left of the wide gully of Tunnel Vision, two buttresses are separated by a snowy amphitheatre. On the better-defined right-hand buttress is the fine line of **Gondola With the Wind**. *The main features of the left-hand buttress are two icefalls which form down the left side.*

Twisted Blood   110m   V,6
C Cartwright and S M Richardson, 4 December 2005
The buttress left of Aquafresh, starting 10m to the left below a shallow gully. Climb to a large sloping ledge (20m). Climb the right-facing corner-line in the series of stepped slabs above, then exit right into the snow basin above to join Aquafresh (50m). Climb the left-to-right stepped groove-line in the tower above. Finish up the left side of the exit bowl of White Shark (40m).

Aquafresh   100m   IV,4 ★
N Marshall and D Ritchie, 26 March 1990
40m left of Tunnel Vision. Climb the left-hand icefall, trending left up mixed ground to finish.

White Shark   110m   IV,4 ★★★
C Millar and R Webb, 27 January 1990
The right-hand icefall – a splendid climb. Climb the shallow gully and a steep slabby corner at mid-height to a ledge. Follow the steep ice pitch which forms down the corner to easier ground.

Jaws   110m   VI,6
S Richardson and C Cartwright, 9 February 2003
The steep buttress between White Shark and Tinsel Town. The right edge of the buttress leads easily to a steep wall, which is passed on the right. Move back left to the end of a sloping shelf and go straight up to easier ground (40m). A shallow gully leads up and right to a belay below a V-shaped prow (30m). A groove just right of the prow leads to the Jaws, a steep chimney-corner above. Climb this until it overhangs, then swing left to steep cracks in the arête (30m). Snow to the top (10m).

Tinsel Town   110m   V,4 ★★
S Kennedy and P Mills, 3 February 1991
Follows the groove-line left of Gondola With the Wind. Start 10m right of White Shark. Follow a groove system just right of the buttress crest, then a chimney to a stance on the left (40m). Go back right to the main groove and climb steep mixed ground to below the cornice (50m). A long traverse right may be necessary to outflank the huge cornice!

Aquafresh and White Shark

White Shark IV,4***

Aquafresh IV,4*

Twisted Blood V,6

Remora
100m III,4

R Reid and R Webb, 24 February 1990

Follow the first pitch of Tinsel Town, then up left below the steep crest of the upper buttress and belay above the icefall of White Shark. Easy snow to finish.

Gondola With the Wind
125m IV,5 ★★

S Kennedy and S Thirgood, 30 December 1989

A good mixed climb up the right side of the buttress, just left of Tunnel Vision, with an exciting finish. Starts up a short groove 8m left of Tunnel Vision, gaining a small amphitheatre and exit on the right (45m). A system of shallow grooves close to the buttress edge is followed, then spiral right round the side of the tower to reach a steep corner (35m), which is followed with difficulty to easier ground (45m).

Maneater
90m V,5 ★★

S Richardson and R Webb, 14 January 1995

The obvious gully between the buttresses of White Shark and Hammerhead Pillar. Ascend the gully to an overhung cave, then steep thin ice on the left wall to a belay (50m). Go up steeply above the belay to join Tinsel Town and the plateau (40m).

Hammerhead Pillar
100m VI,6

C Cartwright and S Richardson, 9 February 1997

Start as for Maneater. From the foot of the amphitheatre follow Gondola With the Wind for 10m up the ramp on the right. Follow a short groove on the left edge to a stance (40m). Climb the steep headwall and grooves above to another stance (30m). Ascend the steep groove in the centre of the wall above, and go left to enter a hanging groove, which is climbed to the cornice.

Tunnel Vision
120m III

S Richardson and R Everett, 22 January 1989

The wide gully between the Ribbed Walls and Central Buttress. Start at the foot of the gully immediately left of Morwind. An initial narrows leads to a snow bay with three possible exits. Climb ice smears up the wall at the back of the bay with interest, in an exposed position, to a steep cornice exit. In full conditions the wall may bank up to a frightening angle and the cornice becomes impassable. The left branch has been climbed (*S Kennedy and S Thirgood, 1990*), and it should always be possible to climb the right branch to reach the easy upper section of Morwind.

Moving right, the area between Tunnel Vision and Left Twin is known as **Central Buttress**. *Some of the finest mixed climbing on the mountain is situated here. The cornice can be massive, but a vague snow arête on the final slopes often provides a possible exit.*

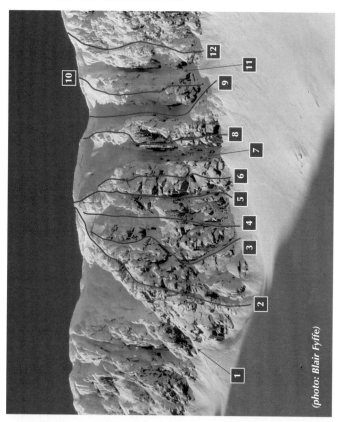

(photo: Blair Fyffe)

Central Buttress

1 Tunnel Vision III
2 Morwind III,4***
3 Turf Walk III,4*
4 Roaring Forties IV,5*
5 Typhoon IV,5***
6 Hurricane Arête VI,7**
7 Left Twin III,4***
8 The Split III,4**
9 Forgotten Twin I/II
10 Siamese Buttress II/III**
11 Right Twin II***
12 The Lost Boys IV,5

Approaching the cornice above Central Buttress

Shelf Route   110m   III

S Kennedy and S Thirgood, 9 March 1990

Start in a small bay up left of the lowest point of the buttress. Move up and right to a steep groove, which is followed to a narrow shelf on the left of the buttress crest and overlooking Tunnel Vision. Follow the shelf until it is possible to break out right onto the buttress crest and follow Morwind to finish.

Morwind   150m   III,4 ★★★

R Everett and S Richardson, 10 January 1988

A fine mixed climb taking a direct line up a series of grooves on the crest of Central Buttress, starting from the lowest rocks about 30m left of Typhoon. A good, technically interesting climb. Climb a short gully leading to a shallow chimney-line with several tricky steps on the crest. This leads to a small bay beneath a cave after two pitches. Exit right up mixed ground to easier slopes beneath the cornice (which could be very large late in the season).

Turf Walk   150m   III,4 ★

RD Everett and C Grant, 25 November 1989

Good mixed climbing on the right-slanting fault line which crosses the front side of the buttress on the left. Start 15m right of Morwind, following a left-slanting gully to belay in a bay below the fault. Follow the fault to ledges leading right. Step right, then up and left, to belay below steep grooves on the left of the central depression. Follow the groove on the left, stepping left onto the exposed prow and continuing to easier ground above.

Roaring Forties   150m   IV,5 ★

RD Everett, SM Richardson and JC Wilkinson, 2 March 1991

A fine varied route which climbs the icefall that forms in the depression in the centre of the face. Not in condition as often as other routes in this area. Start 5m left of the corner of Typhoon. Follow icy grooves to a recess (45m) and climb the steep back wall by a groove on the right (25m). The icefall is followed (50m) to easier ground 20m below the cornice.

Typhoon   130m   IV,5 ★★★

R Everett and S Richardson, 14 January 1989

This excellent climb takes a direct line up the grooves just left of Hurricane Arête. Start 15m left of the deep gully of Left Twin. Climb the lower slabby grooves to a belay at the base of a chimney (40m). Climb the chimney and the groove past an overhang (30m). Continue direct on steep ice to exit onto the final slopes (40m). A further 20m leads to the top.

Note Typhoon and Left Twin are often used as abseil descents to the base of climbs in this area. Please respect any parties already embarked on an ascent of these routes and descend elsewhere.

Hurricane Arête   140m   VI,7 ★★

S Richardson and R Everett, 4 March 1989

The slabby Central Buttress, left of Left Twin, is the highest section of crag in the coire. On its right-hand side is a steep arête, with several overhangs in its upper section, which forms the left wall of Left Twin. This hard climb takes an intricate line through the overhangs just left of the arête. Start midway between Typhoon and Left Twin. Climb iced slabs (30m) to a short left-slanting gully. Climb this, then up right along a narrow ramp to a small ledge (20m). Belay below a prominent overhang, just left of a right-facing corner which is capped by another overhang. Pull over the roof directly above the belay onto a steep slab, and follow a left-slanting crack to reach a prominent spike. Go right below an overhanging wall to a small snow bay (20m). A short but difficult pitch. Climb grooves on the left to the final overhangs, which are climbed by bridging up left towards easier ground (50m). Another 20m leads to the cornice.

Alien Abduction   120m   VII,8

A Powell and A Benson, 22 December 1996

The grooves and stepped corner right of Hurricane Arête. Start up Left Twin to a platform on the left. Climb the right edge of Central Buttress to a stance on the right level with the belay on Hurricane Arête (35m). Go left and climb the right-facing corner and three overhangs. After the third overhang step left and up to a block-belay. The second roof requires rest points and aid (25m). Ascend 5m up left, over a slab and onto easier ground (40m). **Note** The second roof was climbed free by M Pescod and D King in November 2000.

*Right of Central Buttress are two steep narrow buttresses (*Split *and* Siamese*), bordered by three deep gullies. The left side of Split Buttress is characterised by the deep chimney of The Split, containing several jammed blocks which are a good reference point in misty weather.*

Left Twin   120m   III,4 ★★★
R Everett and S Richardson, 22 January 1989
The obvious gully a few metres left of Forgotten Twin and immediately right of Central Buttress. It is climbed direct, with some steep moves left on the final hard pitch. The right side of the gully is steeper and harder than the left and has been climbed on many occasions.

Siamese Twin   120m   IV,5 ★★
The line of ice-filled chimneys on the right side of the gully of Left Twin, climbed in two pitches to easy ground.

The Split   130m   III,4 ★★
S Richardson and R Everett, 19 February 1989
The left-hand side of the buttress left of Forgotten Twin is split by a deep chimney. Start at the foot of the buttress and climb the introductory chimney to snow slopes to the right of Left Twin (25m). Enter the deep chimney and continue under several large jammed blocks until it is possible to exit to the left, some 4m below the final overhang. Continue up the arête to belay (45m). Climb easy snow leftwards to join Left Twin (50m).

Lickety Split   130m   IV,5 ★★
G Mulhemann and SM Richardson, 2 December 1989
A fine varied mixed route. Climb the icefall directly below the gully of Forgotten Twin to a stance below the right-facing corner on the right side of the lower half of Split Buttress (30m). Follow the corner to a stance (20m) and continue up the steep wall above, passing two overhangs to a rock ridge overlooking Left Twin (20m). Go up the ridge to easier ground and the cornice (60m).

Slick Mick's Groove   130m   IV,5 ★
N Hitchings, M Hardwick and AV Saunders, 27 February 1992
A good technical climb. Climb the first pitch of Lickety Split, then move left around

Twins Area

1 Hurricane Arête VI,7**
2 Alien Abduction VII,8
3 Left Twin III,4***
4 Siamese Twin IV,5**
5 The Split III,4**
6 Lickety Split IV,5**

the rib to gain the small left-facing groove left of the crux corner of Lickety Split. Climb the corner (hard) and exit with difficulty onto a ledge. Continue to the final ridge of Lickety Split (40m) and the ridge to the top (60m).

Forgotten Twin   120m   I/II
R Everett and S Richardson, 22 January 1989
The gully between the buttresses of Split and Siamese. A short leftward ramp from the foot of Right Twin leads to an easy gully with a couple of steeper stretches before the cornice exit.

Siamese Buttress   120m   II/III ★★
S Richardson and R Everett, 19 February 1989
The well-defined buttress left of Right Twin provides an enjoyable scramble. Harder (grade III) if started up the steep corners on the left.

Right Twin   120m   II ★★★
S Richardson and R Everett, 22 January 1989
The gully on the right of Siamese Buttress. About 1.5m wide with vertical side-walls, it gives an enjoyable traditional climb, with steep sections at the bottom and at mid-height. Exit left at the top.

The Lost Boys   120m   IV,5
K Howett and A Todd, 17 February 2001
An ice route just right of Right Twin. Climb slabby ice to a belay on the right below steep rocks. Climb ice on the left of the steep rocks, step left onto ledges and move into a shallow corner on the left side of the wall. Go right around a pillar with a crack, and pull over ice on the lip to follow steep ice in a shallow gully to a good belay. Finish up a corner-recess and the snow arête right of Right Twin.

White Noise   100m   IV,5
A Nisbet, 23 February 2007
Start just right of The Lost Boys. Climb to the barrier wall and follow steep ice straight up – or avoid it on mixed ground on the left. Ice and a steeper mixed section lead to the upper slopes. Finish up an arête on the left as for The Lost Boys.

White Light   100m   IV,5
A Nisbet and D Tunstall, 7 April 2008
Start as for White Noise and White Bait to below an ice column (20m). Climb towards the column and pass it by a groove on the right to reach a snow bay (30m). Continue up icy grooves directly above (50m).

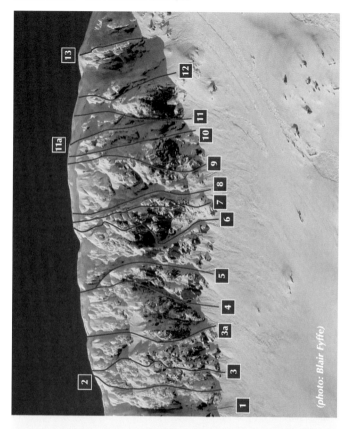

(photo: Blair Fyffe)

North Buttress

1   Right Twin II***
2   The Lost Boys IV,5
3   White Bait IV,5
3a The Slever III,4
4   Golden Promise VI,7*
5   Molar Canal III
6   Slipstream IV,5
7   Grooved Arête V,6**
8   Icicle Gully III
9   Force Ten Buttress III,4*
10 Solar Wind IV,4*
11 Jet Stream IV,4***
11a Jet Stream – Direct Finish V,6
12 North Buttress Route III
13 Foosyerneeps IV,5**

White Bait   100m   IV,5
M 'Ed' Edwards and D McGimpsey, 5 February 2007

Start about 20m right of Right Twin. Climb a short ice groove, then go up and right into an icy bay. From its top gain a narrow ledge on the right and climb through steep walls to a ledge (40m). Continue up, then move right to climb the left side of a large snowy bay (30m). Exit the bay and continue out left, then straight up to the cornice (30m).

White Horses   120m   V,6
A Nisbet and I Parnell, 29 December 2007

The rib on the right. Climb easily up to a large sentry box (20m). Climb a groove on the left, then move back right onto the rib (20m). Move up the rib and pass a steep section on its right to reach the large snowy bay and move right to a rib (40m). A steep groove leads up the crest to the top (40m).

The following four routes start in a large bay about 50m left of **Grooved Arête**.

The Slever   100m   III,4
S Kennedy and D Ritchie, 2 March 1991

The large icefall on the left margin of the bay is climbed in one long pitch to easier ground. Then move right into a small gully and easily towards the cornice.

Pepperpot   100m   III,4
R Lee and N Wright, January 1990

Right of The Slever, in the top left-hand corner of the bay, is a steep icy chimney. Follow this and finish up a gully on the left.

Golden Promise   100m   VI,7 ★
B Davison, S Kennedy and S Venables, 23 February 1992

A difficult mixed route which climbs the steep groove-line at the top right-hand side of the bay. Climb the easier lower snow gully to a large block-belay on the right at the foot of the main difficulties (45m). Climb the steep groove above, pulling over a large bulge at 20m to reach a small cul-de-sac. Exit by a groove on the left and easier grooves above to belay just short of the upper gully of Molar Canal (45m). Climb the gully to the top (10m).

Muck n' Brass   100m   VI,6
A Powell and J Aylward, 4 March 1999

The buttress between Golden Promise and Molar Canal. Climb the front of the buttress, followed by a steep wall and slabs to the left, then move right up a turfy groove to the crest (40m). Follow the crest, then traverse under a wall to Golden Promise in the bay to the left (30m). Cross the upper section of Molar Canal and pass the cornice to the right (30m).

Molar Canal   100m   III

C Jones and S Kennedy, 25 January 1990

Approximately 35m left of Grooved Arête is a gully which is deep and wide in the top section. Climb a short icefall and grooves into the gully, which is climbed towards the cornice. This might be impassable direct, in which case a long traverse left is required.

North Buttress *is the final section at the northern side of the coire. It is separated from Molar Canal by two narrow ribs and is made up of three distinct buttresses, cut by the deep Icicle Gully to the left and the clean groove of Jet Stream on the right.*

Slipstream   140m   IV,5

A Nisbet and J Preston, 23 December 2007

The slot left of Grooved Arête. Climb the easy-angled slot to the overhanging section (50m).Go right on a ledge to the end of a vertical wall above (20m). Two short vertical walls lead rightwards, then move up left to a ledge with a big spike (20m). A short chimney and easier grooves then go left back onto the blocky arête under the cornice (45m). Finish over this (5m).

Grooved Arête   130m   V,6 ★★

S Richardson and R Everett, 26 November 1988

This superb climb takes the narrow arête immediately left of Icicle Gully. Start at the foot of the gully, gain the arête to the left and follow this, easily at first, then with increasing interest up grooves on its left side before moving back right to belay below a steep tower (45m). Climb a series of steep grooves on the crest of the tower until it is possible to move left to a ledge. Climb the short vertical corner above with difficulty, exiting on the right (35m). Regain the crest and continue more easily to the plateau (50m). Excellent technical climbing.

Icicle Gully   130m   III

R Everett and S Richardson, 26 November 1988

The gully between Grooved Arête and Force Ten Buttress. Climb the gully-line with interest to a belay on the right (50m). Take the wider line to the right of a narrow groove (which is bounded by Grooved Arête to the left). Climb this until it narrows and steepens at an icicle, which leads to a snow bay (50m). Continue up the mixed ground above (30m).

Force Ten Buttress   140m   III,4 ★

R Everett and S Richardson, 3 December 1988

This good mixed climb takes the buttress between Icicle Gully and Jet Stream. Climb mixed ground just left of the crest then move right to a belay at the foot of a short chimney where the buttress steepens (45m). Climb the chimney, then step right to climb a short difficult crack (30m). Now climb mixed ground, mainly just to the right of the crest, to join a gully which rises to a col, where the buttress merges into the final slopes (40m). The climb is technically hard for the grade, with several short, difficult, well-protected sections, but the rock is very friendly!

Direct Finish   70m   V,6

B Ottewell and S Wilshaw, 16 February 1993

Instead of going right of the crest after the second pitch, follow snowy slabs up left to a small outcrop overlooking Icicle Gully (50m). Now move up right over slabs to a large block on the arête (22m). Move back left up a turfy corner and the over-hanging corner on the right, which is climbed by a crack on the right. Continue by sustained climbing to easier ground (35m).

In a bay between Force Ten Buttress and North Buttress are two prominent gully-lines which form ice easily and, being in the shade, stay in condition throughout the winter.

Solar Wind   110m   IV,4 ★

RD Everett and SM Richardson, 8 March 1992

Start close beneath Force Ten Buttress and follow the obvious left-hand chimney to a snow patch (45m). Ascend the steep square-cut groove above, exiting left near the top to reach and climb the continuation gully, and belay where Force Ten Buttress merges with the final slopes (40m). 25m remain to the cornice.

Jet Stream   100m   IV,4 ★★★

R Everett and S Richardson, 3 December 1988

This is the narrow gully immediately left of North Buttress (which forms an icicle icefall in its lower part), about 50m left of the northerly bounding coire ridge. Climb the gully over several steep sections to a snow bay (45m). Exit right up a steep awkward wall to easier ground which leads to below the cornice (45m). Go up to the cornice and over the top (10m). Excellent climbing. When fully formed, the icefall which forms in the headwall would make an exciting and fitting direct finish.

To the right of Solar Wind is a chimney which can be used as an alternative start to either of the previous climbs, **Guides Variation** *(45m, IV,4, S Allan and D Etherington, February 1992).*

North Buttress Route 85m III

C Jones, S Kennedy and R Williamson, 25 January 1990

A quick route for the end of the day. Avoid the steep lower section of the buttress, which is characterised by a prominent icefall. Start in a bay 20m up right from the foot of the buttress. Climb grooves up left to the crest, which is followed to the top.

Foosyerneeps 50m IV,5 ★★

A Clark and J Davis, 13 April 1998

The clean pillar at the far right of the coire. Climb via cracks and corners just right of the prow to finish through a hard V-notch at the top.

Perplexed 80m IV,4

P Chapman and P Andersen, 16 February 2006

Follow the rightmost gully until it narrows at half-height and belay against the rock wall on the left (35m). Follow the left side past a spike to a large block on the crest (35m), then easier snow to the cornice (10m).

Aonach Mor West Face

The West Face of Aonach Mor presents several granite ridges of moderate angle 400m high. The steepest of these are directly below the summit cairn and, being in a slightly recessed bay, they are hidden from many viewpoints. The climbs provide excellent mountaineering routes in a wild and remote setting. To locate the buttresses follow the Allt Daim until opposite the distinctive Pinnacle Ridge descending from the summit of Carn Dearg Meadhonach.

Following the floor of the glen alongside the Allt Daim to the main climbing area beneath the summit, parties will pass below a number of shallow gully-lines or iced slabs. On closer inspection these gullies and slabs can provide very good climbing in the right conditions. After the initial steep pitches the ground eases, and it may be possible to abseil and climb another route or, alternatively, continue more easily to the ridge above. These gullies and slabs were climbed on in the 1978–79 winters by Joint Service Mountain Training parties, but never recorded. Further up the glen (1hr) the buttresses become more massive and well defined as follows.

Gendarme Ridge 350m II

M Tighe and party, 1992

The rib to the left of Golden Oldie and the deep gully between. There is a small rock finger near the top, and it provides a straightforward mixed climb.

Aonach Mor West Face

1 Gendarme Ridge II
2 Golden Oldie II***
3 Western Rib II/III**
4 Daim Buttress II/III
5 Solitaire II
6 The Red Eye Routine III
7 Squiggle Gully II

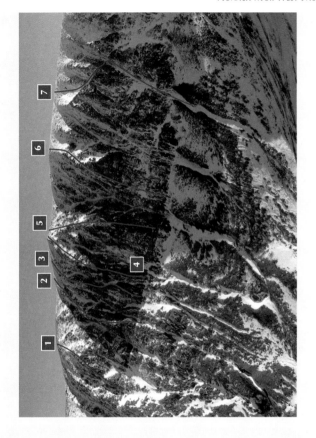

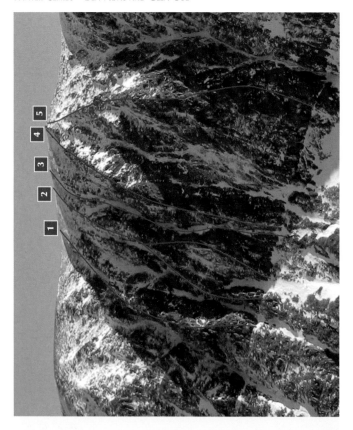

Summit Ribs

1 Golden Oldie II/***
2 Western Rib II/III/**
3 Easter Gully II
4 Daim Buttress II/III
5 Solitaire II

Soldiers' Gully   400m   I/II

JSMTC party, 1978–79

The large gully between Gendarme Ridge and Golden Oldie. It has been skied.

Golden Oldie   400m   II ★★★

A Kimber, 21 December 1979

Follow the leftmost buttress, which becomes better defined and narrower higher up, with deep gullies to the left and right. From below, it appears as a square blocky buttress.

Cave Gully   400m   II ★

The deep gully between Golden Oldie and Western Rib has a large cave at half-height, which is a great place for a brew stop! Exit the cave on the left by an awkward step.

Western Rib   400m   II/III ★★

S Richardson, 17 December 1988

From below, the second buttress from the left appears as a flying buttress joining the third, broader buttress (Daim Buttress), although it is in fact separated by a deep gully. A delightful long route with sustained interest, never very hard. A popular start is on the left side, by an independent rib which then joins the main buttress at a small col.

Easter Gully   400m   II

Lochaber Mountain Rescue Team training party, 1992

The gully between Western Rib and Daim Buttress, including the lower pitches (which are harder and known as Spare Rib Gully – see below). This gully has also been skied, with down-climbing and abseiling on the bottom pitches. This gully finishes close to the summit, if all the right forks are taken in the upper reaches.

Spare Rib Gully   400m   III ★★

C Bailey, M Cooper and R Hudson, 25 January 1993 (first recorded ascent)

Climb the lowest gully between Western Rib and Daim Buttress in three pitches to easier ground (100m). Move left onto Western Rib or right onto Daim Buttress and follow either to the summit.

Daim Buttress   400m   II/III

R Everett, N Barratt and S Richardson, 25 February 1989

This is the third buttress from the left, characterised by a prominent slab just above half-height. Start directly below the slab at the foot of the buttress. The first 200m

Good mountaineering on Aonach Mor West Face

gives enjoyable mixed climbing up snow and rocky corners to ledges at the foot of the slab. Move left and climb cracks on the left edge of the slab to a platform (50m). Take the cracks and corners up the buttress above (50m). Scrambling leads to the top.

Solitaire, Combination Start   110m   IV,4
J Lyall, B Newton, R Willis and P Wright, 22 January 1999
Start 15m left of the original line of Solitaire. Go left of a large roof by ice to a groove, which is climbed to a final bulge and passed by a rib and slabs on the left. Easier ground goes up right to the crest of the original route.

Solitaire   400m   II
RD Everett and SM Richardson, 1 January 1990
The right-hand ridge, starting just left of a deep gully. It is slightly easier than the other routes hereabouts. A good scramble in the summer (Difficult)!!

The Red Eye Routine   400m   III
O Metherell and J Marsham, 13 December 1996
Starts 30m right of Solitaire in a small snow bay just right of a large pink block. Climb the snow bay and exit left awkwardly (30m). Follow the line of least resistance, mostly on turf, to the plateau.

Squiggle Gully   400m   II
J Crook and D Brett, February 1997
A gully at the far right-hand end of the face. If climbed in lean conditions this gully offers a number of grade II pitches, followed by a diagonal ravine and a variety of finishes.

Many more variations are possible in this area.

Sgurr Finnisg-aig – Allt na h-Aire cascade

This water/ice course descends from the Aonach Mor gondola restaurant area in a north-easterly direction and provides good climbing up to grade IV,5 after a prolonged heavy freeze down to sea level. It can be seen from the A82 just south of Spean Bridge. The main fall was probably first climbed by Loch Eil Centre and JSMTC staff in the 1970s and never recorded. Access is from the Nevis Range car park by bike or on foot on forest tracks to GR 196769, then up steeply south to the waterfall. It is possible to climb on the fall and descend from the side-banks back into the forest, or continue up and catch a gondola down, thus saving on knee cartilage!

Esat of Ben Nevis

(photo: Blair Fyffe)

Aonach Beag
North Face

1 North-East Ridge III*
2 Mayfly III*
3 Queen's View III
4 Royal Pardon VI,5***
5 Stand and Deliver V,5**

The main fall, which has been graded IV,5, is **Sgurr Finnisg-aig Fall**, with the last 50m pitch being the crux. Left of the main fall is a diagonal descent line, and left of this two thin ice lines sometimes form. The left-hand one, which is 150m left of the main fall, has been climbed (**Incidental Fall**, *IV,4, S Dring and J Lyall, 1 February 1996*). Taking the left fork at the base of Sgurr Finnisg-aig Fall and going left and right by the easiest line gives **Saints Slip** (*II/III, DWM Whalley, S Coleby and party, 22 December 1996*).

Aonach Beag North Face

Very steep and impressive cascade-style ice climbs form here with sufficient thaw–freeze cycles to allow water to drip down the rocks and ice to form. The climbs are described from right to left as if descending from the Aonach Mor/Beag col. After 100m a wide icefall is seen on the right. This splits below a steep rock headwall, forming a 'Y' shape. Whiteout takes the right branch, Stand and Deliver climbs the prominent central section of the icefall hanging down the wall, and Blackout takes the narrow ice chimney 15m to the right. The routes are difficult to protect, and a selection of rock protection and ice gear is recommended for the harder climbs.

Wipeout   60m   IV,6
M Cooper and C Bailey, 15 April 1994
The icefall right of the first pitch of Whiteout. From rocks on the left of the icefall climb over several steep bulges to rocks directly above.

Whiteout   170m   II
S Richardson and R Webb, 30 November 1985
Follows the wide prominent icefall for 50m to a snowfield. Climb this and exit right via a short icefall to another snow slope. This snow slope leads up to a steep buttress with a deep chimney (Blackout) on its left. Climb the right side of the buttress to a final snow slope.

Blackout   120m   IV,5 ★
J Dunn and RG Webb, 21 February 1987
Climb the deep chimney passed by Whiteout in one long hard pitch on its left wall.

Aquaphobia   125m   VI,6
A Cave and K Cool, March 1999
The slim ice pillar which forms on the buttress to the right of Stand and Deliver.

Stand and Deliver 120m V,5 ★★
C Cartwright and R Clothier, 16 April 1989
The imposing icefall directly above the initial gully of Whiteout. A long and sustained ice pitch.

Sellout 150m III
R Webb and S Richardson, 15 April 1989
A left-hand finish to Whiteout. Where Whiteout traverses right, move left below a steep icefall (Stand and Deliver) to reach an ice pitch to the left of a rock buttress. Climb this (30m) to reach easier ground above.

Sellout Direct 200m IV,4 ★
R Webb and N Wilson, February 1998
Starts a few metres down from the prominent icefall and to the right of Camilla. Follow a chimney through the steep wall to join the original line of Sellout after the left traverse.

About 100m down and left of Whiteout a steep buttress provides some excellent ice climbing.

Camilla 230m V,5 ★★
RD Everett and SM Richardson, 31 January 1993
A serious ice route which climbs the twin icicles that hang down the overhanging right side of the face at mid-height. Start at the foot of the buttress, 25m right of the prominent icefall taken by Royal Pardon. Climb snow and steep ice to the crest of the buttress (40m). Go up the snow slope above and a shallow icy gully to below the twin icicles (50m); belay on the right. Climb the right-hand icicle and easier ground to the crest of the buttress (50m). Continue up ice on the left and a snowfield to the top (90m).

Excalibur 260m VI,6
C Cartwright and S Richardson, 27 January 2000
Start 10m left of Camilla. Go left of a blunt rib to climb an ice wall to easier ground above the rib (50m). Continue to the base of a steep slot (30m). Climb the slot to the base of a large snowfield (20m). Climb to the foot of a left-facing corner at the top right side of the snowfield (40m). Ascend the vertical corner, followed by steep ice, to the crest of the buttress (50m). Easier snow slopes to the top (70m).

Royal Pardon 220m VI,5 ★★★
R Webb and S Richardson, 18 February 1987
About 50m right of King's Ransom is a prominent thin ice smear running down the

centre of the buttress. It is similar to Smith's Route on Gardyloo Buttress, but with steeper and thinner ice. Climb a series of icefalls for 55m to belay at the bottom right-hand side of the smear. Climb the vertical (for 2m) smear (40m); poor belay on the right, or a better one slightly higher (10m). A short pitch up ice leads to a broad snow couloir (20m). Follow the couloir for 50m, then go left up two good steep ice pitches to the summit plateau.

Mean Streak 250m   VII,6

M Hind and R Webb, February 2000

Climbs the thin ice streak to the left of Royal Pardon. From the foot of King's Ransom go up right to an obvious spike (20m). Ascend to an even more obvious spike on the right skyline at the base of a thin ice streak (35m). Climb the streak and ground above to a flake (50m). Go right to a difficult ice bulge, which is climbed to join Royal Pardon above its main pitch (30m).

King's Ransom 250m   VI,6 ★

S Richardson and R Webb, 14 February 1987

Start about 40m left of Royal Pardon. The very left side of the buttress is split by a narrow gully. Follow the gully for two pitches until it fades, passing a large chockstone (possibly behind) and climbing a free-standing ice pillar en route (90m). Belay on a spike below the steep wall on the left side of the buttress. An escape left is possible from here, avoiding the difficulties of the upper pillar. Follow a ramp on the right until it fades, then use aid (has been free-climbed) on the steep wall above to a second ramp, which is followed delicately to the buttress crest. Another 120m of climbing follows a fine snow arête and easier mixed ground to the plateau. A fine and varied route with difficult mixed climbing in places.

The following climbs are less well-defined long mountaineering climbs.

Queen's View 250m   III

P Moores and A Nelson, 8 February 1995

Gain the snowfield in the centre of the face between Mayfly and King's Ransom via a runnel. Leave the snowfield by a narrow gully, which leads directly to the highest part of the face above.

Away from the Crows 300m   II

MJ Munro and P Baillie, 16 February 2007

Follow Queen's View to the snow basin, then climb left over broken ground and head for an open gully left of The Black Prince. Once the gully ends, veer right then left into a large open gully that runs until a snow arête finish.

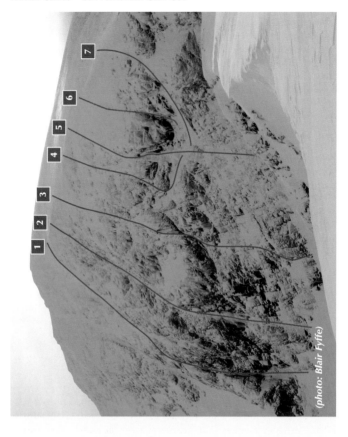

(photo: Blair Fyffe)

Aonach Beag
North Face
(right side)

1 King's Ransom VI,6*
2 Royal Pardon VI,5***
3 Camilla V,5**
4 Sellout III
5 Stand and Deliver V,5**
6 Blackout IV,5*
7 Whiteout II

The White Queen   300m   II
B Davison, 6 April 2000
Start up a slabby buttress left of Queen's View and gain the snowfield. Follow the
ridge to the right of Queen's View from a point where the gully narrows. Gain the
foot of a second buttress on the ridge above a snow slope and follow a turfy right-
to-left ramp to easier ground. Go around the final rock buttress on its right and
follow snow to finish.

The Black Prince   300m   II
A Nisbet, 6 April 2000
Start as for The White Queen into the snow basin, then follow the easiest line up a
wide ridge to the final few metres of the North East Ridge.

Through the Looking Glass   300m   II
S Richardson, 1 January 2009
The left edge of the easier-angled central section of cliff. Start left of The Black
Prince and climb easy-angled ice to join the shallow line that leads up and left to
join the North East Ridge.

Dragonfly   200m   III
M Duff, January 1994
Starts 40m right of Mayfly, up a wide gully to an iceflow, which is climbed. Then go
left up a small steep ice pitch. Move up the broken ridge above, which overlooks
Mayfly to the left.

Mayfly   210m   III ★
K Schwartz, 9 May 1979
There is a large triangular face between the Aonach Mor/Beag col and the North
East Ridge of Aonach Beag. The face has a steep buttress nearest the col, easier gully
area in the centre and a lower rocky section. Just left of the centre (GR 197718), an
initially wide gully, marked on its lower right by a rock rib, leads to above the pinnacles of the North East Ridge. This climb takes the gully. After 90m an 18m-high
and equally wide icefall is reached and climbed on its right side. Continue by a
much narrower gully above, which leads via an awkward ice bulge to the easier
upper section. Finish up North East Ridge to the summit.

Graduate Gully   200m   III
S Richardson and R Webb, 3 January 2009
Climb Mayfly to the foot of the icefall, trend left below its steep section and follow
an icy depression to reach a snow slope. Move left across this for 20m to enter a

231

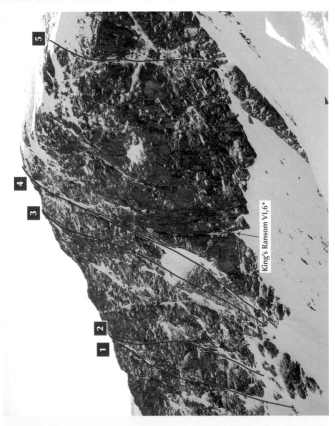

King's Ransom VI,6*

Aonach Beag
North Face
(left side)

1 Mayfly III*
2 Dragonfly III
3 The Black Prince II
4 Queen's View III
5 Stand and Deliver V,5**

well-defined square-cut gully, and climb this for 60m over a chockstone to join the North East Ridge just above the Pinnacles.

North East Ridge
460m III ★

J MacLay, WW Naismith and G Thomson, April 1895

The original climb on Aonach Beag, this long ridge descends well into the coire below Aonach Beag.

From the col (GR 211705) on the Glen Nevis approach, descend for 100m. Head north-north-west for 1½–2km, crossing three burns (second and third burns are gorge-like). Arriving at a fourth burn, the ridge is immediately above (1 hour from the col). The toe of the ridge is also approachable from the Aonach Mor/Beag col. The lower section of the ridge is not particularly difficult, but the middle part of the climb is quite narrow, with several pinnacles at half-height, which may be hard in icy conditions. The pinnacles are turned on the right, and after regaining the crest an overhung nose is passed on the left. The pinnacles may be climbed direct at a much harder grade. A knife-edge snow ridge leads to the broader and easier upper section, finishing about 50m to the north-west of the summit.

Stob Coire Bhealaich and An Aghaidh Gharbh both offer remote and very quiet venues for adventurous climbers in search of solitude. Many routes have been recorded here, but are not included in this guide so that the wild feel to these coires can be maintained.

Aonach Beag West Face

In clear weather the main features of this face are easily seen from the top of North East Buttress or the abseil posts on Ben Nevis, and climbers in that area could help themselves by spying out the lines when on Ben Nevis. Moving south from the Aonach Beag/Mor col, the first feature is a broad gully bounded on its right by Broken Axe Buttress, which has another deep easy gully on its right. Right of this gully is a lot of broken ground, which forms several icefalls before arriving at the most prominent buttress, Raw Egg Buttress (approx. GR 191711), some 700m south-west of the col. The climbs are described as if approaching from the col. An approach from Glen Nevis via Old Steall ruin and the Allt Guibhsachan is also possible (2–2½ hours).

Blind Faith
120m III

E Ewing and T Archer, 18 February 1996

On a narrow buttress up left of the gully to the left of Broken Axe Buttress. Starts up a chimney-groove and follows the crest to the top.

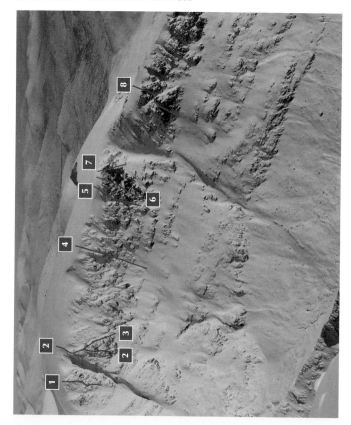

Aonach Beag
West Face

1 Blind Faith III
2 Twinkle IV,5**
3 Aonacrack IV,5*
4 Beyond the Call of Duty III,4
5 Eggsclamation II
6 Raw Egg Buttress IV,4**
7 Ruadh Eigg Chimney IV,5*
8 Prominent Chimney II,6

Twinkle   150m   IV,5 ★★

R Everett and S Richardson, 20 February 1988

An excellent mixed route which follows the crest of Broken Axe Buttress directly. Technically quite hard for the grade, but well protected and with several escapes possible to easier ground. Climb a chimney-groove to the left of the steep wall left of Axeless, then move right to belay above the wall (30m). Climb the open groove above to a small ledge, step right and climb the continuation groove to a small col junction with Axeless (40m). Step right to a steep corner. Climb this and the overhanging chimney above, then continue direct to join the final easy arête (50m). Follow Axeless to the top.

Axeless   150m   III ★

R Webb and R Everett, 16 January 1988

This climb takes an indirect but interesting line up Broken Axe Buttress. Start at a steep wall at the foot of the buttress in a small snow bay. Climb a groove on the right to a ledge overlooking the gully. Step right onto steep ice and climb up to snow, which leads back left to the crest of the buttress at a col. Move left to avoid the steep step above, then trend back right to gain a fine ridge which leads to the top.

Anaconda   160m   V,7

J Currie and S Richardson, 3 March 1996

Climb the first ramp of Aonacrack to the foot of the ice pitch on Axeless (20m). Between Aonacrack and Axeless, climb a steep rib on the left, then back to a wide crack which is followed steeply to its top. Go left up slabs to beneath a steep chimney (50m). Climb the chimney with difficulty to a ledge then go left (20m). Finish along the ridge of Axeless (70m).

Aonacrack   150m   IV,5 ★

J Ashbridge and SM Richardson, 21 March 1993

A good mixed climb which climbs the prominent crack on the right side of the buttress. Start close to the small snowy bay right of Axeless. Follow a ramp awkwardly to the base of the crack (15m). Climb the crack and a steep bulge to a ledge below a huge perched block. Follow a crack on the left side of the block to a belay on the top (25m). Continue in the crack and a steep bulging groove to a ledge (40m). Follow the broken ridge easily to the snow arête of Twinkle (40m), which is followed for another 30m.

Viper Edge   160m   IV,4

S Richardson and J Currie, 3 March 1996

Start at the top right side of the small snow bay of Aonacrack. Follow a short ramp up right, then a tenuous crack-line above to iced-up slabs. Follow the slabs left then right to the right edge of the buttress (45m). Follow the crest by a gully to the top of the tower (35m). Finish along the ridge of Axeless (70m).

Beyond the Call of Duty 150m III,4
R Everett and S Richardson, 20 February 1988
This climb takes the prominent series of icefalls which form in the centre of the face between Raw Egg and Broken Axe buttresses. The first is easy angled; the second is a standing pillar approached from the right; and the third starts steeply but eases higher up. Snow slopes then lead to the top.

West Central Route 150m II
R Everett and R Webb, 16 January 1988
A fine open mountaineering line to the right of Beyond the Call. Follow open grooves to belay at the right end of the rock wall, which is to the right of the second pitch of Beyond the Call. Climb the icefall to the right, then follow snow to a right-facing groove high on the face. Follow this then snow to the top.

Poached Egg 150m II ★★
RG Webb and J Dunn, 21 February 1987
The groove system left of Raw Egg Buttress.

Eggsclamation 150m II
S Richardson and R Everett, 5 April 1987
Immediately left of Raw Egg Buttress is an icy couloir. Follow this over short steps until the main line trends left (Poached Egg). Climb a short wall to gain the steeper direct continuation, which finishes next to the final rocks of the buttress.

Aonach Wall 150m V,6 ★
R Everett and S Richardson, 27 March 1988
This climb takes a direct line just to the right of the left arête of Raw Egg Buttress, taking in enjoyable technical climbing of steadily increasing difficulty. Start to the left of Raw Egg Buttress below the steep tower with the prominent perched block. Climb up and avoid the tower on the right to belay by the notch – as for Raw Egg Buttress (55m). Climb directly up via a short corner to gain snow below a longer corner, which leads to the crest of the arête (40m). Easy snow leads to the base of the headwall (20m). Climb a groove and wide crack straight above to a ledge (20m). Move right to gain the obvious V-groove, which provides the only line up the final wall. Climb this with difficulty to the top (15m).

(photo: Janie Hageman)

Raw Egg Buttress

1 Eggsclamation II
2 Aonach Wall V,6*
3 Raw Egg Buttress IV,4**
4 Top Gun V,6
5 Salmonella VII,8**
6 Ruadh Eigg Chimney IV,5*

Raw Egg Buttress
180m IV,4 ★★

R Everett and S Richardson, 5 April 1987

A good, well-protected mixed climb, with several short difficult steps, which takes a line up the front face trending from left to right. Start to the left of the lowest rocks on the left side of the crag. Climb an icy groove to below an overhanging corner, and then traverse right below a steep wall until it is possible to climb it (30m). Now trend up and left over mixed ground to belay next to a notch in the ridge on the left, formed by a tower with a prominent perched block (50m). Follow the icy groove-line above for two long pitches, always trending right, over several steep steps and corners (85m). The last pitch takes a steep corner to the left of a steep wall and has a difficult exit (15m).

Top Gun
160m V,6

S Richardson and A Mullin, 23 February 1999

Start 30m right of Raw Egg Buttress, 5m up and right of the foot of the buttress. Follow a left-slanting chimney ramp to its top, then up to the barrier wall of Raw Egg Buttress (40m). Climb a short icefall in the wall and go up right via chimneys to a good ledge (Salmonella first pitch finishes here) (40m). Above are three parallel right-trending grooves. Climb the middle groove to a ledge below the right of the headwall. Go left to a belay below a steep corner (50m). The corner above, with obvious flakes on its left wall, is climbed to a ledge (20m). It is a further 10m up the corner to the top.

Salmonella
125m VII,8 ★★

R Everett and S Richardson, 23 March 1991

A very hard mixed climb. Start about 30m up and right of the previous climb, below a prominent right-facing corner which cuts the lower tier and is gained by moderate mixed ground. Climb the overhanging corner for 20m, then continue more easily to a ledge and easy ground (35m). Possible escape down to the right. Scramble up to the obvious V-groove (15m). Climb the groove past a ledge, then continue up a chimney to belay below the prominent overhanging off-width (40m). Climb the off-width to a ledge (10m), then gain an alcove and pull over an overhang to easier ground (25m).

Well up and right (40m) of the previous route is an impressive rock wall which has a couple of good summer climbs on it. The right edge of this wall is defined by a deep gully which steepens into a narrow chimney, capped by three giant chockstones (Ruadh Eigg Chimney).

Stalking Horse
70m VI,7

D Hollinger and A Turner, 18 January 2007

An obvious chimney-corner system left of the impressive rock wall. Climb the wall and chimney-corner, belaying under the overhang. The wide crack is the crux, requiring successive can-opener moves.

Esat of Ben Nevis

Turfy mixed climbing on Raw Egg Buttress (photo: Jamie Hageman)

Blackbeard 70m VII,8

SM Richardson and I Small, 4 January 2008

Spectacular steep mixed climbing up the right arête of the steep wall, just left of Ruadh Eigg Chimney. Start directly below the arête. Climb the first of two corners to a narrow ledge, step right and climb the cracked right edge to a good ledge on the right (25m). Pull through the overhang on the right, then trend left up a steep wall to the regain the arête. Steep cracks on the edge of the buttress reach a left-trending ramp to the top (45m).

Ruadh Eigg Chimney 60m IV,5 ★

R Everett, G Muhlemann and S Richardson, 28 March 1992

Follow snowy steps to the foot of the chimney, then up over the chockstones and ice on the left wall.

Never A Dull Moment
70m   IV,6

R Everett and S Richardson, 1 January 1990

Right of Ruadh Eigg Chimney is another gully, steep at mid-height. Follow the gully past an amphitheatre, then the rock groove on the right, then back left to easier ground.

In the bay 100m south of Raw Egg Buttress is a prominent chimney with buttresses (North Buttress and Crevassed Rib) on either side. The chimney is climbed by **Prominent Chimney***, 100m, III,6, RG Webb and N Wilson, November 1998.*

STOB COIRE AN LAOIGH

Developed relatively recently, this crag in the Grey Coires offers steep mixed climbs on well-featured and turfy quartzite. In fact most of the routes look impossibly steep until the helpful nature of the rock is discovered. A long walk in can be helped by cycling from the end of the public road at Coirechoille (GR 252808), about 3 miles from Spean Bridge. Forest tracks are followed to the dam at the edge of the forest (GR 240765), followed by the east bank of the Allt Choimhlidh, high above the stream, to the stream junction at GR 242755. Cross the east stream (impossible in spate) and ascend the slope between the streams, then bear right to a shoulder from where the crag can easily be seen and approached (3 hours with the cycle). Descent is by either side of the crag.

End Game
50m   II

D McGimpsey and A Nisbet, 24 December 2000

The short blocky ridge starting on the left.

Spider Man
55m   IV,6

D Amos, D McGimpsey and A Nisbet, 14 February 2002

Just right of End Game, this climbs the steep turfy depression. A steep wall leads to the groove, which is climbed for 10m before a traverse right leads to a belay at some more shallow grooves. Climb these to the top (45m).

White Widow
55m   V,6 ★★

D McGimpsey and A Nisbet, 21 December 2002

Climb a short clean cut and undercut corner directly under a groove at 15m. Climb the steep but helpful groove (15m). Go left and back right before finishing up steep walls.

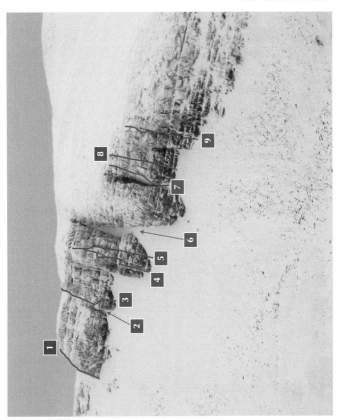

Stob Coire an Laoigh

1 End Game II
2 Easter Sunday Gully I
3 Loopy Louie IV,5*
4 Centrepoint VI,7***
5 Blue Rinse VI,7***
6 Central Gully II
7 Jammy Dodger VI,6**
8 Some Like it Hot VII,7***
9 Taliballan V,6***

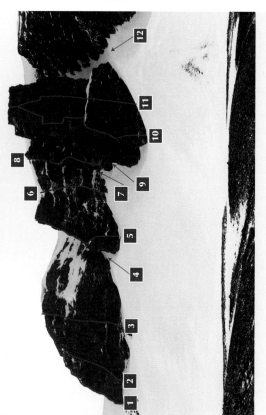

Stob Coire an Laoigh (left side)

1 End Game II
2 Spider Man IV,6
3 Arachnaphobe V,5
4 Easter Sunday Gully I
5 Loopy Louie IV,5*
6 The Wee Grey Man IV,5
7 Tit Gully V,5
8 Slim Jim V,6*
9 Tat Gully IV,4*
10 Centrepoint VI,7***
11 Blue Rinse VI,7***
12 Central Gully II

Tarantula
55m V,6 ★

D McGimpsey and A Nisbet, 2 January 2003

Start at a corner about 10m left of Arachnaphobe, at the left end of ledges leading out from that route. Climb the corner to a ledge and traverse left to a crack in the right side of an arête. Climb the helpful crack to a huge smooth block (30m). Go round the block on the right and finish up the less distinct arête.

Arachnaphobe
55m V,5

D McGimpsey and A Nisbet, 16 February 2002

An ice route up the slab at the right of the leftmost buttress. Reach the icefall by a steep corner to blocks and a traverse left. Exciting moves up and left, then climb the icefall to belay at some rocks (35m). Climb a groove up and right to the top (20m).

The Epithany
60m V,6

J Edwards and G Hughes, 5 January 2003

Start in the middle of the bay at the right end of the buttress. Climb up and move left to the climb on the left side of the bay directly to a chimney. Easier ground leads to a stance below an obvious line, 5m right of Arachnaphobe (50m). The unprotected obvious line leads to the top (10m).

The Alternative
60m IV,5

J Edwards and J Thacker, 11 January 2003

Starting just to the right of the bay, go up and left along a ledge to the right side of the bay, which is climbed moving right to easier ground (35m). A hidden gully leads back left with ease to the top.

Easter Sunday Gully
80m I

S Richardson and J Ashbridge, March 1993

The snow gully right of the leftmost buttress.

Loopy Louie
60m IV,5 ★

D McGimpsey and A Nisbet, 8 February 2002

The arête to the right of Easter Sunday Gully. Start right of the arête, climb an awkward wall and move left to a col behind a small pinnacle. Continue up the short wall and the crest above (30m). Follow the crest, moving left into grooves to avoid steep walls. With little snow at the base there might be an overhanging wall blocking access, in which case approach the col from the left of the arête.

Sloppy Suzie
60m V,5

D McGimpsey and A Nisbet, 16 November 2002

The left-hand groove, right of Loopy Louie, with various variations right and left until a final wall is climbed on the right. Climbed direct (*J Edwards and J Thacker*) it is V,6.

The Wee Grey Man
60m IV,5

N Stevenson and N Wilson, March 1996

Climb a long groove just left of Tit Gully in the face on the left (30m). Traverse left and climb an icefall, then trend left at the top.

Tit Gully
60m V,5

D McGimpsey and A Nisbet, 18 February 2002

Climb the steep ice gully on the left of Slim Jim, moving onto the right at about half-height.

Slim Jim
80m V,6 ★

B Davison, D McGimpsey and A Nisbet, 17 February 2001

The narrow pillar left of the central buttress, approached by a 10m traverse from the gully to its right. Climb just right of the crest to an easing in the angle. Traverse left and go up a chimney on the left of the crest (30m). Climb the chimney and steep ground above to a col behind a pinnacle (not obvious from below). A short awkward wall leads to the top (40m).

Tat Gully
70m IV,4 ★

V Chelton and D McGimpsey, 13 February 2002

The gully right of Slim Jim, climbed over a steep section and up a groove on the right to an awkward belay (30m). Head for the upper right-hand groove by short leftwards traverses and steep grooves (40m).

Popped at the Piste
70m V,6

E Brunskill and D Morris, 16 February 2002

A direct line up the left of the central buttress, starting at the base of Tat Gully. Climb up and slightly right towards a steep slab, and climb the right hand of two parallel cracks. Go up and right to below a chimney (30m). Climb the chimney, stepping right at its top to finish up the edge of the buttress (30m).

New Labour
70m V,6 ★

D McGimpsey and A Nisbet, 16 February 2002

This climbs the left edge of the central buttress. Start round to the left and climb diagonally right to a ledge just left of the edge (15m). Walls and shallow grooves follow a line just left of the edge (35m). Move round to the front face and easily to the top (20m).

Socialist   60m   V,7

D McGimpsey, A Nisbet and J Preston, 2 March 2004

Start on a ledge 6m right of Tat Gully. Climb through an overhang leftwards to a ledge (crux, 10m). Go right along the ledge and up the wall to the highest ledge below the steep wall (25m). Climb the chimney on the right to a ledge and finish up the wall on the right, trending left (25m).

Centrepoint   90m   VI,7 ★★★

D McGimpsey and A Nisbet, 24 December 2000

The central buttress is the most prominent feature of the crag, and this superb route takes the front face. Start at the left of the lowest rocks. Climb diagonally right across a low ledge, then straight up over blocks and a short wall. Move left on turf and up to the top of the lower tier, then walk 10m right to below the leftmost groove in the upper tier (40m). Climb the groove and traverse left to a ledge. After a short wall and groove step left and go up to a wider crack with chockstones. Traverse right, make a long step to a turf ledge, and belay on a higher ledge (25m). Trend rightwards up a wall, then climb a crack to the right of a roof and the top (25m).

Blue Rinse   80m   VI,7 ★★★

D McGimpsey and A Nisbet, 18 February 2002

On the right side of the front face of the central buttress, this route climbs the big roofed corner. Sensational climbing requiring very well-frozen turf. Start to the right of the buttress and climb a big corner leading directly to the base of the corner in the upper buttress (25m). Climb this over a roof and swing left at the second roof (30m). Climb blocks and trend left to finish, as for Centrepoint.

Choc-a-Block   60m   VI,6

J Edwards and G Hughes, 4 January 2003

The first fault in the left-hand wall of Central Gully. The steep fault is climbed on turf to terraces at 25m and 50m, with a further 10m to the top.

The Chaf   60m   IV,5

E Brunskill and D Morris, 9 February 2002

Start about 20m up Central Gully at the second weakness. Climb the groove system in the left wall of the gully up and left to a terrace. Traverse this leftwards onto the front face and a thread-belay below a chimney (35m). Climb the chimney and continue to the top (25m).

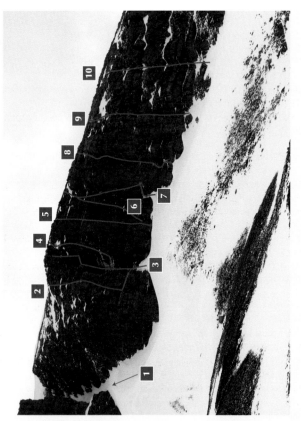

Stob Coire nan Laoigh (right side)

1 Central Gully II
2 The Calf IV,5
3 Cobra Corner VI,6**
4 Jammy Dodger VI,6**
5 Some Like it Hot VII,7***
6 White Heat VI,7*
7 Serve Chilled VII,6**
8 Taliballan V,6***
9 Yee Ha IV,5
10 The White Streak IV,5

Chaf Direct   55m   IV,6
J Edwards and J Thacker, 11 January 2003
Follow The Chaf to the terrace and continue by the corner-fault to a spike. Move right and up to the second terrace (45m). The corner-fault leads to the top (10m).

Central Gully   120m   II
B Davison, D McGimpsey and A Nisbet, 17 February 2001
The biggest gully of the crag, to the right of the central buttress, usually contains a short ice pitch, but can vary from grade I to IV.

Central Wall   50m   IV,4
B Davison, 17 February 2001
An ice line (or mixed at IV,5) on the right wall of Central Gully starting before the narrows. Climb an icy groove to a traverse-line coming in from higher up the gully. A steep narrow groove leads to easy ground at the top of The Calf buttress.

The Calf   75m   IV,5
D McGimpsey and A Nisbet, 4 November 2000
On the buttress to the right of the central buttress, starting up Cobra Corner. Climb the gully and traverse left along a narrow ledge to below wedged blocks (25m). The blocks lead to a ledge on the left, then go back right up a stepped ramp to a good ledge (20m). Climb steeply up and left around the crest to mostly easier ground (30m).

Cobra Corner   80m   VI,6 ★★
B Davison and A Nisbet, 13 December 2002
The huge roofed corner to the right of Central Gully is slow to freeze, and is another line that is more amenable than it looks. The gully is climbed over two steps (20m), followed by the corner, then a right-trending line to a turf ledge and groove to another steep corner (30m). The corner and its continuation lead to an escape on a ledge to the left.

Jammy Dodger   85m   VI,6 ★★
D McGimpsey and A Nisbet, 3 February 2002
Mostly climbed on ice on the first ascent this route takes the right wall of the huge roofed gully of Cobra Corner. Start as for The Calf up the gully and continue over another step until level with the large slab on the right (20m). A serious traverse on turf rightwards then make steep moves up to a ledge 5m from the arête (20m). Climb a short crack and move right to the arête, continue around the arête and climb a steep groove until an easier traverse left can be made to an alcove (40m). A final bulge on the right leads to the top (5m).

Some Like it Hot   70m   VII,7 ★★★
M 'Ed' Edwards, D McGimpsey and A Nisbet, 13 February 2007
Steep and sustained, starting about halfway along the wall, below and just right of a
right-facing corner 20m up. Climb over a short wall into a V-groove, go left and step
back right on to a 'diving board' above the roof of the V-groove. A steep wall leads
to the corner (25m). Climb the corner.

White Heat   65m   VI,7 ★
M 'Ed' Edwards, J Edwards-Lihocka and A Nisbet, 20 March 2007
The left-facing corner and its sensational right arête. Start as for Some Like it Hot
and climb into its roofed groove, but pull out right onto blocks. A shallow groove
on the right leads to below the corner (15m). Climb the corner to stand on a block
below overhangs. Step out right, move up to a small platform on the arête, and
climb blocks and cracks, mostly just left of the arête, to a ledge below a roof (30m).
Move right into the finishing groove of Serve Chilled. Go up this for 10m, but move
left and finish up the rib on the left (20m).

Serve Chilled   70m   VII,6 ★★
D McGimpsey and A Nisbet, 6 February 2002
A very serious ice route that takes the groove just left of the rib between the roofed
gully of Jammy Dodger and the chimney of Taliballan. Climb a short chimney and
traverse right into the groove. Climb the groove, trending slightly left, then a vertical
sheet to an excellent belay in a niche (40m). Continue up the groove through a slot,
then left and up another groove leading slightly rightwards to the top.

Pentagon   50m   VI,7
S Allan and A Nisbet, 16 April 2005
The left side of the rib left of Taliballan. Take the short chimney and right traverse,
as for Serve Chilled (15m). Climb up left for 6m, as for Serve Chilled, before a short
traverse right gains a ledge. Reach a second ledge, then go slightly right and back
left over a bulge to gain a shallow corner which leads to the base of a big left-facing
flake-line (20m). Climb the flake-line, then a corner on the right, to pass a smooth
wall and finish back in the original line (15m).

Full Frontal   60m   VII,8 ★
T Stone and V Scott, 22 November 2008
The rib left of Taliballan and the overhanging off-width at the top. Steep and
exposed. Halfway along the wall left of Taliballan, climb a corner to a ledge. Take
another short corner above, then move left up cracks to a block on the arête. Go
up from this left, then back right to beneath a left-facing groove (25m). Climb

the left-facing groove and traverse the wall beneath a roof to a second left-facing groove, which leads to a turf ledge. Climb a bulging groove on the right, a steep wall and a slab to blocks above, with sustained interest, to a large ledge. A steep corner leads to the overhanging off-width, which is exited on the right (45m).

Taliballan   70m   V,6 ★★★
D McGimpsey and A Nisbet, 27 December 2001
A superb mixed route and a modern classic, climbing the bottomless chimney blocked by a large roof. The turf needs to be well frozen, and there can be variable quantities of ice. Climb towards the chimney to a vertical wall, traverse left 5m and climb a cracked ramp back into the chimney (20m). A steep turf bulge starts the chimney, which is climbed to the big roof (20m). Cracks in the right wall lead around the roof to a good stance (10m). Continue to a chockstone below a steeper groove, traverse left and go up and right over blocks into the less steep groove to finish (20m).

Yee Ha   70m   IV,5
D Amos, D McGimpsey and A Nisbet, 14 February 2002
The ice line left of White Streak, starting up an iced corner, then a shallow chimney and a deeper chimney. Exit right and continue to easier ground (50m). Follow an easier groove above to the top (20m).

Switchback   60m   IV,5
D McGimpsey and A Nisbet, 4 January 2004
Start as for Yee Ha and climb a steep flaky corner up and right, then more easily to belay as for Jaws below the V-groove (35m). Continue diagonally rightwards, then traverse left to the top of a groove. Steep turf to the top (25m).

Jaws   60m   IV,5
A Nisbet and J Preston, 24 February 2004
Start as for Yee Ha but climb the wall on the right into an obvious widening crack. Climb the chimney and corner above to a V-groove 10m left of The White Line (35m). The groove leads over an overhang to the top (25m).

The White Streak   50m   IV,5
B Davison, D McGimpsey and A Nisbet, 17 February 2001
Near the right end of the crag, this can be an obvious thin straight white line. Climb an icy groove directly up from where a rightward-slanting ramp leads to a terrace.

Tidal Groove   80m   III

D McGimpsey and A Nisbet, 27 November 2000
The right-slanting ramp and slabby groove at the right end of the crag.

A LONG WAY DOWN by Mike Pescod

It's difficult to choose which tale to tell. There are many to choose from, but one stands out, reminding me of how to approach climbing on Ben Nevis.

After 15 years of climbing on Ben Nevis I still haven't climbed Castle Ridge in winter. That's not to say I haven't spent some time on it, though. Many years ago I set out to climb the ridge with a few friends, with a relaxed approach and little haste as the route is quite short. Entertaining grooves, slabs and chat took us up the crest with little thought as to what might be happening beyond our bubble of camaraderie. On reaching the crux, a step right above the void of the North Face into a steep groove, the gales forecast to arrive many hours later appeared early and abruptly. This wasn't part of our plan for a gentle day of climbing and we decided upon a retreat.

As with the majority of British mountaineers unused to down-climbing, descending the ridge did not appeal to us. Neither did abseiling down the ridge with all the snag hazards on the easy angle rocks and the wind blowing the rope around.

So we elected to abseil down the North Face of Castle Ridge, thinking we were very clever to realise this was the best option to get out of the wind and make it easier to retrieve the ropes on the abseils. We were right, we did get into relative shelter quickly and the ropes did pull each time. One abseil later and we felt quite smug, then another pitch completed. But the ground appeared no closer, especially as it was now dark.

Abseiling down this face is not popular and finding anchors was not easy, a job made even more difficult using a headtorch. Going straight down should, on the face of it, make the route easy to find, but this didn't seem to work out either. Running out of slings to leave behind added to the feeling of things not going our way.

Six abseils later and a few hours after dark we walked away from the foot of the face with the resolve to learn how to down-climb, Ben Nevis appearing to be much bigger than when we started.

GLEN COE

Descending Broad Gully, Stob Coire nan Lochan

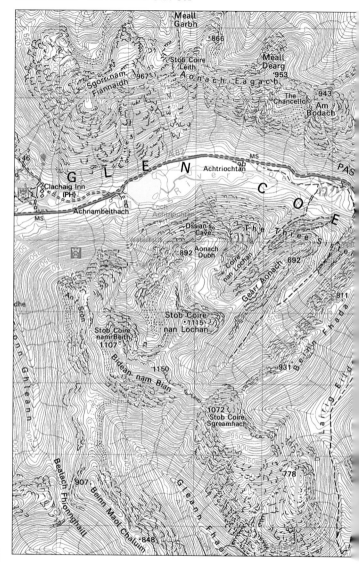

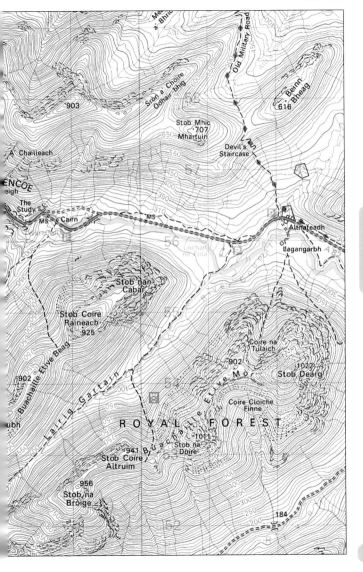

CENTRAL AREA

Steep mixed climbing on Tilt, Stob Coire nan Lochan

The varied and complex peaks of Glen Coe are all lower than those of Ben Nevis and the Aonachs, and good conditions are therefore less certain. Nonetheless, this area provides a wide range of route choice – from mixed routes on the buttresses to cascade-style ice climbs. The ridges which abruptly separate the deep glens and coires are all fine outings, whilst the ridge and coire walls provide excellent winter climbing to all standards. Only in recent years has Ben Nevis superseded the 'Coe' as the leading edge of modern winter climbing on Scotland's west coast, especially where mixed routes are concerned. However, the quality of the climbs here is still very highly regarded.

Many climbs in Glen Coe are rocky mixed climbs requiring a good freeze and snow and rime to make the crags white. Generally the ice climbing in Glen Coe, when in condition, will be of the frozen waterfall/drainage weeps variety, unlike Ben Nevis, which provides more frozen atmospheric rime ice cover due to its higher elevation. There are a few snow-ice gullies in Glen Coe, which are very popular when in condition.

Another major advantage over Ben Nevis are the shorter approaches, especially when starting from higher up the glen. Some routes on The Buachaille, for example, can be started after only an hour's walk. Descent routes from all of the peaks should be treated with extreme care due to the steep and rocky nature of this area. The complex nature of the crags also allows the formation of small pockets of windslab in many locations, which can easily catch out unwary climbers. The area is well covered by either of two maps, OS Landranger Sheet 41, 1:50,000, or Harvey Superwalker, Glen Coe, 1:25,000.

CLIMBS FROM COIRE NAM BEITH

The magnificent northern coire of Bidean is contained in the horseshoe ridges linking Stob Coire nan Lochan, Bidean nam Bian, Bidean's West Top, Stob Coire nam Beith and the nose of An-t-Sron. The main cliffs are the Diamond and Church Door buttresses on the North Face of Bidean nam Bian, the westward-facing cliff on the flank of the north spur of the west top and the immense cliff cone leading to the summit of Stob Coire nam Beith.

The main approach for this coire starts from the road junction (GR 137566) through a gate immediately west of a road bridge spanning the River Coe. The path climbs steeply to the south (beware of an icy patch on the path) and after about an hour levels off into a short gorge. At this point it is better to descend to the streambed and follow either side of the stream uphill to avoid steep slabs below the deteriorating path. You soon arrive at a stream junction. Straight ahead, the left (east) bank of the main stream can be followed towards the col between Stob Coire nam Beith and An-t-Sron. From this col a steep but straightforward approach can be made to the summit of Stob Coire nam Beith: the west and main tops of Bidean. It also provides a good method of descent from all routes starting in this coire.

A glance at the map (Sheet 41 – 1:50,000) will reveal three streams departing from the junction previously mentioned (GR 138554). If the vague central branch is followed it leads up into Summit Gully (described below). This stream approach can provide a good reference point for parties climbing on the complicated cliffs of Stob Coire nam Beith. The left-hand stream can also be followed in a south-easterly direction through a steep band of rock bluffs into the coire beneath the cliffs. A waterfall will be encountered on this approach and is best avoided to the right (west).

The coire continues up to a higher basin (often referred to as the Bidean Coire) beneath the Church Door and Diamond buttresses. Leading up steeply on either side of these two big buttresses are easy slopes to the cols between Stob Coire nan Lochan and Bidean, and between Bidean and the West Top. Both of these give descent routes, but care should be exercised, as they can become very icy. The right (west) of this upper basin is another subsidiary coire, which leads up between the cliffs of the West Top Spur and Stob Coire nam Beith to a shallow col between the two summits. This gives another descent route, although one should not glissade, as there are a number of small rock outcrops in the coire which may be hidden from above.

This route should be treated with care, especially if avalanche conditions prevail on north-facing slopes. In good conditions it is best to head well right in descent until an open snow slope is seen, avoiding any cliffs.

An-t-Sron

1 Sac-o'-Coal Couloir III
2 Smashed Spectacles Gully II/III
3 Cold Turkey IV,4

An-t-Sron, 834m

This mountain lies up to the right of the main approach to Coire nam Beith. On the north side of An-t-Sron are the following climbs.

The Chasm of An-t-Sron   360m   IV,4 ★
HM Brown, J Matyssek, RK Graham and M Smith, 2 January 1963
The great gully which splits the North Face. The first pitch is normally turned, but the other pitches higher up in the right-hand branches give good sport in icy conditions.

Blind   80m   III
M Duff and R Nowack, 14 February 1996
On the right wall of The Chasm, three icefalls sometimes form at approximately one-third height. This route climbs the lowest of these and is approached by abseil.

The following climbs are on the East Face of An-t-Sron (ie. the right wall of the subsidiary coire between Stob Coire nam Beith and An-t-Sron). There are several easy gullies further right towards the mass of crags. The right-hand section includes a big prominent smooth slab. To the left of this is a snow bay at a slightly higher level, from which rise steep twin diverging couloirs. The following first two obvious lines give the climbs.

Sac-o'-Coal Couloir   150m   III
J McArtney, D Selby, B Payne, J Lines and G Drayton, 18 February 1969
The left-hand line leads to a very steep and awkward corner exit before a final easy slope leads to the summit ridge.

Smashed Spectacles Gully   150m   II/III
I Clough, F Jones, R Fox and C Wood, 18 February 1969
The right-hand line gives a short ice pitch in the first section, and then follows a very steep chimney capped by an ice bulge before an easier continuation leads to the top.

Cold Turkey   130m   IV,4
A Nelson and A Paul, 25 February 2000
Opposite Hidden Gully (Stob Coire nam Beith). Climb the clean-cut corner/groove on the right of the prominent slab to mixed ground and a belay on the right under a roof (50m). Climb a sloping shelf and mixed ground above (80m).

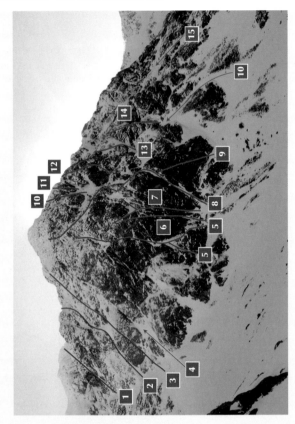

Stob Coire nam Beith

1 The Corridors III/IV,4*
2 Broken Gully II/III
3 Number One Buttress II/III*
4 Arch Gully III*
5 Central Gully IV,4**
6 Crack Climb III
7 Deep-Cut Chimney IV,4***
8 Number Four Buttress II
9 Isis VI,8**
10 North-West Gully III**
11 The Mummy IV,5
12 The Sphinx IV,5**
13 Cleftweave II/III
14 The Pyramid III*
15 Summit Gully II**

The climbing on this mountain offers length, quality and variety. It will test the ability to find a route without a detailed description, especially higher up the climbs, where many different options will be found. A fine peak for middle-grade mountaineering routes.

The base of this massive and complicated cone of cliffs swings through a great arc, so that all the climbs cannot be seen from the junction of the stream on the approach route. The most obvious feature here is the long Summit Gully. The slabby 90m Pyramid and (above and left of it) the bigger and steeper Sphinx Buttress form an indefinite ridge which bounds Summit Gully on the left. To the left of these is the region where the vague North West Gully winds its way through the broken rocks of Number Four Buttress. The topography of the important central section can be seen in the diagram – the unmistakable Deep-Cut Chimney, the rightward-slanting ramp gully start of Number Four Buttress, the chimney-groove line of Crack Climb and the long shallow ice course of Central Gully. Beyond Central Gully the cliffs on the left-hand side of the cone fall back and eventually form a very big bay. Arch Gully runs up the right-hand side of the bay, and to the left of the lower part of this is a big rock rognon split by a narrow chimney-line, the start of the so-called Number One Buttress. Above this rognon is a broad sloping snow shelf and the continuation of the Number One Buttress chimney-line, which leads up the rocks at the back of the bay. A shallow gully curls up and round the left-hand side of the rognon to the snow shelf. This is the approach to Broken Gully, which has two forks and lies in the left-hand recess of the bay. It leads up to the left to emerge on a shoulder. Beyond Broken Gully the final bold projection below the shoulder is called Zero Buttress.

Zero Buttress   115m   IV,4 ★

S Kennedy and R Hamilton, 26 February 2006

Based on the prominent right-facing corner in the buttress immediately left of The Corridors. Climb directly into the base of the corner, then traverse to slabs right of the corner (25m). Cross the slab diagonally rightwards to a large block on the right edge, overlooking The Corridors. Surmount the block and follow an open groove to a short wall (45m). Climb a steep slab just left of the wall, then mixed ground, before moving left on snow to finish by an easy groove (40m).

The Corridors   160m   III/IV,4 ★

I Clough, MA Hudson, C Hutchinson, C Williamson and D Davies, 12 February 1969

To the left of Broken Gully the face of Zero Buttress is cut by two shallow square-cut gully sections: the first ending at a ledge about 45m up, and the other starting from this ledge a little further to the right and leading to the top of the buttress. This gives the line of the climb. The first corridor is often only filled with powder snow, so a better alternative is to take the ice ribbon leading directly up the lower slabs to the second corridor. This should then give a couple of steep pitches leading to easier ground.

Broken Gully   160m   II/III
Mr and Mrs I Clough, 13 January 1966
The gully goes left up into the recess above the broad terrace which splits Number One Buttress into two tiers. After about 30m a shallow gully on the right is followed until an easy leftwards traverse leads to the top of Zero Buttress. The left fork is a direct continuation and is separated from the normal route by a rock rib. It is steeper and holds more ice (grade II/III).

Number One Buttress   270m   II/III ★
I Clough and party, 9 March 1967
The chimney-line up the rognon left of Arch Gully and the upper tier above gives a series of short ice pitches leading to the shoulder on Arch Gully.

Arch Gully   270m   III ★
CM Allen and JHB Bell, December 1933
To the left of Central Gully is a shorter buttress, Number One Buttress; dividing the two is Arch Gully. The first section is generally banked up and leads to a couple of steep pitches, which are climbed direct to a shoulder. Continue to the summit or traverse off to the left.

Central Gully   450m   IV,4 ★★
J Clarkson and J Waddell, 12 January 1958
To the left of Crack Climb an ice trap can form. Climb the ice trap and follow the gully above past three to four steep pitches to easier ground. A fine climb.

Crackwork Grooveplay   150m   IV,4 ★★
A Nelson and T Blakemore, March 1999
Climb a slab between Central Gully and Crack Climb to the base of a steep crack and left-facing corner. Ascend the corner and V-groove above to a chockstone and easier ground in the upper section of Central Gully.

Centre Route   450m   II/III
JG Parish, D Haworth and D McIntyre, February 1945
A rather indefinite climb starting round to the left of the lowest rocks to the right of Central Gully. Zig-zag up the buttress for the initial 90m until the angle lessens.

Crack Climb   450m   III

LS Lovat and N Harthill, 12 January 1958

Follows the obvious chimney-groove on the projecting side-wall to the left of Deep-Cut Chimney, starting about 25m up. The line leads to the foot of a steep 10m wall which may be hard – but escape to the right is possible into the amphitheatre of Deep-Cut Chimney.

Deep-Cut Chimney   450m   IV,4 ★★★

WM MacKenzie and WH Murray, April 1939

The obvious deep narrow gully starting just to the left of the slanting ramp is a classic climb. The lower part gives two or three steep pitches leading at 130m to a small amphitheatre, from where escape right is possible. Go up left from the amphitheatre over iced rocks to a long steep crack-line, which leads to easier ground. A further 200m to the summit.

Pharaoh's Rib   150m   III,4

A Clarke and J Main, 19 December 1992

The crest just right of Deep-Cut Chimney via off-widths, wide cracks and grooves to easier ground on Number Four Buttress. Hard to start.

Number Four Buttress   450m   II

The indefinite crest to the left of North West Gully starting from the top of the slanting ramp.

Isis   60m   VI,8 ★★

R and C Anderson and R Milne, 23 March 1991

Starts just up left of the lowest rocks of the big wall left of North West Gully. Climb an obvious groove and steep flake-crack to a recess (45m). Climb a short crack to easier ground (15m). Descend by abseil or the slanting gully of Number Four Buttress.

Scarab   70m   IV,5

J Blyth and S Lampard, 14 November 1992

Starts just left and down from North West Gully and right of Isis. Climb up and to the left side of a large flake, then up to a small ledge down and right of an inverted flake; belay (35m). Go up the crux rib above and left at an overhang to finish (35m). Descent as for Isis.

North West Gully   500m   III ★★

Glover and Worsdell, April 1906

Sometimes mistaken for Summit Gully to its right, but distinguished by its lack of real entry and by a ramp cutting in from the left below Number Four Buttress. Open to considerable variation. The best start is by the slanting ramp, but steep and harder direct entries can be used. Easy snow then leads to a fork. The left branch lacks interest, so go right to another fork amid impressive scenery. From here go to a shoulder, from where a steep wall leads to easier ground.

The Mummy   60m   IV,5

A Clarke and J Main, 20 December 1992
The steep tower which splits the right branch of North West Gully. Follow grooves to a belay on the left, then cracks to the top.

*On the right side of North West Gully are two buttresses, one above the other. These form a ridge on the left of Summit Gully. The wedge-like lower buttress is **The Pyramid** and above is **The Sphinx**. Immediately left of and higher than The Sphinx is the steep column of The Mummy.*

The Sphinx   135m   IV,5 ★★

JR Marshall and I Douglas, 12 January 1958
Climb North West Gully until below a long black cave about halfway up. Start below and left of this cave by a shattered wall, and climb to a small basin below the cave. Go right to a platform under the steep upper rocks. Climb high-stepped walls to reach the obvious chimney above (20m) and gain a tiny recess 3m up to the right. Grasp the top edge of a pinnacle-flake on the right-hand side, swing into space and start climbing for the top (75m); sustained!!

The Sphinx – Direct   205m   IV,7 ★

R Anderson and R Milne, 28 December 1997
Ascend North West Gully to a short leaning wall 30m below the ordinary route. Go left around the edge and up a chimney-groove and crack before trending right to belay beneath a groove in the blunt crest (45m). Follow the groove for 5m, then go left to an open groove which leads to a ledge with a clean-cut groove above. Step left and climb grooves on the left before moving back right to a ledge on the crest (40m). Above is a prow of rock with a wide fault on the right. Enter the fault from the left, climb a short chimney, then go right to a shallow recess on the right of the fault. Climb out on the right by using a pinnacle flake on the original route and go up right to a stance at the foot of a corner (50m). Climb the corner to a belay (20m). In the buttress above is a fault which is gained from the left and climbed to easier ground. Easier ground and different options now lead to the top of the mountain.

Cleftweave   450m   II/III

B Clarke and A Strachan, January 1972

Well to the right of North West Gully, follow a series of gullies which wind up left of The Pyramid to overlook Summit Gully. A steep short ice wall on the left is followed to gullies and a snow bowl. Follow a gully and ice pitch on the right to exit on summit slopes.

The Pyramid   90m   III ★

JR Marshall and I Douglas, 12 January 1958

Begin at the lowest rocks above the start of North West Gully and follow the north ridge to the top.

Vertex   130m   IV,5 ★★

B Hamilton and S Kennedy, 6 December 2008

A line close to the right edge of Number Six Buttress overlooking The Causeway. Start behind a huge detached block. Climb an obvious groove-line just left of the edge to a large flake below a steep wall. Climb the slabby wall on the left, then move back right and continue up a groove to a detached flake and thread on the edge overlooking the gully (45m). Climb a wall on the left into a groove which leads to a slabby corner. Climb the steep wall just right of the corner and continue up short steps to easier ground (45m). Further short walls lead to the final steepening, which is avoided by a short traverse left to the edge. A narrow snow arête leads to the top of the buttress (40m).

The Causeway   450m   III

A Findlay, S Kennedy and A Nelson, 24 March 1996

Climb into the gully on the right of The Pyramid, and halfway up it traverse right along a ledge onto the buttress. Ascend the buttress to a snow arête which looks into Summit Gully on the right. Continue up the arête to a small buttress just right of the central cleft of Cleftweave. Ascend the right side of this buttress to the top of the cleft, and from a large chockstone go left (crossing Cleftweave) along an obvious narrow spiral terrace to the buttress edge. Go up an awkward cracked wall and steps to the top of Sphinx Buttress. Finish up Cleftweave on the right and easier ground above.

Summit Gully   500m   II ★★

The great long gully which starts just to the left of the lowest rocks of the Stob Coire nam Beith cone of cliffs. This route is often mistaken for North West Gully. If snow has obliterated the vague streambed mentioned in the earlier approach description, look for the most obvious and continuous gully-line of least resistance descending from just right (west) of the summit. This is seen well from the stream junction of the approach route. The route is generally straightforward, with a possibility of ice steps to start with. A large cave pitch at mid-height might be impossible, but can be turned by a right-hand gully branch 50m lower down. Above the cave it is straightforward to the exit, which is just right of the summit cairn.

The following mixed routes lie between the lower section of Summit Gully and Adagio, on a prominent steep slabby buttress. An abseil descent is possible; alternatively, go down Summit Gully or finish up the easier upper ridge of Adagio.

Voie Crombie   160m   III,4

S Kennedy, M Thomson, R Hamilton and A Paul, 19 February 1996
Follows the banana-groove on the left side of the buttress. Climb the groove from a recess to a wide ledge and block-belay on the right (The Junction) (50m). Make a difficult move off the left end of the ledge to a ramp leading to the left edge of the buttress. Move up right to a block-belay (40m). Go easily up right to a narrow chimney, which is climbed to the Adagio ridge (70m).

Team Machine   90m   IV,5

J Grieve, P Harrop, A Paul, S Kennedy and A Nelson, 17 March 1996
Just right of Voie Crombie is a buttress with a chimney-groove. Ascend either the chimney or the rib on its left to gain the upper groove and The Junction belay (50m). Climb the initial difficult moves on Voie Crombie to the left, but then go up right by a narrow ramp and a slab to a groove which is climbed to a block-belay (40m).

The Gathering   95m   IV,5 ★

S Kennedy, A Paul and A Nelson, 24 March 1996
Start 10m right of Team Machine and go left to a thin hanging corner on the right edge of the slabby buttress (10m). Climb the sustained corner to The Junction (45m). Ascend a blocky wall to the right, then go horizontally right to a groove which is climbed to a ledge. Go back left over a short steepening to the block-belay on Team Machine (40m).

Arthur's Corner   95m   IV,5 ★

A Paul and G Reilly, 31 March 1996
Ascends the open right-facing corner on the right side of the buttress to the right of The Gathering. Hard moves at the start and to finish.

Adagio   400m   IV,4 ★

H MacInnes, R Birch, D Chen, P Judge and R O'Shea, 5 March 1969

Climbs the obvious narrow and steep gully in the crest of West Buttress which lies to the right of Summit Gully. Go up easily to a steepening with a thinly iced left wall. Ascend the corner on the right followed by a left-rising traverse round the corner to twin icy chimneys. The left-hand chimney is climbed for 6m, then the right-hand one above a bulge and onto easier ground. Follow the main gully, keeping left and climbing a cave direct towards the easier ground on the ridge to the right of Summit Gully.

The following three climbs lie on the left (east) wall of the subsidiary upper coire between Stob Coire nam Beith and An-t-Sron. To reach these climbs follow the left bank of the stream (gorge) towards the An-t-Sron/Stob Coire nam Beith col, until above a large rock island. **Hidden Gully** *is the obvious gully lying across to the left, while* **Bootneck Gully** *is 75m higher up.*

Bootneck Gully   245m   III

H MacInnes, I Duckworth, P Wells, R Ward and J Parsons, March 1969

Take the central chimney-line for two pitches until a steep ice wall has to be climbed. Above are easy slopes.

Alleyway   105m   III ★

KV Crocket, D Jenkins, C Forrest and J McEwan, 23 March 1969

The left-slanting gully right of Hidden Gully, which can be used as an alternative start to that route. Mixed ground (30m) followed by easy snow leads to a very narrow alley capped by a large chockstone. From the top of the alley descend 10m into Hidden Gully below the difficulties.

Hidden Gully   180m   IV,4 ★★

L Lovat and W Greaves, 13 February 1955

Climb snow to a cave and exit to easy ground via the left wall. Continue past another cave to a narrowing with two exits, either of which can be taken steeply to the ridge overlooking Summit Gully.

West Top of Bidean nam Bian

Slightly higher up the coire, these cliffs are on the western flank of the spur that descends northwards into Coire nam Beith from the West Top of Bidean nam Bian (ie. the highest point of the ridge between the summits of Bidean and Stob Coire nam Beith, GR 141542). The lower end of this ridge ends at Bishop's Buttress (GR 142544).

(photo: Donald King)

Bidean nam Bian

1 Central Gully I**
2 West Chimney Route V,6***
3 The Fang V,6
4 Closer IV,5**
5 St Peter's Well VI,7**
6 Return of the Nedi IV,5**
7 Parthian Shot V,7
8 The Gash IV,4**
9 The Hash III
10 Hourglass Gully I
11 Dubiety IV,5*
12 Minute Man IV,5*

Under the Weather 60m VII,7

G Hughes and J Edwards, 28 December 2004

The right-facing corner and overhang 5m left of the arête on the left of Bishop's Buttress starting at an open V-slot. Climb the slot to a ledge at 10m, reach to corner and climb this past an overhang, then follow steep grooves to a large ledge (45m). The right-slanting crack leads to easy ground (15m).

The Crook 50m VI,7

D King and A Nelson, 28 December 2003

The prominent crack-line up the centre of the North Face of Bishop's Buttress. Climb the crack to a right-sloping ledge and follow this into a bay. Climb a left-slanting groove and short wall to reach another bay with a rocking block (35m). Climb the corner above and exit left (15m).

Ambush 75m VI,7

B Fyffe and D Hollinger, 23 January 2003

On the West Face, 12m right of the edge of the buttress, climb a line of weakness past jammed blocks to a stance (10m). Move right to a corner and go up past a ledge to a groove to a stance on the right (25m). Direct to the terrace. Difficult with awkward protection.

The Gallery 80m III/IV

R Hamilton, S Kennedy, A Nelson and M Thomson, 1 February 1998

Climbs diagonally left from just below the narrows of The Fang. Go left along narrow ledges to a snow shelf beneath the steep upper wall (45m). Continue in this direction to another steep wall near the edge. Climb up the wall for 3m, then go left along a narrow exposed ledge to finish (35m).

The Fang 75m V,6

B Ottewell and I Sutton, 26 March 1994

The prominent gully right of Bishop's Buttress. Follow the iced corner and leave it to the right at the icicle. Climb over bulges to a cave belay (40m). Move left and up the steep ice wall, then back right to the gully before exiting up an icy corner and bulge to the left. An exit right is possible.

Closer 75m IV,5 ★★

C Dale, A Kassyk and D Talbot, 18 February 1982

Starts some distance below The Gash beyond broken ground. A prominent steep chimney with an icefall beneath it. Climb the icefall, chimney, bulges and chockstones to the top.

St Peter's Well   50m   VI,7 ★★

B Davison, S Kennedy and D Wilkinson, 13 January 2001

The left of three corner-lines approached by a short steep groove on the left. Two hard sections in the corner lead to icy grooves.

Return of the Nedi   90m   IV,5 ★★

S Kennedy and A Nelson, 29 December 2000

The central corner-line gives good sustained climbing.

Parthian Shot   90m   V,7

S Kennedy and A Nelson, 8 March 1998

The first open groove-line 25m left of The Gash, the right hand of three corner-lines. Start from the wide snow shelf which girdles the face and ascend the groove-line, which is initially fairly hard (45m). Continue up a steep groove on the right to finish just left of the top of The Gash.

The Gash   120m   IV,4 ★★

I Clough, M Hadley and M Large, 22 March 1959

The steep cliffs below Hourglass Gully are split by a narrow deep-cleft gully gained by a rising traverse leftwards from Hourglass Gully, or it may be reached directly. This gives a series of short bulging pitches barred at the top by a chockstone. Climb this on the left to a cave below a second huge chockstone. An intriguing through-route should be possible.

The Hash   125m   III

H MacInnes and AN Other, February 1971

The obvious narrow gully to the right of The Gash, formerly known as Caradhras Cleft. Start as for The Gash and gain the gully direct, or move in from Hourglass Gully. Follow the gully to the top, with a bulge where it narrows.

Surely   60m   II/III

I Sutton and B Ottewell, 24 March 1994

Starts 25m up Hourglass Gully on the left wall. Climb via ice and a shallow gully to a rock wall (40m). Follow a corner to the top (20m).

Hourglass Gully   120m   I

I Clough and party, February 1966

The long tapering gully right of The Gash which opens into a snow fan near the top. Steep but straightforward.

Hourglass Groove   60m   III

S McFarlane and A Clark, 16 February 2003

Halfway up Hourglass Gully, take the groove on the right below a notch in the skyline, going slightly right then back left into the big groove.

Dubiety   110m   IV,5 ★

F Yeoman and J Mathie, 23 February 1987

An obvious line on the steep right-hand wall of Hourglass Gully. Start 30m up the gully and climb the steep iced corner-chimney to finish on the summit.

Minute Man   120m   IV,5 ★

M Hamilton and R Anderson, February 1983

The obvious groove in the buttress, right of the foot of Hourglass Gully. Gain entry into the groove over a roof and follow it to the top.

BIDEAN NAM BIAN, 1150M   GR 143542

The summit cliffs of Bidean consist of two main buttresses divided by a gully, Central Gully. The right-hand buttress is called Church Door Buttress; the left-hand one Diamond Buttress. Collie's Pinnacle is the square buttress at the foot of Central Gully, dividing the gully in two.

Diamond Buttress

North Route   210m   III ★

J Clarkson and F King, 6 February 1955

Skirts round the left end of the buttress following a series of chimneys and scoops which lead to a final rocky arête. Easy escapes are possible to the left. A slightly more difficult start (*III, LS Lovat and W Harrison, March 1955*) is to follow an obvious steep scoop near, but to the right of, the normal route, which leads to an arête on the right. The arête is followed by a traverse into another scoop, and then the line goes up and left to join the normal route at about 80m.

Diamond Route   255m   V,6 ★

D Rubens and G Cohen, 9 February 1986

Start in a bay midway between the toe of the buttress and Collie's Pinnacle. Gain the left-trending ramp, follow it and go further left (40m). Climb steeply to belay

Glen Coe Central

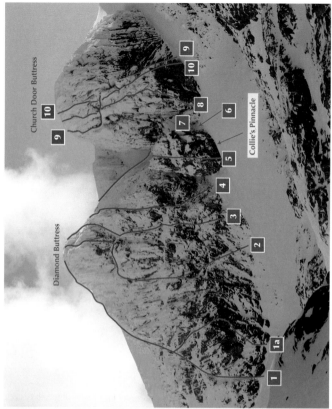

Diamond Buttress

Church Door Buttress

Collie's Pinnacle

Diamond Buttress and Church Door Buttress

1 North Route III*
1a North Route – Direct Start III
2 Diamond Route V,6*
3 Direct Route V,6**
4 Koh-i-nor V,7*
5 Fever Pitch V,7
6 Central Gully I**
7 Crypt Route IV,6***
8 Knights Templar VII,8**
9 West Chimney Route V,6***
10 Critical Mass VII,7

below a short V-chimney (30m). Avoid the chimney awkwardly to the right and go straight up, continuing to the upper girdle ledge (65m). Go right to the end of the ledge (60m). Climb a short difficult chimney to an arête and then to the top (60m).

Winter Route   250m   VI,6 ★

K Spence and J McKenzie, February 1983

Start in a bay midway between the toe of the buttress and Collie's Pinnacle at a left-trending ramp. Climb the ramp for 10m until it is possible to break up right on steep mixed ground to a snow slope, which is climbed to a rock wall. Go left and descend a little way, then climb slabby ground to a corner at the foot of a snow basin. Break out right by a steep groove on the right wall to a belay. Easier ground leads to the middle ledge, where a groove is climbed. Continue up a groove to gain the upper girdle on the left. Go 30m left to the foot of a short wall, which is climbed up and left to easier ground. Continue leftwards to gain the ridge.

Direct Route   150m   V,6 ★★

M Noon and J MacLean, January 1959

Find a way up the central wall of the buttress to gain the right end of a long ledge which cuts across the face. Continue by grooves up, and then to the right, to emerge on the right-hand ridge shortly below the summit. A solid coating of good snow/ice is essential for this route.

Koh-i-nor   185m   V,7 ★

R Anderson and R Milne, 20 February 2005

Start at the foot of the left branch of Central Gully and climb the obvious slabby line up and left to below a small crest (30m). Climb a stepped turfy corner up and right, and step left just below its top to reach the end of the big terrace ledge (30m). Go up into a recess, swing right and then right again into a groove which leads to ledges. Climb the obvious chimney above (50m). Continue in the obvious line up and right, climbing the right side of an obvious narrow chimney (50m). Easy ground to the top (25m).

Diamond Edge   130m   IV,5 ★

M Robson and B Ottewell, 14 April 1994

Starts in the left branch of Central Gully, at the narrows before the top of Collie's Pinnacle. Follow a groove for 20m, then go left across a large block and up ice above, trending left to easier ground (50m). Continue up to belay below icy grooves (35m). Climb any one of the grooves and go right to the top.

Crazy Diamond
110m   III

J Lyall, 27 January 2004

From the beginning of the narrows in Central Gully move left along a ledge, over a bulge, to climb a turfy fault to easier ground.

Choker
100m   III

J Lyall, 27 January 2004

The narrow gully in the left wall of Central Gully, 15m higher up.

Collie's Pinnacle

Found at the base of Central Gully, splitting its left and right starts.

North Chimney
50m   IV,5

S Taylor and J Danson, 31 January 2004

A good short route.

West Face
50m   IV,6

R Cross and D Hollinger, 30 January 2004

The cracked corner-line obvious from the bottom of Central Gully right-hand start. Climb the corner, step right into an off-width slot and squirm up this to exit left. Easier walls and ledges to the top.

Fever Pitch
60m   V,7

D Hollinger and R Cross, 30 January 2004

The steep groove up the left side of the West Face. A difficult move out of an overhung slot leads to a rest, before another hard move gains the turfy groove. Easier ground leads to a huge boulder, followed by an easier second pitch to the top.

Central Gully
180m   I or II ★★ (depending on the route followed)

A fine route, but with some avalanche risk. Start to the right of Collie's Pinnacle and continue directly to the top up easy slopes. By taking a start to the left of the pinnacle and using the right fork near the top, a good climb of grade II standard will be found.

Church Door Buttress

To the right of Collie's Pinnacle at the foot of Central Gully a wide spur divides this buttress into two facets. The East Face overlooks Central Gully and West Face towers above the easy, but steep snow slopes ascending towards the summit of Bidean.

Church Door Buttress

1 North Route III*
2 North Chimney IV,5
3 Un Poco Loco VII,7**
4 Flake Route IV,6*
4a Flake Route – Right Hand V,7**
5 Knights Templar VII,8**

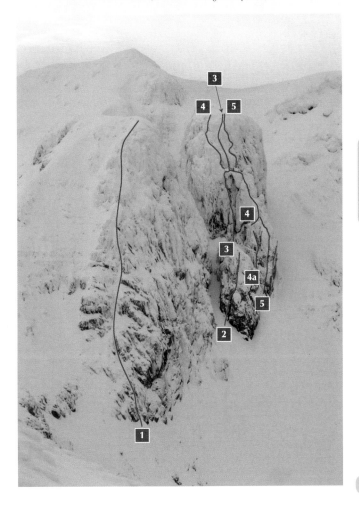

Redemption   75m VI,6 ★
R Anderson and R Milne, 13 February 1994

Starts in Central Gully, 75m higher than the foot of Crypt Route. Climb the obvious groove, starting on the left, then on the right, passing a small recess to an easing. Go left and climb the groove and around a snow crest to a bay (30m). Go right and up a stepped groove, pass a bay, and go up a shallow leftward groove to finish (45m).

Un Poco Loco   120m VII,7 ★★
A Cave and M Duff, March 1994

Follow Crypt Route for 20m. Go left below the Arch by cracks to the left end of the span. Swing left into the groove and ascend extremely steeply to the ledge and a belay in the middle of the span (35m). Go directly above the span to a groove and flake-crack, then trend gradually left (25m). Easier to the top (40m). The Arch was threaded directly by E Tresider and I Lewis (*14 February 2005*), reached by a shallow right-facing corner, hard and steep VII,7.

Crypt Route   60m IV,6 ★★★
H MacInnes and party, February 1960

An unusual route winding its way through passages in the right wall of Central Gully. Climb the first pitch of Central Gully and move right to climb a steep chimney in the buttress. Where it closes step left and move through the Crypt to emerge at the Arch, a platform above the initial chimney. Finish as for West Chimney Route. Not a route for larger people. Take a torch!

Flake Route   130m IV,6 ★
GR Scott and FW Cope (combined tactics), 18 March 1942

10m right of Crypt Route a huge flake is split from the buttress by a crack. Climb the crack, or ascend the other side of the flake by a traverse around it 15m lower down the gully. From the col behind the flake go up and right awkwardly, then straight up broken ground until it is possible to traverse left to the Arch. Cross the Arch and climb a shallow chimney (crux), followed by grooves and walls to the top.

Flake Route, Right Hand   190m V,7 ★★
R Anderson and R Milne, 26 February 2005

Starting at the entrance of the Right Hand Start of Central Gully, this route climbs the right-hand side of the huge flake. Just below the chockstone in the gully, climb a series of corners on the right to ledges, and continue to belay at the fork in the chimney above (40m). Follow the widening left fork over chockstones, then tunnel under the huge jammed blocks to belay at the col on Flake Route on the other side (25m). Follow Flake Route to the top.

Dark Mass 140m VI,6

M Bass and S Yearsley, 4 March 2000

Start at the back of the bay just up from the lowest rocks of the face. Climb a narrow crack between the buttress wall and a detached pinnacle (10m). From the top of the pinnacle ascend a steep crack past the left-hand end of a narrow slot, which is climbed awkwardly to an exit on the left and easier ground (35m). Continue to a junction with Flake Route (East Face) and on to the bouldery traverse ledge of West Chimney Route (30m). Above the ledge climb a wall by left-trending cracks (8m), then up right and climb a shallow chimney-groove. Exit right at the top and cross a difficult slab to reach a peg. Follow discontinuous ledges down right from the peg to the arête. Go around the arête and ascend two short corners direct to easier ground, then right (5m) to below a steep corner (40m). Follow the corner, then exit right and up a groove to the top (25m). **Note** Part of pitch 4 on this route may coincide with Un Poco Loco.

Knights Templar 150m VII,8 ★★

I Small and B Fyffe, January 2007

A fine direct line following the crest of the buttress and cutting across West Chimney. Start just to the left of the toe of the buttress. Climb a wide crack and the wall to the left to a terrace (20m). Climb the obvious groove to a steep exit, then easier ground to a hole/cave where Flake Route comes in (40m). Continue up moderate ground to belay by the boulder on West Chimney Route above the arch (50m). Climb a steep groove in the arête, just behind the boulder, to a shelf. Climb up a groove at the left of the shelf, step right at a spike to another groove, and follow this to a chimney-groove. Climb this to easier ground (40m).

Critical Mass 130m VII,7

I Small, T Stone and G Hughes, 11 December 2008

A direct line up the steep front of the buttress, finishing straight up the headwall. Start at the right side of the front face, left of the recess where West Chimney Route begins. Climb steep right-facing corners to easier ground and a block-belay where West Chimney through-route emerges (60m). Climb the rib above to belay on the large block at the start of West Chimney's traverse (30m). Follow Dark Mass until above the shallow chimney-groove, then move left into a groove leading to a ledge below a steep wall. Pull steeply leftwards over this into a niche, and take grooves to finish up an off-width crack (40m).

West Chimney Route 180m V,6 ★★★

A Fyffe and H MacInnes, 8 February 1969

Up to the right of the lowest rocks of the buttress is a snowy bay leading to an obvious deep chimney, which is followed past two difficult chockstones to a cave where there is a through-route to the Crypt. Beyond another chimney, a bouldery ledge-system leads left to the top of the Arch, an airy platform formed by two huge jammed boulders. Above a hard 10m corner-chimney, the route continues up left to the summit.

Crusade   115m   VII,8

S Chinnery and S House, March 2005

Steep, sustained and well-protected climbing up the wall above West Chimney. Start 15m right of the chimney and go left up ramps to a large square chockstone above the start of the chimney (15m). Climb the flake-line above for 25m, step left at the top, then back right to reach good ledges (50m). A bulge on the left leads to easier ground, trending right to a steep open corner (50m).

The Gangway   70m   II

An obvious line high up on the right-hand wall of the buttress, slanting up to the left to reach the top.

AONACH DUBH

The right hand of The Three Sisters is the spur to the north of Stob Coire nan Lochan. It is very steep on all sides and has a complex array of buttresses.

West Face of Aonach Dubh

The West Face of Aonach Dubh, which faces Clachaig Inn, is a vast and complex series of buttresses and gullies. If the snow level is low the face comes quickly into condition, and so provides one of the more popular cliffs in the glen. The buttresses are split horizontally into three tiers by Middle Ledge, between the lowest and middle tiers, and The Rake, between the middle and upper tiers. Splitting the face vertically are six main gullies numbered from left to right, and there are two scoops which split the main mass of the middle tier. The best approach is from the bridge (GR 137566) on the main road at the Clachaig road end and up to the right of the stream until above the waterfalls. Cross the stream and gain access to the climbs. The safest descent is to go over the ridge and down into Coire nan Lochan or right into Coire nam Beith, but the quickest way, in good visibility, is by the easy upper part of Number Two Gully and the lower part of Dinner-Time Buttress.

Aonach Dubh
West Face

1 Dinner-Time Buttress II**
2 Number Two Gully
3 Number Three Gully III***
4 The Smear IV,4*
5 The Screen IV,5*
6 The Flute V,5*
7 C-D Scoop II**
8 Amphitheatre
   Scoop Direct V,5***
9 Amphitheatre North Ridge II
10 Number Four Gully IV,4*
11 Number Five Gully III*
12 Elliot's Downfall V,6***
13 Number Six Gully IV,4***
14 Chaos Chimney III*

Dinner-Time Buttress   335m   II ★★

Lies on the left-hand side of the face below the col, between the Nose of Aonach
Dubh and Stob Coire nan Lochan. It is defined by the vague Number One Gully on
the left and by the deep watercourse of Number Two Gully on the right. Except for
the final section, it is mainly grass with short sections of scrambling. Can be used to
approach the climbs on Stob Coire nan Lochan. A good bad-weather route.

   Various options can be found on reaching the final rocky section, and all are
worthwhile:

- traverse left into Number One Gully (grade I/II);
- climb a short awkward chimney in the frontal face of the buttress between
  Number One and Number Two gullies; followed by some interesting
  scrambling (grade II);
- traverse right into Number Two Gully (grade I);
- climb an icy gully up left at the point where Number Two Gully is entered
  (grade II).

*The following two routes are on the North Face of B Buttress overlooking Number
Two Gully.*

Bumblebee   140m   V,7 ★★

P Moores and A Nelson, 6 March 1998

Look for the obvious feature of a central rib, seen in profile when ascending from
the lower part of Dinner-Time Buttress. Start to the right of a deep crack in the rib
and follow a system of grooves on the right side to a final crack, which is climbed
to the top. A good route if the weather higher up is grim.

Silent Running   120m   IV/V,5

M Duff and R Nowack, 7 February 1986

An ice smear forms on the north wall of B Buttress where Dinner-Time Buttress
joins Number Two Gully. Gain the smear by a ramp.

Middle Ledge   II

Gained from Number Two Gully, the ledge gives an exposed if easy traverse.
The only difficulty lies in the initial pitch out of Number Two Gully. On reaching
Number Four Gully, ascend the middle section of the gully without difficulty and
escape left along The Rake. Impressive scenery.

Cyclops   105m   IV,5 ★

H MacInnes and party, January 1970

At the start of Middle Ledge a steep corner goes directly up B Buttress. Climb this to easier ground. Take the chimney-line above to gain an eye in the buttress. From the other side of the eye climb iced rocks to the top.

The Pinnacle Face   90m   III/IV,4 ★

KV Crocket and C Stead, 31 January 1971

Start 10m right of a chimney, which itself is just right of the groove of Cyclops. Just left of the buttress edge follow a slab awkwardly up left to the crest. Climb the crest for two pitches to a steep wall, which is climbed on the right to the easier ground of The Rake above.

Number Three Gully   300m   III ★★★

Crofton and Evans, March 1934

This gully, immediately right of B Buttress, is shallow and rather indefinite except where it cuts through the middle tier. Often gives a good ice pitch at the start. Can bank out and become easier. The top part, often avoided by The Rake, is well worth doing.

The Smear   75m   IV,4 ★

I Clough and party, 26 March 1969

This icefall lies on the right wall of Number Three Gully, where it cuts the middle tier. A pleasant climb which can provide a suitable continuation to The Screen.

The Screen   75m   IV,5 ★

D Bathgate and J Brumfitt, February 1965

The obvious large icefall which forms over the lowest tier of rocks to the right of Number Three Gully. Climb for 25m to an icicle recess (good runner), step left and move up to rock-belays on the left. Trend right to Middle Ledge. An enjoyable and popular route.

The Flute   75m   V,5 ★

D Cuthbertson and W Todd, 30 January 1979

Just to the right of The Screen is a narrow icy chimney which gives the line of the climb.

C Buttress   150m   II

J McArtney, A Smith, A Thompson, A Taylor and K Withall, February 1969

Enter by the lower part of B Buttress and Middle Ledge, and climb the middle tier by a short wide chimney. Continue up the well-defined crest.

C-D Scoop   150m   II ★★

D Bathgate and J Brumfit, February 1965

The easy gully splitting the middle tier above The Screen.

Glen Coe Central

Aonach Dubh
West Face
(right side)

1 Amphitheatre
  Scoop Direct V,5***
2 Number Four Gully IV,4*
3 Southern Death Cult V,5**
4 Number Five Gully III*
5 Elliot's Downfall V,6***
6 Number Six Gully IV,4***
7 Chaos Chimney III*

D Buttress   150m   II/III

I Clough, J Choat, J Friend, P Mallinson and D Power, 18 February 1969

Climb a steep icy gangway just to the right of C-D Scoop from the Middle Ledge. Above, zig-zag ramps and ledges lead to the crest, where a steep grooved wall leads to easier ground.

Amphitheatre Scoop Direct   240m   V,5 ★★★

IS Clough, G Lowe and J Hardie, February 1966

To the right of the middle tier of D Buttress is a well-defined gully with a steep ice pitch above Middle Ledge. Start beneath the lower tier directly below this gully. Climb the lower tier by a steep ice chimney (crux) and continue by the ice pitch to gain the easy upper gully. One of the best climbs on the face.

Amphitheatre North Ridge   100m   II

I Clough and party, 27 January 1969

Starts above and slightly right of the easy upper gully of Amphitheatre Scoop, and goes up a series of cracks and grooves in the fine crest.

Number Four Gully   300m   IV,4 ★

J Brown and D Whillans, December 1952

The obvious deep gully near the centre of the face has several pitches in the lower part, but unfortunately rarely has its deep-cleft finish in true condition. Gives an interesting route when combined with Christmas Couloir.

Christmas Couloir   240m   IV,4 ★

I Clough and DG Roberts, 25 December 1965

From the easy middle section of Number Four Gully, move up and right to the foot of the icefall which drops from an obvious couloir to the right of Number Four Gully onto The Rake. Climb the icefall by a long pitch and continue more easily to a choice of three steep finishes.

Christmas Eaves   90m   III/IV,4

A variation to Christmas Couloir which takes a central line into a corner when opposite the base of the ramp leading onto The Rake. Climb up rightwards to regain the main route on the snow slopes above.

Southern Death Cult   150m   V,5 ★★

J Tinker and K Howett, 3 February 1984

Start at a recess 15m left of Number Five Gully and follow the overhanging fault diagonally right, via vegetation, to a hanging stance under the roofs at their right

The first pitch of Number Six Gully

end (30m). Climb icicles through the roof and exit right to a shallow cave below a rock barrier (40m). Go up left to an ice weep which cuts through the bulge and groove, and continue up easy slopes past trees to the upper rock band. Belay below the iced chimney (The Vent, Severe) (35m). Ascend a vertical icicle in the chimney and overhanging groove, then continue up snow to a large cave (45m). Easy gully to the top.

Number Five Gully   300m   III ★

A Fyffe, C MacInnes and N Clough, 18 February 1969
A gigantic icicle forms on the overhanging wall directly below this gully, so start to the left at the short leftward-slanting gully. Climb this gully (crux) to a cave. Exit by a steep ice wall on the right and head up right to the main gully. This leads, with one steep short pitch, to easy slopes.

Elliot's Downfall   115m   V,6 ★★★

D Cuthbertson, February 1979
The gigantic icicle below Number Five Gully gives an extremely steep and serious lead. Two easier pitches then lead to Number Five Gully. It was the downfall of Elliot's proclamation that it would never be climbed that gave the route its name, not the fact that it is prone to collapse when it is climbed!

Number Six Gully   240m   IV,4 ★★★

D Munro and P Smith, 30 March 1951
The long gully on the right side of the face usually gives about four good pitches, the last one being the crux. A popular climb and recommended, but the rock below middle ledge is very poor for belays, and snow anchors will be necessary. A quick descent can be made by climbing up right via a chimney, 50m after the crux pitch, to a series of ledges, which lead right above steep ground and descend into Coire nam Beith opposite Deep-Cut Chimney.

Chaos Chimney   135m   III ★

A Fyffe, E Vveash, B Jenkins, P Hardman and J Snodgrass, February 1969
The chimney-gully going slightly right from the foot of Number Six Gully can be difficult in a poor build-up. Generally it offers three short sections.

Squaddie's Climb   130m   III

P Moores and party, February 1980
An iceflow often forms on the ground to the right of Chaos Chimney, giving unserious practice in front pointing. The belays are, however, poor.

Glen Coe Central

Aonach Dubh
North Face
(left side)

1 Divergence IV,4
2 Darwin's Dihedral VI,6**
3 King Cobra V/VI,6
4 Venom IV/V,5*
5 White Snake IV,4**
6 Findlay's Rise IV,5*
7 The Corridor
8 Ossian's Close III*

North Face of Aonach Dubh

The face is dominated by the huge dark recess of Ossian's Cave. The cave itself is situated above a terrace, Sloping Shelf, which slants up from left to right and starts at the apex of the approach triangle. The right leg of this approach triangle is formed by a gully containing many waterfalls and lying to the left of the vegetatious terrace walls that rise from the floor of the glen to Ossian's Cave. The left leg is a slanting grassy ramp topped by cliffs which are split by a huge Y-shaped gully, Ossian's Close. The main climbs lie on either side of Ossian's Close, but to the left of Ossian's Cave. The path up the right side of the triangle is often icy, so the recommended approach is along the grassy ramp (as the climbs are described) after crossing the River Coe, as for the direct walk into Stob Coire nan Lochan.

To the left of Ossian's Close is a broad corridor which slants up right into the top of the gully. The icefall of Findlay's Rise starts at the foot of The Corridor and rises on the left wall. The steep and grassy nature of the approaches to all of the climbs provides a potentially dangerous base for avalanches after heavy snowfalls or during thaw conditions.

Darwin's Dihedral   240m   VI,6 ★★
D Cuthbertson and M Lawrence, 28 December 1981
Towards the left end of the cliffs is a Y-shaped feature, obvious from the road. Climb the icefall beneath and the large right-facing branch of the corner, which is to the left of the gully of Venom.

Divergence   170m   IV,4
A Nisbet, C Murray and S Taylor, 21 January 1984
Climbs the left branch of Darwin's Dihedral, avoiding the crux of that route. Take the buttress on the left of the ice to gain the higher basin and follow the deep chimney of the left branch.

Venom   240m   IV/V,5 ★
A McAllister, M Duff, R Anderson and D Brown, January 1979
Start about 30m left of Findlay's Rise below a steep chimney in the initial buttress. Climb the long chimney to trees and move left to gain and climb the gully left of White Snake. To the left of the initial pitch is a less obvious chimney, which can be taken as a direct start to the main gully (**Viper Start**, *IV,5*, R Anderson and D Brown, February 1979*).

Aonach Dubh
North Face
(right side)

1 Ossian's Close III*
2 Midnight Special V,5*
3 Midnight Cowboy V,6**
4 Shadbolt's Chimney IV
5 Against All Odds VI/VII,7**
6 Fingal's Chimney VI,7***
7 Fall-Out VII,7***
8 Deep-Gash Gully IV

King Cobra 280m V/VI,6

M Duff and R Nowack, 17 February 1986

Take the Viper Start to Venom (120m). Ascend the chimney/gully to a point where an ice seep is seen on the steep left wall (25m). Climb the seep to a stance beneath the roof and right of icicles (35m). Traverse left to an icicle, which is climbed, followed by a left-trending ramp then a steep groove to a block-belay (60m). Easier ice to the top (40m).

White Snake 240m IV,4 ★★

R Anderson, A McAllister, D Brown and M Duff, January 1979

Climb the icefall just to the left of Findlay's Rise to a cave formed by a huge block. Follow a left-slanting ramp, then continue more easily up a gully to a roof. Traverse left to avoid the roof, regain the gully and continue to the top.

Findlay's Rise 240m IV,5 ★

I Nicholson and party, 1978

Start at the icefall at the foot of the left wall of The Corridor. A fine water-ice climb. Move steeply left onto the foot of the ice, and climb less steeply to a small cave and belay. A long pitch leads to the top of the icefall, from where mixed ground gives access to the summit.

Two Shakes 250m III

M Duff and A Greig, 24 January 1984

The buttress right of Findlay's Rise.

Ossian's Close 240m III ★

H MacInnes and C Williamson, February 1979

Above and slightly to the left of the apex of the approach triangle is a huge Y-gully. An unusual route, not as hard as it looks. Climb above the path to gain the gully at 15m. Easy ground leads to an ice wall going left to a cave. The upper section of the gully is gained by a through-route leading to an easy exit.

Midnight Special 300m V,5 ★

I Clough and K Spence, 1969

The prominent depression to the left of Ossian's Cave, starting just up to the right from the apex of the approach triangle. From the bottom of the depression climb a steep pitch (crux) to reach a shallow gully. Climb this and bear left to reach the summit slopes, or finish directly by the line of the depression.

Glen Coe Central

Midnight Cowboy   370m   V,6 ★★

D Knowles, Dud Knowles and W Thomson, 1974

Follows the line of an obvious gully running straight up, left of Shadbolt's Chimney. Start midway between Shadbolt's Chimney and Midnight Special. Follow iced walls and a chimney into the deepening gully, which is followed with difficulty and poor protection to the top.

Shadbolt's Chimney   300m   IV

D and R Goldie, 13 February 1955

A deep chimney goes up from Sloping Shelf to the right of Midnight Cowboy start, and not far below and to the left of Ossian's Cave. This gives the first 45m of the climb. The route then uses the grassy buttress on the right to avoid a loose section, before a difficult 10m chimney leads on to an amphitheatre on the direct finish of Midnight Special. Finish up this. Rarely in condition.

Against All Odds   150m   VI/VII,7 ★★

M Fowler and C Watts, 14 February 1988

A prominent line right of Ossian's Cave and left of Fingal's Chimney. Start left of the weakness at a tree. Go up right and tension to a bendy sapling in the fault, then climb an overhang on turf tufts to a niche and exit right to climb up to a nut belay (30m). Go up a short wall on the right and the overhang above in the corner. Climb on tufts, just right of the corner, and gain a ramp coming in from the right, then continue to a belay ledge (30m). Climb on minimal ice smears and tufts right of the wide crack to beneath the overhanging section. On the first ascent, three pegs were used to reach the next tufts leading steeply to snow. Gain a belay below a snow-filled chimney which slants up left (30m). Keep going in line with the lower pitches on minimal tufts and ice and protection to easier ground and a snow slope which ends 15m below Pleasant Terrace (45m). Follow a ramp on the left to Pleasant Terrace (15m). Either descend Pleasant Terrace or take easy slopes on the left.

Fingal's Chimney   190m   VI,7 ★★★

W Tauber and D Gardner, 1969

A fine sustained mixed climb requiring a lot of snow to be in good condition. One of the longest chimney climbs in the area. Very few ascents. Right of Ossian's Cave are two narrow chimneys cutting the big wall. Climb the right-hand one. From the base of the chimney a series of ledges runs down rightwards, terminating by a pinnacle. Start at the pinnacle and climb its right edge. A delicate traverse left beneath overhangs is made to a ramp which leads to the base of the chimney (45m). Climb the chimney in three long pitches to Pleasant Terrace. Either continue easily up the chimney or traverse left into Shadbolt's Chimney, which can be followed to the top.

Pleasant Terrace   270m   III ★

J McArtney, I Clough and party, 4 January 1969

This climb and Deep-Gash Gully both start from the upper right-hand end of Sloping Shelf. The Shelf itself may give difficulty in icy conditions, and the best route may be to cross the gully to gain the ridge on the right. Deep-Gash Gully is obvious immediately above the end of The Shelf. Start from a bay to the left of Deep-Gash Gully and climb two pitches to gain The Terrace. This soon narrows to a thin and sensational ledge, leading horizontally left for a long way. After a slight descent the ledge broadens again below a deep chimney. Climb this with difficulty to the top.

Fall-Out   125m   VII,7 ★★★

G Taylor and R Anderson, 23 January 1988

Start below the narrow chimney at the foot of Deep-Gash Gully and climb a corner and wall to belay just right of the chimney (30m). Climb the chimney to belay beneath a huge chockstone (25m), and continue up the chimney to a ledge (25m). Move right along the ledge to another chimney (possible belay), which is climbed to the foot of a short chimney/crack (40m). Move up then left to easier ground and back right to grooves, short walls and a ledge (40m). Continue up left to easier ground.

Deep-Gash Gully   65m   IV

J Cunningham and M Noon, 24 February 1957

This short gully at the top of Sloping Shelf can give a hard technical problem, but often banks out with snow.

Above Loch Achtriochtan is an impressive hanging garden of trees, heather and mosses, easily seen from the road. A good long freeze at a low level is required, and could provide the exploring climber with good sport! Descend by traversing right at the high-girdle ledge towards Dinner-Time Buttress, or maybe abseiling from trees.

North Face Route   600m   III

K Spence and R Anderson, February 1982

A central zig-zag line.

North West Face Route   450m   II

K Spence and Co., 1971

Up the right side of the face.

Mr Softee   325m   VI,6

M Fowler and A Saunders, 1983

An isolated vertical icefall high on the face towards the left side.

Glen Coe Central

Amazonia
325m   V,5

A Clarke and C Smith, 1996

A continuous varied ice and mixed fault line right of Mr Softee. A fin of rock obscures the route for much of its length. The entry is overhung and avoided by a turfy ramp on the right.

Conquistador
300m   V,5

A Clarke and L Collier, 14 February 1996

On the right side, this climbs on the upper two-thirds of the face. Approach from Dinner-Time Buttress and traverse in on the second terrace. The climb starts on the left of the initial icefall, which was insufficiently iced on the first ascent. Finishes on the girdle ledge.

East Face of Aonach Dubh

On the opposite side of the stream to the approach path to Stob Coire nan Lochan there is a huge area of steep rock forming many buttresses. In very cold weather many cascades form amongst these buttresses, offering a variety of good short ice climbs. Low down on the right of the face is the Lady Jane Wall. Higher up and to the left are the Weeping Wall and Barn Wall. Left again is a small hanging coire with the far Eastern Buttress on its left.

The following climbs are found on the **Lady Jane Wall** *and require a very good freeze to form. Even then, they are all steep and thin cascades with poor protection but a quick walk in. Approach is by the good path towards Stob Coire nan Lochan to where it heads steeply up hill at the entrance to the coire. Follow the old path right to a huge boulder in the stream, cross the stream and reach the crag directly. The four excellent routes are described from left to right.*

Dangerous Curves
25m   VII,8

D MacLeod and B Fyffe, 14 January 2010

A few opportunities to bridge make this not quite as hard as it looks.

Exellerator
25m   V,5

W Todd, February 1986

Often fatter than it looks, but steeper than it looks.

Jane's Weep
25m   VIII,8

D MacLeod and B Fyffe, 13 January 2010

Unprotected for the first half.

(photo: Blair Fyffe)

Lady Jane Wall

1 Dangerous Curves VII,8
2 Exellerator V,5
3 Jane's Weep VIII,8
4 Reasons to Leave VI,7

Glen Coe Central

Steep cascade climbing on Exellerator (photo: Blair Fyffe).

Reasons to Leave   25m   VI,7

B Fyffe and D MacLeod, 13 January 2010

The steep crack and ice pillar on the right side of the crag.

*The **Far Eastern Buttress** is best approached from the stream crossing at the trian-gular boulder on the Stob Coire nan Lochan path, one hour from the road. Traverse right to the foot of the buttress from this point. Descent is best made by reaching the floor of Coire nan Lochan first. The climbs are all mixed routes requiring a good freeze and frozen turf with some ice.*

Orient Express   85m   IV,5 ★

R Anderson, C Anderson and R Milne, 2 February 1991

The thin chimney in the middle of the face just left of the more obvious corner of Eastern Slant. Climb straight up on ice to the belay of Eastern Slant (40m). Climb the steep chimney above and left (25m). Continue to a boulder at the top (20m).

Eastern Slant   120m   III,4 ★

R Anderson, C Anderson and R Milne, 16 February 1992

The obvious rising corner-line. Climb the corner (40m), then follow the traverse-line left around an edge and across a slab to a corner and belay on the left (40m). Continue in the same line to finish up a short chimney (40m).

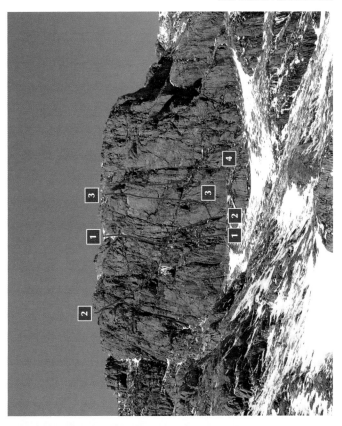

Far Eastern Buttress

1 Orient Express IV,5*
2 Eastern Slant III,4*
3 Nirvana Wall VI,8**
4 Yen VI,7

Nirvana Wall   75m   VI,8 ★★

D King and M Pescod, 21 December 2003

Based on the summer line up the striking crack in the steep slab high on the buttress. Start up Eastern Slant and break out right to climb the front of the buttress to a ledge (35m). Continue up steep cracks to another good ledge (10m). Climb the crack with awkward moves at the top through a buldge (30m).

Yen   100m   VI,7

R Anderson and C Anderson, 9 February 1991

The cracks on the right of the Nirvana Wall. Follow an obvious chimney and traverse up and left to a short corner (40m). The corner and cracks lead to a ledge (20m). Step left and continue up the groove (40m).

STOB COIRE NAN LOCHAN, 1115M   GR 148548

This magnificent peak dominates the view between Aonach Dubh and Gearr Aonach. It is best seen to the south-west from a lay-by on the A82 (GR 168569), from where all approaches can start.

The cliffs high in the north-east-facing coire immediately below the summit of Stob Coire nan Lochan usually give good winter climbing even when lower-level cliffs are spoiled by thaw. The floor of the coire is at about 800m, and the cliffs, which have an average height of 165m, are arranged in a semi-circle below the summit and the shoulder extending northwards from it. The topography of the coire is relatively simple. Below the summit of Stob Coire nan Lochan is Summit Buttress. This name applies particularly to the steep right-hand face; the open face and broken rocks of the left flank can be climbed anywhere at grade I standard. To the right of Summit Buttress are Broad Gully and Forked Gully. To the right again are the South, Central, North and Pinnacle buttresses, all separated by narrow gullies.

Probably the most attractive approach is by the ridge of Gearr Aonach, reached by climbing the Zig-Zags up the North Face of Gearr Aonach, but the quickest is up the coire. The bridge over the River Coe at GR 167566 is gained from a big lay-by on the south side of the road, east of Achtriochtan (GR 168569). A long steady ascent up the valley eventually leads over the final lip to the floor of the coire (2 hours). Another possible approach is by Dinner-Time Buttress or another climb on the West Face of Aonach Dubh.

Stob Coire nan Lochan

1 Boomerang Gully II*
2 Broad Gully I*
3 Dorsal Arête II,3***
4 Forked Gully I/II* or II/III*
5 Twisting Gully III,4**
6 SC Gully III,3***
7 NC Gully II**
8 North Gully I/II

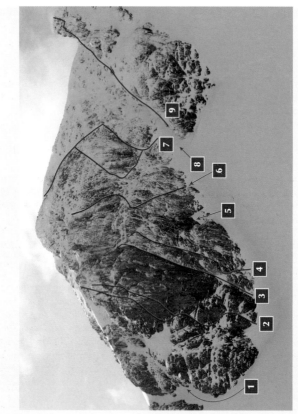

Stob Coire nan Lochan Summit Buttress

1 Boomerang Gully II*
2 Summit Buttress –
  Ordinary Route IV,5**
3 Scabbard Chimney V,6*
4 Spectre V,6**
5 The Tempest X,9
6 Innuendo V,6**
7 Langsam II/III***
8 Broad Gully I*
9 Dorsal Arête II,3***

Boomerang Gully
210m II ★

J Black, RG Donaldson and WH Murray, January 1949

This route curls round to the left of the steep rocks of Summit Buttress (and right of an indefinite rocky ridge which bounds the left flank) and swings back to finish by the ridge leading on from the top of the buttress to the summit of the mountain. The first long tapering gully slope is followed up to the left from the foot of the steep rocks until an entry pitch on the right, rocky and frequently iced, leads up into the main couloir. If the entry pitch is missed, the initial slope leads out onto the face of the left flank. The main couloir curves rightwards and leads to the final rocky arête.

Boomerang Arête
210m III ★

J Clarkson and R Keltie, 24 December 1956

Traverse right onto the buttress from the entry pitch of Boomerang Gully. Climb a short wall and grooves to a ledge. Turn the steep wall above on the right and the next steepening also by a chimney on the right, which may form an ice pitch. **Note** Very loose in a thaw.

Ordinary Route
130m IV,5 ★★

K Spence and party, February 1971

Start just left of Scabbard Chimney and climb direct to a snow shelf then left to a corner. Follow the corner past a block and a snow shelf up left beneath the main buttress. An escape is possible into Boomerang Gully at this point. Ascend to the long right-trending groove-and-crack system and stepped ledges to the top. A harder variant (V**) is possible from the point where an escape can be made into Boomerang Gully by climbing an awkward short wall on the right which leads to a ledge-system. Traverse the ledges rightwards, including a mantelshelf to a higher step and sensational block-belay. Sustained climbing up the tapering groove above, then a short ramp and chimney, leads back left to easier ground (*M Duff, N Kekus, A Nisbet, 7 January 1986*).

The Dual
133m IX,9 ★★★

D Cuthbertson and R Anderson, 24 February 1999

A modern test-piece of the highest order. Climb up from the right of Scabbard Chimney, which is crossed to gain a ramp which leads to a block-belay (30m). Clip the poor in-situ gear up on the left before going back down to the foot of the wall, which is climbed up right to a break at the overhangs. Ascend the corner and move right (ignore peg/krab) to the edge, which is climbed up and around to the foot of the upper ramp (40m). Go up the ramp and wide crack to a chimney and terrace above. Large gear is useful on this pitch (35m). Climb the left hand of three corners to easier ground (25m).

Glen Coe Central

Scabbard Chimney

123m V,6 ★

LS Lovat, JR Marshall and AH Hendry, 12 February 1956

The obvious deep chimney which starts near the lowest rocks of the steep Summit Buttress and slants up to the right. The crux is a 'sentry box' at about 65m. Above the chimney, a gully on the left leads up to the final arête. A good plating of snow and ice is essential to make this climb feasible. The crack leading up the left wall from just after the sentry box has been climbed (*M Garthwaite, January 2003*) at VII,7. The continuation buttress above the abseil point and right of Scabbard Gully has also been climbed (*N Bullock and M Tweedly, January 2003*) at V,5 (45m).

Spectre

120m V,6 ★★

K Bryan and J Simpson, 12 January 1958

Follows a steep shelf 12m right of Scabbard Chimney. Climb Scabbard Chimney and traverse right across slabs from the foot of its first chimney to a point where an awkward descent gains the long shelf. Alternatively, climb directly into the shelf-line. Climb an icy bulge and groove, followed by a steep slab and bulge, to easier ground. Continue to a broad ledge and the narrow gully of Scabbard Chimney.

The Tempest

30m X,9

N Gresham, 12 January 2001

First climbed using a redpoint style with pre-placed protection, this route takes the wall on the left of the foot of Broad Gully straight to the spike commonly used to abseil from Spectre and Scabbard Chimney. The fixed gear was removed in 2010, and the route first climbed with leader-placed protection by A Turner in March 2010. Soon afterwards, the first on-sight was by D MacLeod, who down-climbed from near the top on his first try after realising he had insufficient protection for the last few metres. He went back with the right gear to complete the climb with no use of the rope at all.

Death or Glory

50m VII,7

S Paget and A Mullin, 4 March 1999

Start in the obvious snow bay 5m left of Innuendo. Climb the corner at the back of the bay, and pass a small roof on the left to a small groove and ledges (20m). Continue in the groove and go left of a large pinnacle (20m). Ascend a short wall and corner on the left to easier ground (10m). Abseil descent or continue to the top by Scabbard Chimney.

Innuendo

150m V,6 ★★

H MacInnes, R Birch, P Judge and R O'Shea, 1969

Starts above Broad Gully, opposite and level with the foot of Dorsal Arête, below an obvious chimney-groove which leads to a ledge cutting across the face. Climb the chimney-groove past a ledge (36m) into an overhung bay. Exit by an awkward chimney on the right and ascend more easily rightwards to a block-belay below the upper wall. Traverse right beneath an overhung chimney until it is possible to climb steep cracks and gain the chimney by moving left above the overhanging section. Follow more easily up the chimney to the top.

Innuendo Direct Finish   50m   V,6
N Wilson and S Campbell, 9 March 1997

Above the awkward chimney of the second pitch ascend directly to the foot of the leftmost groove/chimney system (25m), which is climbed until it is possible to step left into an overhung bay (10m). Climb the overhanging chimney and capstone above to easier climbing.

Nessie   120m   IV,5
D Jarvis and B Ottewell, 27 January 1993

Starts as for Innuendo, then follows a groove-line on the right wall, with a step left to the foot of a blank wall, then right to a large block beneath the hanging chimney of Innuendo (55m). Climb up right of the chimney and take a steep direct line up the ice wall above (45m). Alternatively, climb up right from the block under a capped chimney (10m), then climb a corner to finish up left and above the chimney (50m).

Langsam   200m   II/III ★★★
H MacInnes, MC MacInnes and party, March 1969

Starts up the gully from Innuendo and follows the snow slope until under a rock wall. Then either traverse left on steep snow and up right to a short gully and the top, or climb a chimney on the right under the wall and continue the traverse up left to steeper snow then easier ground.

Pearly Gates   150m   II ★
I Clough and party, 17 April 1966

Leaves Broad Gully at about half-height, where the side-walls of Summit Buttress become more broken and a notch is seen in the left-hand skyline. Zig-zag ramps lead up to this feature in 45m, and after passing through the 'notch' a shallow fan of snow leads directly to the summit.

Broad Gully   150m   I ★

A very easy route which often provides the best means of descent into the coire and rarely forms a cornice, but care may be required in icy conditions.

Glen Coe Central

Stob Coire nan Lochan (North, Central and South Buttresses)

1 Forked Gully I/II* or II/III*
2 Twisting Grooves IV,5**
3 Twisting Gully III,4***
4 Tilt VI,7***
5 Unicorn VIII,8***
6 SC Gully III,3***
7 East Face Route VI,7**
8 Central Grooves VII,7***
9 Central Buttress –
   Ordinary Route IV,4***
10 NC Gully II**
11 Evening Citizen V,7**
12 Intruder VI,7**
13 Crest Route V,6***
14 North Gully I/II
15 Pinnacle Buttress,
   North-East Face III

Dorsal Arête   120m II,3 ★★★
J Black, T Shepherd, J Allingham and J Bradburn, 28 January 1951
Start a few metres up Broad Gully and climb the arête on its right. The route becomes increasingly interesting as height is gained, finally tapering to a very narrow and well-defined arête that should be climbed direct on the crest but can be bypassed on the left. There are good rock-belays but the blocks can be a little loose on the arête, after which the route goes either up right by a snowy ramp or left into a steep groove in the final buttress (III). The climb is very useful in bad conditions, and many harder direct starts are possible on the lower front face of the buttress between Broad and Forked gullies.

Forked Gully   Left Fork   135m I/II ★
                   Right Fork   130m II/III ★
The gully to the right of Dorsal Arête gives a steep but normally straightforward snow climb by the Left Fork. The Right Fork (right of a 60m rock rib which splits the upper section) is steeper and often iced.

Twisting Grooves   130m IV,5 ★★
W Sproul and T Carruthers, 11 March 1962
Starts 30m to the left of Twisting Gully and follows a line of corners. Ascend the first corner to a small snow patch and continue up a crack topped by an overhanging chockstone (25m). Continue to a snow patch above the first pitch of Twisting Gully (30m), followed by snow to the bottom of a chimney (55m). The chimney leads to broken rocks near the top (20m).

Twisting Gully   150m III,4 ★★★
WH Murray, D Scott and JC Simpson, December 1946
One of the classic Scottish snow climbs, although the interesting sections are short lived. This route takes a shallow gully immediately to the left of South Buttress and is separated from Forked Gully by an indefinite rocky rib. The first 30m lead up into a deep recess, from which there are two continuations. The normal route follows an icy chimney on the left until it bulges, where a short left traverse is made across the gully wall to gain the left rib. There is an awkward mantelshelf move on the short arête, which leads to easier ground. Above this crux pitch, about 30m of snow leads to another short ice pitch, which can be turned on the right if necessary. The gully continues without difficulty to the final wide fan and a choice of steep exits.

Glen Coe Central

South and Central Buttresses

1 Twisting Grooves IV,5**
2 Twisting Gully Right Fork IV,5**
3 Moonshadow IV,5**
4 Chimney Route VI,6***
5 Tilt VI,7***
6 Unicorn VIII,8***
7 East Face Route VI,7**
8 Central Grooves VII,7***

Twisting Gully Right Fork   150m   IV,5 ★★

JR Marshall and ID Haig, January 1958

A more difficult and direct variation on the middle section of the normal route. From the deep recess, a very steep pitch up an ice corner on the right is followed by a continuation runnel (separated from the original route by a broken rib), which joins the normal route below the final fan.

Moonshadow   150m   IV,5 ★★

K Crocket and C Stead, January 1972

An interesting finish to the right fork of Twisting Gully. From the ice corner above the first main pitch, climb the right wall to a belay in a corner (36m). Climb this corner/groove past a chockstone to the top.

Chimney Route   125m   VI,6 ★★★

Start opposite the foot of Twisting Gully at the left end of a snow ledge. (This good route is often climbed in mistake of Tilt.) Climb steeply up the chimney (25m), then continue and go slightly right up turf to the left end of the upper terrace (45m). As for Tilt, a wall and a V-groove lead to the crest (25m), then easier to the top (30m). A variant is possible on pitch 2 by going straight up into the wide chimney of Inclination. This is separated from the upper terrace by a huge fin of rock.

Tilt   140m   VI,7 ★★★

M Hamilton, K Spence and A Taylor, January 1980

A steep mixed climb with little ice and reasonable protection. This climb follows a very prominent chimney-line just left of the blunt buttress crest. Follow iced cracks to the obvious chimney and groove (40m). Climb the groove until above an overhang. Move right with difficulty and climb a wall to belay on a large flake, or continue by following more grooves (delicate) to a terrace. Finish by a chimney and obvious V-groove on the left.

Inclination   145m   VII,8 ★

R Anderson, C Anderson and R Milne, 17 February 1991

Belay at the start of Tilt. Move right to gain and climb a right-slanting stepped groove on the right side of the crest to a ledge and large block (20m). Climb the ramp on the left and carefully step up right onto a small block and climb cracks in the wall to a chimney. Climb the chimney and easier ground to join Tilt on the crest (20m). Climb up left onto the unlikely looking wall, and finish up a short groove (20m). Ascend the wide fault above (Chimney Route), but go left up into a wide chimney whose right side is a huge fin of rock. Climb the chimney to belay on top of a boulder choke (45m). Move up left onto a chockstone, then right to easier ground and the top (40m).

Glen Coe Central

Unicorn   125m   VIII,8 ★★★

C MacLean and A Nisbet, 24 January 1985, FFA C Smith and L Collier, February 1999

The obvious corner gives a sustained and outstanding climb. Three pitches lead to a shattered ledge from where a fourth pitch up a chimney then the wall on the right gain the top.

SC Gully   150m   III,3 ★★★

PD Baird, L Clinton and F Clinton, March 1934

The steep gully between South and Central buttresses is another classic and a serious route requiring good conditions. Early in the season a steep ice pitch often bars entry to the gully. If it is too formidable, the rib on the left may give an easier alternative. Steep snow then leads up into the bed of the gully proper. The route then traverses up to the right to gain and follow a steep ice gangway, which often has a bulge shortly before the top. A long run-out will normally be required to reach a satisfactory belay above the pitch. Beyond this, steep snow leads to the cornice, which may be quite difficult.

The classic SC Gully

East Face Route   130m   VI,7 ★★

M Hamilton and R Anderson, 20 March 1982

On the East Face of Central Buttress overlooking SC Gully are two parallel chimney systems. This route climbs part-way up the left-hand one before moving into the chimney on the right.

Climb the chimney and move left onto a pedestal (20m), then go back right and climb past the left end of a roof in the corner to belay in a shallow recess (15m). Gain the right-hand chimney system by difficult moves across the wall, around the arête, then up and right (30m). Follow the steep chimney to a belay on its left wall (45m). Go right to the crest and the finish of Ordinary Route (20m). The right-hand chimney was climbed in its entirety, including the clean-cut corner-crack in the headwall, to give a very sustained icy mixed route, possibly one of the best of its type in Scotland (*VII,8, P Benson and G Robertson*).

Central Grooves   120m   VII,7 ★★★

K Spence and J McKenzie, February 1983

A well-protected hard mixed route. More difficult than Tilt in that is technically the same, but more sustained. To the right of SC Gully is Central Buttress. The climb starts at the lowest rocks and follows an obvious groove just left of the crest throughout.

Central Buttress   135m   VII,7 ★★★

K Spence and M Hamilton, 12 February 1981

From a distance, an elongated S-shaped crack can be seen starting from the foot of the buttress. This is the route. Start as for Central Grooves pitch 1 (30m). Traverse right, climbing the wall to a corner, which is followed to a ledge on the crest (20m). A short wall above is followed by easier ground rightwards to the edge. Go right and climb a pinnacle to a small snowfield (40m). Follow the chimney above before breaking out right below the top, and climb the last part of Ordinary Route (45m).

Central Buttress – Ordinary Route   150m   IV,4 ★★★

H Raeburn with Dr and Mrs C Inglis-Clark, April 1907

Starts from the bay to the left of the lowest right-hand spur and goes up to the right to gain its crest. The ridge leads to a tower, which is best turned on the right, regaining the crest by a short chimney. A good route with splendid situations. **Note** It is possible to bypass the initial long pitch by a traverse in from the lower reaches of NC Gully. The first pitch is, however, very good!

The Douglas Pebble   50m   V,7
J Edwards and G Hughes, 1 February 2003
An alternative start to the Ordinary Route up the overhanging corner into the snow-field above, followed by the right-hand chimney. Steep but well protected.

NC Gully   155m   II ★★
The gully between Central and North buttresses generally gives a steep but straight-forward snow climb. Early in the season it may have short pitches. A good introductory gully.

The Day After   70m   VI,7 ★
A Nelson and D Ritchie, 4 April 2000
There is an obvious deep chimney formed by a pinnacle on the right side of NC Gully. Climb the left wall of the chimney, then go left to a ledge, which is easily gained from higher up NC Gully (40m). Climb the prominent V-groove above the ledge, left of an overhang, in two pitches (20m and 10m).

People's Friend   105m   VI,7
A Nisbet and M Duff, 31 December 1985
The steep groove-line just to the right of The Day After. Start at the foot of NC Gully and go up a groove, then left beyond Evening Citizen to a stance below a 3m pinnacle above the NC Gully chockstone (35m). Ascend the pinnacle and difficult small recess above, exiting by the top-left corner (20m). Climb the well-defined groove above, which eases as height is gained (50m).

On the right wall of NC Gully is an obvious tower with a roof at half-height, which helps in locating the following three climbs.

Evening Citizen   95m   V,7 ★★
K Spence, H MacInnes and A Thompson, 1971
Left of the roofed tower is a well-defined corner/chimney which gives the route to the crest.

Para Andy   90m   VI,7 ★★
A Cunningham, A Nesbit and A Newton, 8 January 1988
Climb the big corner/groove right of the roofed pillar. Climb direct to the groove (35m). Climb the groove until tight against a roof (loose), and traverse left to a mantelshelf. Belay ledge on the front face above the roof. Pass the short wall above to the left and back right to a crack-line in the centre of the face, which is climbed until it is possible to move left to a ledge and blocky arête leading to the top.

Intruder   100m   VI,7 ★★

R Anderson and G Nicoll, 14 February 1988

Climbs the slimmer right-hand groove right of the tower, starting at the lowest rocks. Go up left passing Financial Times to the bottom of the groove (15m). Ascend the groove with difficulty, passing two pegs to a flake, and continue to a ledge beneath the flake of Financial Times (25m). Gain the groove on the left and climb it to the top of a pinnacle. Go up, then right, to climb a short groove, then right to belay by a perched block (35m). Easy to top (25m).

Financial Times   135m   IV,6 ★

R Anderson and A Taylor, 19 February 1981

A line near the crest which starts at the lowest rocks. Gain then follow a right-trending groove to a pedestal-belay at large blocks (40m). Go up and left to the edge, then up a flake-crack to pull around to a ledge in the centre of the face below a pinnacle (25m). Climb the large pinnacle, starting on its right (10m), and gain the groove of Intruder to the left, which is followed to the top (60m).

Crest Route   115m   V,6 ★★★

R Anderson and M Hamilton, 24 November 1985

To the right of NC Gully is North Buttress. This climb follows an obvious groove just right of the buttress crest and starts at the lowest rocks. Climb broken stepped ground, a short wall and cracks to belay on a pedestal (35m). Climb a flake-crack above, and move right across a slab to gain a corner, which is followed to the crest. Step left at a large spike onto a ledge (30m). Follow the groove and easy ground to the top; a short wall is overcome by a stepped flake-crack on the right. Well protected, but sustained.

Tuberculosis   50m   VI,6

D Hollinger and G Willet, 7 February 2004

The steep groove right of Crest Route. Start up a short chimney at the top of the snow bay. After a few moves a difficult swing left gains the groove, which is followed to the steep corner and snow ramp to the top. A little loose unless well frozen.

Black Box   100m   IV,5 ★

S Kennedy and A MacDonald, 19 February 2005

Climb the broken buttress to the right of Tuberculosis to a large snow ledge where North Face goes left. Cracks and steep slabs left of a corner pass a large flake to a ledge (55m). Climb the right-facing corner on the left to the top (45m).

Glen Coe Central

North Face   90m III

LS Lovat and K Bryan, 29 January 1956

The groove running up the right side of the buttress from the lowest rocks. Go up and right to a snow ledge in North Gully, then climb to a recess high up on the face. From the left end of a ledge, climb a steep groove and go left to a nose and easier ground.

Note This route and those further right (Pinnacle Buttress) have a disposition towards loose rock!

North Gully   75m I/II

Divides North Buttress from Pinnacle Buttress. It is steep, sometimes gives a short pitch, and often carries a heavy cornice.

Pinnacle Buttress Groove   60m III ★

LS Lovat and NG Harthill, 5 January 1958

Follows a steep groove on the North Gully flank of Pinnacle Buttress to the left of a prominent arête. Start on the right near the foot of North Gully. An excellent short climb in icy conditions.

The Struggler   60m V,7

A Clarke and N Gresham, 24 February 1995

Climbs the off-width crack in the prominent arête, followed by a chimney to a pinnacle (25m). Climb the V-groove opposite, then finish up the awkward chimney on North East Face route (35m).

Leaning Jowler   70m III,4

M Duff and J Knowles, 26 February 1993

Right of the prominent arête is a corner system which is climbed awkwardly, then over flakes to a ledge (35m). Go up the sharp corner above, then right and up to another ledge (20m). Go right for 5m to a steep groove and climb it.

Pinnacle Buttress, North East Face   90m III

I Clough and JR Woods, 26 January 1967

Starts at the lowest rocks and climbs up right, then left, up a short groove to a steep wall. An icy corner-crack on the right leads to a ledge, and a higher ledge is gained up to the right. From the left end of this upper ledge an awkward chimney leads to the roof of the buttress.

To the right of Pinnacle Buttress are some short gullies and rocky outcrops which can provide good practice on a short day.

Gearr Aonach
West Face

1 Ciotach Route II/III
2 Rescue Team Gully II/III*
3 Jim's Gully II/III
4 999 III**

Glen Coe Central

West and North Faces of Gearr Aonach

The huge North Face of Gearr Aonach dominates the ridge running between the Lost Valley and Stob Coire nan Lochan. The first two climbs described lie to the right side of this face, while the remainder are situated on the steep buttress on the West Face below the highest point of the ridge. All the climbs are easily reached from the path running up the east side of the stream on the approach to Stob Coire nan Lochan.

Avalanche Gully   300m   IV,4 ★

H MacInnes and party, 1960

After crossing the bridge over the River Coe the main path strikes up towards the North Face of Gearr Aonach before veering up to the right. The lower-stream way of this gully crosses the path at this point. In hard weather conditions, the lower part gives a series of short water-ice pitches. The gully follows a rightward slant and leads to the summit of the Nose. Take the right forks at the lower and upper branches. The lower left branch is short, steep and interesting (grade IV). The upper left fork, when in condition, is grade IV.

Farewell Gully   150m   II/III

J McArtney and party, February 1969

From slightly higher up the path from Avalanche Gully, the climb goes up in a direct line to meet the finish of that route. Several short pitches, but little of interest.

The following four climbs are on the buttress below the highest point of the Gearr Aonach ridge on its east side. Although short, they have the attraction of easy access. The best approach is to follow the Stob Coire nan Lochan path until it passes a natural overhung shelter (1 hour). The gully to the right of this welcome spot drains from the vicinity of the routes. The climbs described are various finishes to the approach gully, and are described from left to right.

Ciotach Route   90m   II/III

H MacInnes and party, January 1959

This lies higher up the access gully on the left and climbs an icy section to the ridge, with variations possible.

Rescue Team Gully   85m   II/III ★

H MacInnes and party, March 1966

The left-hand branch is a steep icy chimney with a through-route chockstone at its foot. Two good pitches.

THE THREE SISTERS

Lost Valley — Gearr Aonach — Avalanche Gully IV,4* — Stob Coire nan Lochan — Far East Buttress — Lady Jane Wall — Aonach Dubh North Face

Gearr Aonach East Face

McArtney Gully III

The Graduate, IV,4*

Gearr Aonach zig-zags

Jim's Gully   106m   II/III

J McArtney and party, March 1968
The central branch emits an icefall landing near the start of the previous route.
Above this icefall the gully is easy.

999   135m   III ★★

H MacInnes and party, February 1969
The right-hand branch gives a series of enjoyable short steep pitches in caves and
up chimneys, finishing in a steep chockstone-capped corner. The line trending even
further right gives easier climbing.

*The following climbs lie on the area left of the imposing rock nose of Gear Aonach
which faces the road. They have the attraction of a short approach and quick
descent. Climb the first ledge on the Zig-Zags to where they turn left. Go around the
corner to the right to access the following three routes.*

Trumpeting Elephants   130m   III

M Duff, I McLeod and A Owen, 10 February 1988
Start as for White Rhino (see next) and follow the recessed chimney-line.

White Rhino   150m   IV/V,5

A Cave and M Duff, February 1988
From the end of the first right-trending rake of the Zig-Zags, walk right along a ledge
to a small chimney and tree in an exposed position. Climb a very obvious diagonal
rake for two pitches. Go into the gully above (steep) to a recess below overhangs.
Move steeply left, with difficulty, and climb ice-covered slabs and grooves to easier
ground and the Zig-Zags descent.
    Note The name of this route relates to the avalanche which was seen on the
descent (top of Zig-Zags) after the first ascent!

Zig-Zag Direct   150m   III

From the end of the first right-trending rake of the Zig-Zags, continue around the
corner for a short distance (5m) until it is possible to climb the walls above. The
first pitch (50m) leads to a good belay on a large ledge overlooking the Zig-Zags.
Follow a hidden chimney up to the left, then scrappy ground to regain the Zig-Zags.

Zig-Zags   200m   I

A popular route up the left side of the steep North Face of Gearr Aonach that can
be used as an approach to Stob Coire nan Lochan. After crossing the bridge below
the Meeting of Three Waters (GR 173561) and following the track up towards Coire

Gabhail (Lost Valley) as far as the beginning of the gorge section (about 0.5km above the bridge), the route cuts up to the right, aiming for the cliffs of the East Face of Gearr Aonach some distance to the left of the Nose. Although marked by occasional cairns the route is not too easy to follow, and it is wise to try and pick it out from well below. Careful inspection will reveal two obvious slanting terraces, up to the right and then back to the left, winding up through otherwise sheer cliffs. The Zig-Zags are gained by walking leftwards up a grass slope below the cliffs until the start of the first terrace is reached in a corner immediately to the right of a 15m prow of rock. After about 30m of scrambling, the terrace leads gently up to the right under some steep cliffs to an easy slope, which is followed for another 30m or so before taking a short slab and gully corner on the left. This leads to a second big terrace, which is followed to its left-hand end. After a short ascent, another long rightward-rising traverse and a brief tack back to the left leads to the top of the Nose of Gearr Aonach. The ridge is then followed until an easy traverse can be made into the floor of Coire nan Lochan (about 2½ hours from the road).

This route is difficult to find in descent. Without prior knowledge, and certainly in bad visibility, the descent down from Coire nan Lochan should be made.

CLIMBS FROM COIRE GABHAIL   GS 1655, THE LOST VALLEY

Starting from lay-bys on either the north or south side of the road a path leads down to the footbridge over the River Coe near the Meeting of Three Waters (GR 173564). It continues up into the coire, first through a gorge, eventually crossing the stream and passing the Lost Valley Ice Slabs on the left, then a rough path, to reach the floor of the coire, a flat 500m of shingle and grass (45 minutes). The gorge path is exposed to the drop to the stream and can be icy, in which case the path at a higher level is recommended and reached from the entrance to the gorge. The walk so far is very interesting and worthwhile for its own sake on an off-day. At the entrance to the coire floor is the 10m Boulder – a useful landmark. Beyond the coire floor there are two paths to the right of the stream and at different levels. The highest is the better of the two and makes a gradual ascent along the side of the valley, with the East Face of Gearr Aonach cliffs up to the right. The main stream is crossed beyond its deep gorge bed (accidents often occur here).

The track disappears soon above this point, and the two main approach/descent routes bifurcate. One route continues straight ahead to the col at the end of the valley – between Stob Coire Sgreamhach, 1070m, on the left (east), and Bidean nam Bian to the right (west). The slope is easy, but there may be fairly large cornices. The other route bears up right into a subsidiary coire, which leads up to the col

At the top of the Zig Zags

between Bidean and Stob Coire nan Lochan. Either of these are good descents, but care may be required near the cornices. The cliffs of Stob Coire nan Lochan may also be reached by bearing back in a northerly direction, beyond the cliffs of the Upper East Face of Gearr Aonach, obliquely across the hillside to reach the shoulder where the Gearr Aonach ridge rises steeply towards the summit of Stob Coire nan Lochan.

East Face of Gearr Aonach

These climbs are all on the right-hand side of Coire Gabhail beyond the Lost Valley Boulder. They are particularly useful when conditions are poor at higher levels, and for their relatively short approach. However, many of them are fine climbs in their own right, and some rank with the best in Glen Coe. Icy conditions are preferable. The best descent is by the Zig-Zags (if the team is competent and the visibility good) on the nose of Gearr Aonach, but most people prefer to walk towards Stob Coire nan Lochan and descend into the upper part of the Lost Valley or Coire nan Lochan. The routes are described from left to right, and climbers new to the area should try to locate the more obvious gullies of Ingrid's Folly and Rev Ted's as useful reference points when exiting from the gorge section of the approach walk onto the flat area below the climbs.

Gully C   230m I
Probably Glencoe School of Winter Climbing (GSWC) parties
A long shallow couloir on the extreme left before the cliffs fade out entirely. It may contain a few short pitches. Competent climbers may find this route useful as an approach to Stob Coire nan Lochan.

Gully B   230m II
Probably GSWC parties
The next gully to the left of Gully A is straightforward except for one large chock-stone pitch.

Gully A (Left Branch)   235m IV,4
H MacInnes and GSWC party, February 1970
This is the branch of the gully which starts as a very steep ice pitch slightly to the left of the main Gully A. Follow the gully-line throughout (escape is possible halfway up on the left), and take either the chimney-line above or break out right up steep iced rock.

Gully A (Central Branch)   230m IV
D Haston and J Stenhouse, January 1969
Gully A divides at the start of the main pitch, and this variation takes a line directly up a steep ice scoop.

Gully A   235m IV,4 ★

H MacInnes and D Crabbe, January 1964

Starting some distance beyond where the path rises from the floor of the Lost Valley. It runs the full height of the face, is indefinite in its lower part, deep-cut in the middle and becomes a steep straightforward slope in the upper section. It faces south and is hidden until immediately below it. A pitch climbed on the left leads into the gully, which is followed to the right to a bulging groove, the crux of the climb.

Lost Leeper Gully   300m III,4 ★★

H MacInnes, A Gilbert, P Debbage, D Layne-Joynt and D Allwright, 13 February 1969

The shallow indefinite gully which comes down immediately to the left of the Mome Rath Face and reaches the lower slopes of the valley above the gradually rising path. The route weaves its way up through the lower crags, giving interesting route-finding, and the more distinct upper gully should give at least two good ice pitches. The belays in the main part of the gully are poor.

Given the right conditions the upper cliffs to the left of Rev Ted's Gully give some of the most sensational ice climbing in Glen Coe. The terrace below the upper wall can be reached by the lower sections of Rev Ted's or Lost Leeper gullies. The upper wall (Upper East or Mome Rath Face) has high up a long barrier of overhangs. In exceptional conditions much of the face becomes masked with smears of ice, and the overhang is decorated with a fantastic fringe of icicles which can attain 10–15m in length.

Rainmaker   100m VI,5 ★★

D Cuthbertson and M Duff, February 1980

At the left-hand end of the upper face, next to Lost Leeper Gully, is a large ice-cased corner. Climb a long pitch up ice smears to the left of the corner and belay in a recess. Now climb the corner with a short excursion on the left wall.

Snowstormer   100m VI,5/6 ★

D Cuthbertson, A Paul and C McLean, January 1984

This route follows close to the exposed edge right of Rainmaker. Climb to a belay on a pedestal above an obvious V-notch (27m). Follow icy corners above to beneath the overlap overlooking the corner of Rainmaker; belay. The vertical corner of the second pitch is well protected. Easier climbing leads to the top.

Outgrabe Route   115m V,5 ★★

R Anderson and R Milne, January 1980

A direct start and variation finish to Mome Rath Face Route (see below), creating a virtually independent line. Start 10m left of Mome Rath Face Route and climb directly to a gully/chimney-fault, which is climbed in two pitches, keeping left of the icicle fringe on the second pitch.

Newsholme's Groove   140m V,5 ★★
G Hornby and C Schaschke, February 1986

A broad groove between Mome Rath Face Route and Snowstormer, a bold line. Start at an open bay, move up right then left and climb a thin vertical step; belay. Follow the open groove above and move right along the icicle to finish up the last groove left of Mome Rath Face Route. Belays on ice screws may be necessary.

Mome Rath Face Route   135m V,5 ★★★
A Fyffe and J McArtney, 16 February 1969

The general line of the route is a long leftward slant. It starts below the icicle-fringed overhang by an obvious broad ramp and continues the line up to the left into a chimney. This is followed for about 20m before going left again into another chimney, which leads to a bay. A slabby ice-plated rib on the left is followed by a short steep corner-chimney. Again this route combines sustained technical climbing with a high degree of exposure.

Jaberwock   135m VI,5 ★★
A Paul and D Cuthbertson, January 1984

Climbs the obvious icefall between The Wabe and Mome Rath Face Route, taking in the ice fringe at the top.

The Wabe   135m V,5 ★★★
I Clough, H MacInnes and J Hardie, 16 February 1969

Approximately follows the line of a prominent icefall to the right of the icicle fringe. A short wall is climbed. Belay on a snow ledge above the main terrace. The route then goes up slightly to the right before making a long diagonal leftward traverse across the icefall towards a prominent nose and a stance at 45m. After passing below the nose (immediately above an overhang) the route veers right then left to reach a pedestal stance below the right edge of the icicle fringe. Then move back right to climb the icefall where it passes through a recessed panel; good stance on the right above this section. The final pitch goes diagonally right and then back left. The route is sustained throughout and extremely exposed.

Whimsy   120m IV,5 ★★
R Clothier and D Hawthorn, January 1984

The icefall a few metres right of The Wabe.

Mimsy 120m IV,4

P Moores and A Paul, 24 January 1995

Near the right end of the terrace and approached from Rev Ted's Gully. Start 6m right of a right-slanting groove at a crack, which is climbed, followed by broken ground to a ledge. Climb a shallow gully, then go left and climb a steep crack, followed by broken ground and a short steep section.

Rev Ted's Gully 300m III ★

H MacInnes and Rev Ted, February 1960

Follows the obvious long couloir which slants leftwards up the full length of the face. The lower pitches are usually straightforward and lead to an obvious junction in the upper cliffs. Several alternatives are available. The best is either to follow an ice chimney-line just to the left of the icefall at the junction, or to take the icefall direct. If the easy right branch is followed, another steep chimney-line will be found leading up from a bay – interesting but awkward. From the same bay an easy escape right can be made, reducing the whole climb to grade I/II.

Between Rev Ted's and Ingrid's Folly and Peregrine Gully, the cliffs of Gearr Aonach give broken crags in the lower half, leading to an almost continuous wide horizontal terrace. Above the terrace is a series of steep walls, unpleasantly grassy in summer, but which give good winter climbing. The first big break in these upper cliffs is a large rightward-facing corner – McArtney Gully.

Frostbite Groove 200m IV,5

H MacInnes and GSWC party, February 1969

At the point where Frostbite Wall traverses back across the obvious ledge, take the ice chimney/groove-line up and slightly right. Break out left after one pitch, over the ice bulge to gain the ice scoop. Climb the scoop and small chimney to the top.

Frostbite Wall 200m V,5

H MacInnes, A Gilbert, P Debbage, D Layne-Joynt and D Allright, February 1969

Take the main line of the ice ribbon up the wall, gaining it first by a rightward traverse from the bottom of it, then back left to it some 50m up via a ledge. Climb the ice ribbon direct to the top.

Note This route is usually in condition when the ice ribbon is complete from top to bottom of the cliff.

McArtney Gully 175m III

H MacInnes and GSWC party, 3 February 1969

The lower half of this big corner-gully is reasonably straightforward, but the upper part is very steep. A vertical chimney is followed to a diagonal groove and corner, which gives the crux.

Ingrid's Folly and Peregrine Gully   300m   III ★

GSWC party

The foot of Ingrid's Folly is only about 5 minutes' walk diagonally up the slope to the west of the Lost Valley Boulder. It is a well-defined gully tucked away in a corner, much better than its appearance might suggest. The long grassy buttress to its right (and immediately left of The Graduate) is John Gray's Buttress, grade II. Ingrid's Folly consists of several relatively easy rock pitches, which give good sport when veneered in ice. Above the last pitch, where the gully gives an easy slope to the top, a 100m traverse to the left leads into Peregrine Gully. This gives further pitches, another cave with a through-route and an easy passage below a gigantic block which forms an archway just before the steep exit.

John Gray's Buttress   300m   II

H MacInnes, January 1968

Follow the easiest line up the buttress just right of Ingrid's Folly. A good freeze is needed.

The Graduate   175m   IV,4 ★

DA Knowles, J Loxham, D Wilson and A Wilson, 8 February 1969

The boulder field which blocks the entrance to the floor of the Lost Valley is the result of a great landslide which has left a huge deep recess in the cliff of Gearr Aonach. Follow the great right-angled corner at the left-hand side of this recess. It is most easily reached by going up and slightly rightwards from the Lost Valley Boulder. Rarely in condition.

Bunny's Route   95m   III ★

I Clough and CG Kynaston, 29 March 1967

Not often in good condition, this route can provide a fine outing with a short approach if avalanches are likely on higher cliffs. Starts about 50m up left of the lowest rocks just left of the Zig-Zags. The main feature is a fault leading to a prominent chimney. Descent by the Zig-Zags.

Lost Valley Minor Buttress

The smaller and left hand of the two prominent buttresses at the head of the valley and below the middle of the ridge leading up from the col to Bidean. Routes are described from left to right.

Lost Valley Minor Buttress

1 Left Edge Route III,3
2 Chimney Route III/IV,4*
3 Minor Issue IV,6
4 Central Scoop IV,4
5 Right Edge IV,4**
6 Minor Adjustment IV,5*
7 Right-Hand Gully I

Left-Hand Gullies   75m I

To the left of the buttress are two easy gullies separated by a rocky rib.

Left Edge Route   76m III,3

J Moffat and C Dale, February 1984

Start to the left of Chimney Route. Follow the obvious gangway up left to a short corner, which is climbed to the top.

Chimney Route   75m III/IV,4 ★

R Marshall and J Moriarty, January 1959

The obvious deep chimney to the left of the centre of the face. A series of chock-stone pitches can give considerable difficulty.

Minor Issue   80m IV,6

R Anderson and G Taylor, 10 January 1988

Climbs the corner-groove line left of the buttress edge between Chimney Route and Central Scoop.

Central Scoop   85m IV,4

I Clough and Mrs N Clough, February 1969

This is the chimney-line between Chimney Route and Right Edge. The chimney (short) starts from a platform some 13m up, and the route takes this corner/chimney, then follows the buttress to the top.

Right Edge   120m IV,4 ★★

JR Marshall, J Stenhouse and D Haston, February 1959

At the right-hand side of the face a broad snowfield-ramp leads up rightwards below overhangs. Access to the ramp is gained by an icy chimney below its left end, and an arête leads from the top of the ramp to the summit.

Minor Adjustment   115m IV,5 ★

R Anderson and C Greaves, 19 February 1989

The obvious groove and corner just up the gully from Right Edge. A direct line which joins that route after its upper traverse. Climb the groove steeply to a small ledge and spike, then go steeply left up a ramp around the edge to ledges. Traverse right back into the corner and belay higher up (45m). Climb the corner, move right and climb a short groove and step right below a small roof. Follow the snow ramp to a belay above a short wide crack (25m). Climb to the top (45m).

Over the Influence   90m   IV,4 ★

R Anderson and C Anderson, 10 January 1999

Follows a line of corners and grooves just left of Chimini Minor in two pitches. Start just right of the chimney and move left into the corner-line.

Chimini Minor   75m   IV/V,6 ★

R Anderson and R Milne, 15 November 1998

Starts just up the gully from Minor Adjustment and climbs a thin chimney-crack to a small ledge (25m). Up the groove to easier ground (50m).

Old Farts Corner   80m   IV,5 ★

R Milne and R Anderson, 23 January 2000

Just right of Chimini Minor is a left-facing corner which is climbed to easier ground (50m). More easily to the top (30m).

Right-Hand Gully   75m   I

Probably GSWC parties

The gully immediately to the right of the buttress gives a straightforward but steep climb and often has a large cornice.

Grannies Groove   70m   III

The right-hand branch of the gully to the right of the crag, which sometimes has an overhang that should be passed to the left.

Lost Valley Buttress

The large right-hand buttress is in two distinct sections: an easier-angled left-hand portion, but very steep and set back at a higher level on the right. The routes are described from left to right. Neanderthal remains the most sought-after climb on the crag and very much worth the long walk.

Left-Hand Gully   90m   I

Probably GSWC parties

The gully is bounded on the left by a broken indefinite rib of rock. Straightforward climbing to a steep corniced exit.

Sabre Tooth   135m   IV,5 ★

I Clough and H MacInnes, 9 February 1969

There is a prominent vertical 45m corner towards the right-hand side of the left-hand section of cliff. This has been climbed (Delusion), but gives a much more

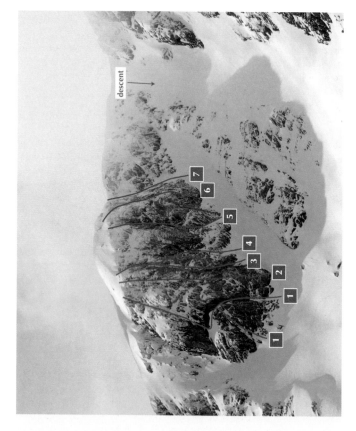

Lost Valley Buttress

1 Sabre Tooth IV,5*
2 Directosaur VI,7*
3 Pterodactyl V,6/7*
4 Moonlighting V,6*
5 Neanderthal VII,7***
6 Barracuda V,7**
7 Right-Hand Gully II

difficult start which would elevate the general standard of the climb to grade IV/V.

Starting to the left of the corner, the route goes up into a recess and breaks out rightwards, eventually arriving on a terrace above the big corner. The terrace leads back left to the foot of a steep shallow 15m corner (good belays on the left). The corner is hard for a climb of this standard, but well protected. Above it, a line of grooves is followed to the top.

Tiger Feet   165m   IV,5
R Anderson and R Milne, 16 January 2000
The icefall running through Sabre Tooth. Climb into the recess of Sabre Tooth, then climb a thin left-facing iced corner to the Sabre Tooth belay below the corner, which is above the terrace (45m). Climb the icefall on the right wall to a belay above the corner (50m). Ascend to the small upper buttress and climb a leftward-slanting groove in this to easier snow (50m). Continue on to the top (20m).

Prehysteria   190m   VI,7
R Anderson and R Milne, 1 November 1998
Starts just left of the buttress edge and Directosaur, and follows a system of corners. Climb a short corner and wall to a ledge (15m). Go up left then above the belay, followed by two short corners on the left to the base of the main corner (20m). Climb the left-leaning corner (20m). Step down and right, then follow a blocky corner and fault line (55m). Go left to a shallow fault line, which is followed to easy ground (60m). Continue to the top (20m).

Directosaur   160m   VI,7 ★
G Ettle, R Anderson and R Milne, March 1989
Start at the lowest rocks and climb the serious shallow groove just left of the edge. Go left and up to a ledge which leads back right to the edge. Climb a steep flake-crack on the left and easier ground to below the corner of Tyrannosaur (45m). Climb the corner and grooves up the right side of a huge block-like feature to its top (30m). Go right and climb a short groove to regain the crest and snow grooves leading to the upper rocks and final slopes.

Tyrannosaur   150m   VI,7 ★
I Clough, D Morrish and ES Taylor, 5 March 1969
Takes the well-defined right edge of the left-hand area of the cliff. Starts on the right wall well below the corner of Pterodactyl and 10m up from the lowest rocks. Climb a shallow chimney and the thin continuation crack, trending slightly left over the edge to a snow bay. Climb the steep corner and grooves up the left side of a huge block-like feature to easier grooves which lead to the top.

Glen Coe Central

Velocyraptor   160m   V/VI,7
R Anderson and R Milne, 6 March 1999

The crack-line between Tyrannosaur and Cold Feetus. Immediately right of the shallow chimney of Tyrannosaur is a thin crack-line, which is climbed past a niche and an off-width to a large block-like feature (60m). Continue as for Directosaur up right (50m). Easy to the top (50m).

Cold Feetus   80m   V,6
M Garthwaite and N Gresham, 24 February 1996

Starts from the foot of a deep cleft up right of Tyrannosaur. Ascend via a slim groove on the left wall to the foot of a steep corner (20m). Climb the corner and finish up Directosaur (60m).

Klu Klux Cleft   100m   V,7
M Garthwaite and N Gresham, 28 November 1996

On the left of Pterodactyl is a rib with a deep chimney on its left. Climb into the deeper part of the chimney, which is climbed, then out right onto a stance on the rib (30m). Follow the groove-line of Pterodactyl to a belay at the foot of an overhanging chimney-groove (10m). Ascend the chimney-groove for (10m) and grooves above to the top (50m).

Pterodactyl (Moonlight Gully)   110m   V,6/7 ★
H MacInnes and D Crabbe, January 1964

Follows the line of the shallow gully lying in the corner that divides the two sections of cliff. The overhanging entry to the upper couloir is difficult but relatively short. The route follows a steep corner to a stance beneath the overhang, which projects for 2m then climbs to gain the upper couloir using the crack to the left of the main icicle formation.

   Note The central section of this route is climbed on aid and is out of character with the rest of the route. In years of good icing it may be possible to climb steep ice on the right of the central section. Chockstones have fallen out of this section.

Moonlighting   120m   V,6 ★
R Anderson, G Taylor and N West, 27 January 1988

An obvious line right of Pterodactyl at the top of the bay. Gain the groove and a ledge at the foot of a wall (35m). Move up the steep flakeline on the left and go left at its top to the edge overlooking Pterodactyl, then move up right to a shallow groove which leads to a short wall (35m). Move into the gully of Pterodactyl, which is followed to the top (50m).

Neanderthal   125m   VII,7 ★★★

R Anderson and G Nicholl, 14 February 1987

An improbable-looking line up the huge corner, 30m right of Pterodactyl. Very good climbing according to those who have done it! Go easily up the gully and left wall to a platform, traverse right and climb a chute to belay at a cul-de-sac (35m). Traverse right until it is possible to climb to the base of corner and a small ledge (21m). Follow the corner to the right side of a square roof. Move left underneath this and follow the recessed wall above towards an obvious narrow slot on the skyline (27m belay). Easier climbing soon leads to the top.

Savage   80m   VI,8 ★★

G Taylor and R Anderson, 31 January 1988

Climbs the obvious monolith on the wall right of Neanderthal, gained from the leftward ramp which starts at the edge of the buttress. Climb the ramp to a belay at the foot of the monolith (20m). Climb the corner-crack on the right side of the monolith, with difficulty, to a belay on its top (10m). Stepped walls and grooves are climbed above until forced into a traverse right around the buttress edge into a shallow groove. Climb the groove, then the rib just left of the steepening on Barracuda. Go right and finish on Barracuda (50m).

Barracuda   80m   V,7 ★★

R Anderson and R Milne, January 1988

Another steep and difficult mixed climb, although the easiest of the harder routes on this crag. Goes up the obvious steep crack-line which springs from the left-trending ramp-line right of Neanderthal. Start at the edge of the buttress. Follow the ramp to a belay at the foot of the crack. Climb the crack (with very hard initial moves) to the buttress crest. Climb the gully above to the top.

Barbarian   80m   V,6

M Gray and R McAllister, 29 December 1995

Start 8m right of the ramp of Savage/Barracuda and follow a groove for 10m (Trilobite?), then go around an overhanging bulge on the left to a block at the foot of a chimney-crack running up right of Barracuda. Follow this to a belay (30m). Continue up the chimney rightwards to the top (50m).

Dislocation   85m   III

CJS Bonington and F Mitchell, 1969

Starts about 15m up right from Barracuda and follows grooves rightwards to a snow patch and a broken chimney above to the top.

Glen Coe Central

Trilobite
60m III

H MacInnes and I Clough, 9 February 1969

On the side-wall of the buttress, leaving Right-Hand Gully where it begins to narrow and opposite a ramp which goes up steeply out to the right, Trilobite follows a very steep groove which runs directly up the gully wall to the top of the buttress.

Right-Hand Gully
90m II

Probably GSWC party

A steep gully with a big cornice, often containing a small ice pitch. About 30m up, below the steepening and narrowing to the pitch and level with the runnel of Trilobite, is a variation sloping steeply up to the right – The Ramp (grade I/II).

Descent Gully
I

Separated from Right-Hand Gully by a rocky rib. Straightforward and usually corniced.

Beinn Fhada (GS 1654) and Stob Coire Sgreamhach (GS 1553)

These two peaks link a fine ridge crest and form the steep slopes which enclose Coire Gabhail to the south-east. The ridge is steep and rocky on all sides and gained most easily from the east below point 811m (GR 172553). Ascent to this point is also possible from Coire Gabhail, starting up the steep and tedious slope 200m beyond the large 10m Boulder. Take the line of least resistance and arrive at a bealach after 1–1½ hours of upward toil! The ridge is followed with continual interest to a rocky step (GR 157538), which should be turned on the left before ascending to the summit of Stob Coire Sgreamhach. This fine outing is similar in parts to the Aonach Eagach (grade III). In descent the easiest route is via the bealach at GR 151537. Care should be taken on this slope. The cornice can be large and the avalanche potential is considerable at certain times.

The North Face of Stob Coire Sgreamhach provides long and interesting approaches to the summit at grade II, depending on the line you take. Access to this face is best by the track up the west bank of Allt Coire Gabhail as far as the stream junction beyond the gorge (GR 154543). From here, strike up the steepening slope to the south beneath the summit cone.

Lost Valley Ice Slabs – West Face of Beinn Fhada

On the east side of the stream, emerging from the boulder field below the flat part of the Lost Valley approach, are tiers of slabby wet rock that quickly freeze in a cold winter. Several good pitches have been made on these steep slabs. The steepest central icefall hereabouts is **Bop Till You Drop** (*105m, IV,4, M Garthwaite and A Foster, 6 December 1981*). Various trees can be used for belays and abseil points.

North Face of Beinn Fhada

Easily seen from the road and with a short approach, these routes offer good sport when freezing levels are low. When the conditions are right the stream crossings on the approach should be frozen and low. The climbs start above the big gully at GR 175560. The easiest approach is to follow the east side of the stream downhill from the cottage at GR 175566, then uphill to the big gully. Cars should be left in the lay-bys 500m west or east of the cottage. Descent from most routes can be made by abseil. Climbs are described from right to left.

Time for Tiffin   150m   IV,4
P Moores and A Paul, 27 January 1996
The rightmost icefall.

Time for Tree   150m   III/IV,4
P Moores and A Paul, 28 January 1996
The central ice smears.

Solicitor's Slot   150m   IV,4 ★
P Moores and A Paul, 29 January 1996
St Valentine's Climb for one pitch, then go right into an obvious rocky chimney.

St Valentine's Climb   150m   III,3 ★★
P Moores and A Paul, 28 January 1996
Next line on the left.

Andy's Folly   140m   IV,4 ★
P Moores and A Paul, 31 January 1996
Ascends the uppermost ice smear at the top of the rocky parallel gash, after an initial mixed rocky pitch.

Kriter   120m   IV,4
P Moores and A Paul, 1 February 1996
The lower ice smears in the central part of the parallel gash as seen from the road.

The following route lies on the East Face of Beinn Fhada.

The Bubble   60m   III/IV,4 ★★★

S Kennedy, C Macleod and M Slater, 2 January 1982

Well seen from the road, if in condition, at approximately GR 177556. A good little route.

The icefall to its right has also been climbed at grade III.

BUACHAILLE ETIVE MOR – STOB DEARG, 1022M   GR 223543

Buachaille Etive Mor is a long ridge with four tops. Stob Dearg is the north top, a beautifully symmetrical cone as seen from the junction of the roads leading down into the glens of Etive and Coe. It is the highest of the four tops, and the only one which gives much climbing, and it is generally referred to as The Buachaille.

The mountain is an excellent summer rock-climbing area, whilst in winter its natural ridge and gully-lines are amongst the best in Scotland. The view from the area surrounding Curved Ridge is one of the most striking panoramas of any British hill.

The most popular routes are all on the central section of the mountain above the Waterslide Slab, but many fine climbs can be found on the area overlooking Glen Etive between D Gully Buttress and The Chasm.

Many of the climbs start from Crowberry Basin – below Crowberry Ridge and Gully. The most usual starting point is from Altnafeadh (GR 222563) on the main road. The River Coupall is crossed by a bridge leading to Lagangarbh. Beyond the hut, a track leads south-eastwards, gradually rising, to cross the foot of Great Gully after about 1.5km. From this point one can take a shortcut by following the lower easy part of North Buttress with some scrambling, bearing left into the basin below Crowberry Ridge. Alternatively, one can continue following the track below North Buttress, which rises slowly to meet the prominent Waterslide Slab. From this slab ascend straight up the steep and loose scree slopes to its left. Higher up, a delicate traverse right must be made above steep rocky ground in order to gain the foot of Crowberry Gully or Curved Ridge (1½ hours). Routes to the left (south) of D Gully Buttress can also be approached via the Glen Etive road. For climbers new to this area, it is advisable to drive along the main road towards the Kingshouse in order to view the main features of the mountain before choosing a route.

Beware! Many avalanche incidents have occurred in the Great Gully and Crowberry Basin areas.

DESCENT

There is only one reasonable descent route in winter. From the summit (GPS NN22363 54311) follow the fairly level ridge for 300m bearing 250° grid, or to GPS NN22104 54113. Then change course to 270° grid and descend to reach a shallow cairned col (GPS NN21637 54157) at the head of Coire na Tulaich. This section can be particularly difficult in white-out conditions. There are occasional cairns, but it may be necessary to stay roped up and take both front and back bearings to keep on course. The most common mistake is to continue too far south-west and descend into Glen Etive. This slope is not too difficult, but it is a long walk back on the road. Care should be taken not to stray to the north too early, as there are some large crags at the head of Coire na Tulaich. From the col a steep initial slope leads down into the coire. This slope is often in a hard icy condition and it may be best to wear crampons and to belay. Even in soft conditions it is better not to glissade, as there are often boulders and screes exposed lower down. There have been many accidents here. The lower part of the coire (there is a track down the left-hand, west, side) leads easily down to Lagangarbh and the road. In this coire there are good opportunities for climbing when a short approach is required or the conditions on the higher crags are affected by bad weather. Do, however, be careful if the avalanche hazard is high, as a number of significant, fatal slides have taken place in this area.

It is also possible to ascend slightly from the col to point 903m (GR 214542) and descend north by the ridge to the west of Coire na Tulaich. All the large outcrops on this descent are avoidable by moving left, and this descent is recommended when there is significant avalanche hazard in Coire na Tulaich. The routes are described from left to right.

Stob Dearg from Glen Etive – South East Face

The area between Central Buttress and The Chasm is both complicated and huge in scale, requiring good judgement and climbing skills. No easy exits exist until the summit or Curved Ridge is reached. This section of the mountain is recommended to experienced climbers who savour the challenge of long routes with an 'Alpine' feel about them. Due to its south-easterly aspect this part of the mountain often produces good névé when other cliffs are covered in powder. Snow conditions can change as height is gained, and a wary eye should be kept on potential avalanche conditions.

The Chasm   450m   IV,4 ★★★

This route is approached from the Glen Etive road (GR 233531), 2.5km from the main road junction. At this point two streams can be seen on the map joining by the road, and The Chasm drains into the northmost one. It forms an obvious gulch on the hillside to the right (west), and is blessed with a short approach. During winters of heavy

Glen Coe Central

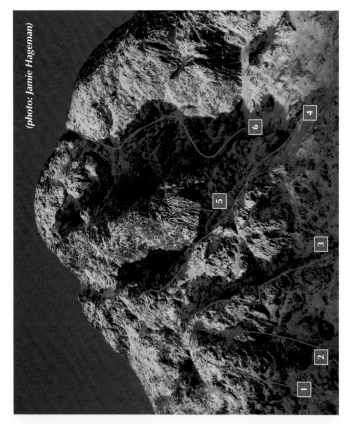

(photo: Jamie Hageman)

Buachaille Etive Mor South East Face

1 The Veil V,5**
2 Alpen IV,4*
3 D Gully Buttress IV,4**
4 Curved Ridge II/III,3***
5 Agag's Groove VI,6***
6 North East Zig-Zag III*

snowfall this climb may be straightforward. In leaner conditions several pitches will be present, and the nature of the climb becomes hard and time-consuming. Several variations exist higher up the gully, with the direct continuation being the most difficult. Escapes from the gully can be made at a number of points, most easily to the left.

The Chasm North Wall   360m II ★

JHB Bell, JW McGregor, J Napier, RG Napier, December 1895
Takes the rock walls bounding The Chasm on the right. Start 100m above the first pitches on The Chasm. Two steep buttresses are encountered.

The Chasm to Crowberry Traverse   1000m II ★

Easily seen from the Glen Etive road, this expedition starts at the edge of The Chasm below the first high wall of the previous route at an altitude of around 550m. An obvious feature is an undercut cave at the halfway mark. The line can be followed towards the top of Curved Ridge, or harder, more direct variants taken towards the summit. An excellent day out for explorers!

Lady's Gully   240m IV,4 ★★

JR Marshall, ID Haig and GJ Ritchie (Left Fork)
LS Lovat and WJR Greaves (Right Fork)
Easily seen on the hillside to the west of a stream junction (GR 240537), this gully is the first one north of The Chasm. It can be approached by continuing left from the Waterslide Slab on the Curved Ridge approach path. Not often in good condition, but when it is (during winters of heavy snowfall and good build-up), the climbing is very good. Follow the line of the gully to a steep wall (45m). Climb the wall, which can be difficult (45m), and several more difficult pitches to a fork in the gully. The left fork is the best option. This leads to easier ground beneath the summit ridge. Finish either by gaining the summit or by traversing left above The Chasm and descending into Glen Etive. If the right fork is followed, the top of Curved Ridge can be gained beneath Crowberry Tower.

Waterslide Gully   90m IV,5 ★★

T McAulay and C Murray, 9 February 1986
Left of The Veil, a shallow icy channel. Climb to a hanging stance (50m) then continue straight up (40m).

The Veil   180m V,5 ★★

T Brindle and A Moore, 20 February 1986
Climb the icefall right of Waterslide Gully in two pitches. Another pitch up a snow bay leads to a vertical column of ice, which is climbed to easier ground.

Glen Coe Central

Right of the previous two climbs is the main mass of **Central Buttress**. *The right side forms a steep narrow buttress of rock, and on the left it is bounded by the shallow Waterslide Gully. It is a two-tiered crag lying low down on the south-east side of the mountain.*

Direct Route   95m   IV ★

T McAulay and D Sanderson, 21 January 1984

This route lies on the South Face of Central Buttress and is reached by traversing left under the lowest rocks of Central Buttress beneath a distinctive yellow cave and climbing up to a small pinnacle. Pass the pinnacle on the right or left and climb to a ledge, which is followed up right to a 6m chimney, which is followed to Heather Ledge. Descend from Heather Ledge as in the following route.

Kinloss Corner   120m   V,6 ★★

A Paul and D Sanderson, January 1984

A short technical and sustained route which starts 15m left of and below North Face Route, where a slab leads to a corner. Climb the slab and corner, and a second easier slab leading to a short open corner. Climb the corner, then a rib on the left of another corner, which leads to an easier ledge (Heather Ledge). It is possible to traverse right on the ledge and either abseil or climb down rightwards to easier ground between Central Buttress and D Gully Buttress.

Spindrift on D Gully Buttress

Central Chimney   75m   IV
A Paul and D Sanderson, February 1992
This route is on the upper tier and starts from Heather Ledge 20m left of the buttress edge. It can be accessed either by climbing Kinloss Corner or the lower part of North Face Route. Follow the left hand of two inset corners, and then a corner on the right of the left-hand rib to the top of the buttress.

North Face Route   220m   V,6 ★★
JR Marshall and J Stenhouse, January 1958
A sustained and difficult mixed route. Climb a series of steep corners, walls, chimneys and cracks on the right (north-east edge) side of Central Buttress. These lead to an easier-angled ledge (Heather Ledge). A large white scar may be seen on the North Face above, with a recess beneath it. Gain the recess by traversing round two pillars. Continue the traverse rightwards, descending to a ledge. Climb an awkward 3m wall to a right-slanting ledge, which is followed to a 20m chimney. Climb the chimney to gain a platform, then traverse left to short steep crack near the north-east edge. Follow the edge to the top. Traverse rightwards across the top of D Gully onto Curved Ridge.

Special K   85m   IV,4 ★
R Anderson and A Russel, 21 January 1984
Starts higher up the open easy gully from which Alpen starts, and climbs the obvious icefall to the right of a prominent fin of rock at the top of the gully. Climb the icefall with difficulty to a belay (40m). Climb the same line, slightly left and trending left to the top of Central Buttress (45m).

Alpen   245m   IV,4 ★
S Belk, I Fulton, KV Crocket and C Stead, March 1972
Follows the chimneys and small gullies, as mentioned below, to the left of D Gully Buttress. Start halfway up an easy gully which trends left between D Gully Buttress and Central Buttress, at the foot of a wall. Climb steep turf ledges to the foot of a corner (45m). Continue up the corner to a cave belay (20m). Climb the right wall of the cave (10m), then a chimney, and trend more easily left to a small spike-belay (40m). Traverse left and belay below the right hand of two parallel chimneys (15m). Climb this chimney and rightward ramp to a belay (40m). Move up left in the gully (40m) and finish up right to the buttress top (45m).

*Left of **D Gully Buttress** is **Central Buttress**, and the two are separated by a wide open bay, from the back of which springs a line of chimneys and small gullies. An approach towards Central Buttress can be made by continuing horizontally on a faint track for a further 500m from the Waterslide Slab mentioned in the approach*

Glen Coe Central

to the Crowberry Basin. This approach will put the climber below the rocks of Central Buttress. It is also advisable to drive down Glen Etive for a mile or so in order to sort out the various routes on this complicated face. If a descent into Glen Etive is envisaged, the approach from Glen Etive is, in fact, shorter.

Stob Dearg – North East Face – Lagangarbh approach

D Gully Buttress   150m   IV,4 ★★

The buttress is narrow, and defined on the right by the deep D Gully and on the left by indefinite rocks merging with Central Buttress, with which it forms a right angle. The start of the buttress is vague, and entry is usually made from the foot of D Gully. A prominent steep smooth step high up the buttress is a useful landmark. The first section is fairly easy, apart from one steep short wall climbed by good cracks. The way is then blocked by the steep smooth step. Turn this on the left by a shallow chimney and gully leading back rightwards to regain the crest, very narrow at this point. Above, a long slabby section gives the crux, climbed at its right edge. After a further 30m or so the buttress ends on a shoulder, from where a right traverse should be made to gain Curved Ridge below its crux tower.

D Gully   150m   II
GT Glover and Collinson, April 1898
The gully below and to the left of Curved Ridge rarely has much snow. Usually easy, but it can give several short pitches. At the top, traverse up and right to Curved Ridge.

Curved Ridge   300m   II/III,3 ★★★
                                   (but can attain grade III after heavy snowfall)
GT Glover and RG Napier, 11 April 1898
A magnificent route and by far the most popular climb to the summit of the mountain. It passes through grand rock scenery, is a good general viewpoint and gives interesting climbing under almost any conditions (it is especially well sheltered from a south-west gale). Certainly the most useful winter climb on the Buachaille, and it can be quite hard. The line follows the crest of the ridge throughout. Easier options are available in the gully to the right of the crest (beware of avalanches).

Climb slightly left out of the Crowberry Basin by any of the several variations and pass beneath the Rannoch Wall of Crowberry Ridge (two short steep pitches) to reach a final big cairn at the top of Curved Ridge proper and below the foot of Crowberry Tower. From the cairn a horizontal left traverse for about 30m brings you onto a snow slope with two gully exits.

Buachaille Etive Mor

1 D Gully Buttress IV,4**
2 D Gully Buttress IV,4**
3 Curved Ridge II/III,3***
4 Crowberry Gully IV,4***
5 North Buttress
  (West Route) IV,4***
6 Raven's Gully V,5***
7 Great Gully II/III*
8 Great Gully Buttress
9 Broad Buttress

Glen Coe Central

Fresh snow on Curved Ridge

1   The gully slanting back to the right reaches the Crowberry Tower Gap, and from there a short groove leads left, then right, to the top of Crowberry Gully and the final summit slopes.

2   The gully going up slightly leftward leads directly to the summit rocks. It is probably the quickest, but not the most interesting way.

If time permits, an ascent of the Crowberry Tower can be included if the first route is followed. From the gap a short corner is climbed to a ledge on the left, then an easy rising spiral traverse leads to the top. There are more interesting routes up the tower, but this is the easiest and best in descent.

Agag's Groove   105m   VI,6 ★★★

H MacInnes, C Bonnington, K MacPhail and G McIntosh, 8 February 1953
The obvious corner ramp-line cutting up and left across Rannoch Wall on the left side of Crowberry Tower. It is a very good and highly regarded rock climb in summer and should be kept that way. Only attempt an ascent in perfect winter conditions. Start at a detached block at the bottom right side of the face. Climb the deepening corner in two pitches to a block-belay and good ledge (60m). Climb the ramp above and step left to climb the nose up a steep hidden crack (25m), or climb the ramp and continuation groove direct (harder). Traverse left and follow corners to the top.

Line Up   75m   VII,8

A Nelson, A Sharpe and K Grant, January 2010

Just left of Route I, start to the right of a red slab. Climb up to an overlap, cross it and continue to the left of a slab. Go right and up to belay (25m). Climb the 5m corner above, step left and continue to a roofed corner (25m). The large blocky corner above and the roof lead to the top (25m).

Route I   70m   V,6 ★

H MacInnes and partner, February 1972

The natural line of weakness in the middle of Rannoch Wall, starting 15m above the cave pitch in Easy Gully to the right of Curved Ridge. Climb a chimney and trend right up a slanting narrow shelf to slabs under a 4m wall. Climb the wall (crux) and the long upper groove back left.

Crowberry Ridge (Naismith's Original Route)   200m   IV,5 ★

From the narrows at the foot of Crowberry Gully proper move left onto the obvious Pinnacle Ledge at the foot of two chimneys. The left-hand chimney is followed. Climb up to the right, and as soon as possible take the easiest line back left to the crest. Continue up the crest, with easing difficulty, to the Crowberry Tower.

Shelf Route   200m   IV,6 ★★

WM MacKenzie and WH Murray, March 1937

A superb and sustained climb if good conditions are present. A shallow chimney-line running up the left wall of Crowberry Gully. Start low down in Crowberry Gully and traverse left to the foot of two chimneys. Climb the right wall and rib of the middle chimney to a shallow trough above. Follow the scoop above between the steep left wall and a small pinnacle. There are possible escapes over iced slabs to the ridge on the left. The direct line continues to a recess under the pinnacle, from where an awkward right traverse is made to gain icy grooves which lead up to the ridge below Crowberry Tower. Either climb the tower direct and descend its right side to the col (Crowberry Gap) or traverse left towards the top of Curved Ridge.

Crowberry Gully   300m   IV,4 ★★★

H Raeburn, WA Brigg and HS Tucker, April 1909

A magnificent classic climb of considerably quality. Unfortunately it is not often in good condition and can be dangerous due to avalanches. Conditions vary remarkably and can change in a short space of time. It may be completely banked up with snow except for an ice pitch at the junction (where a rightwards-rising traverse is made from the foot of the deep recessed Left Fork) and another pitch at the exit from a cave near the top of the gully. The cave will usually give the crux of

Heading for the sun on Curved Ridge

the normal route climbed by the right wall, which is invariably of green ice and 10–15m in height. If attempted when out of condition (particularly early in the season) there could be many more pitches, and Junction and Cave pitches may be all but impossible with only a thin veneer of verglas.

Crowberry Gully, Left Fork   IV,5 ★★

CMG Smith, RJ Taunton and IC Robertson, 18 March 1949

The Left Fork leads steeply out of the main gully to Crowberry Tower Gap. The deeply recessed gully soon becomes a narrow iced chimney, which is capped by a large overhanging block. The capstone will always be difficult, but good protection is available. Although it is a hard technical problem, this fork is very short and shouldn't require as much time as a complete ascent by the normal route (rarely climbed). On the first ascent, a third member of the party could not be pulled over the capstone after the second man had stood on his head to gain elevation!

Crowberry Gully, Centre Rib Finish   IV,5

M Robson and T Ward, 9 March 1996

Go right from the foot of the Left Fork by a crack, right of a chockstone, leading to a groove, then past a downward-pointing spike to a belay in the right fork. Climb up to the right edge of the rib, and when possible go left to its crest, which is followed to the top.

North East Zig-Zag   100m   III ★

JR Marshall, AH Hendry and GJ Ritchie, 1957

An interesting climb in open surroundings which has many variations and is clear of the avalanche problems in Crowberry Gully. Start from the left end of a broad terrace above and right of Crowberry Gully. Move up left and then back right by the simplest line to gain the upper section of North Buttress.

North Buttress (West Route)   300m   IV,4 ★★★

The first winter ascent is not recorded, but for an account of an early ascent of the route (and several others in this guide) see *Mountaineering in Scotland* (1962) by WH Murray. This is the huge buttress to the left of Great Gully and right of Crowberry Gully. From the foot of Great Gully two alternatives are possible. The first aims straight up easy ground for the line of chimneys splitting the middle section of the buttress. After 160m these lead onto easier-angled slopes with the odd difficult step. An easier approach is to continue along the path past the Waterslide and climb the lower reaches of Crowberry Gully to the Basin. From here traverse rightwards to join the chimneys of the first approach. The climb itself is possible in virtually any conditions and is safe from avalanche once on the route.

Glen Coe Central

The cave pitch of Crowberry Gully in thin conditions

Slime Wall *is the very steep rocky cliff left of Raven's Gully and overlooking Great Gully.*

Misty High   195m   V,5 ★★

A Paul and D Sanderson, 17 March 1979

This climb follows an icefall on the extreme left side of Slime Wall. Go up the ice-fall and follow the right-hand chimney. Climb easier ground to a short chimney and under a chockstone to North Buttress. Follow an icefall on the right for two long pitches to easier ground.

Guerdon Grooves   180m   IX,8

D Cuthbertson and A Paul, 28 January 1984

Technical and very serious, with poorly protected leads on steep rock and ice. The belays are satisfactory! The obvious icy grooves to the left of Raven's Gully are fol-lowed for three pitches into Raven's Gully. From the flake-belay in Raven's Gully the left-hand finish is taken.

Raven's Gully   135m   V,5 ★★★

H MacInnes and C Bonington, 14 February 1953

The dark slit high up on the North Buttress (left) wall of Great Gully. When in condition (fairly often) the crux is soon reached, a large chockstone. Above, three or four long difficult pitches lead to the top. A popular classic. The Direct Finish is rarely in condition.

A descent into Great Gully can be made after finishing Raven's Gully. This is advised only if avalanche potential is low and daylight is available to find a route down.

Raven's Edge   150m   VI,7 ★★★

S Allen and B Sprunt, 24 January 1984

Start at the foot of Raven's Gully. Climb the left edge of the buttress to a large block 10m above the chockstone in Raven's Gully (30m). Climb the vertical wall above, then traverse left to a prominent corner, which is followed to a ledge (25m). Climb a rib on the right of the corner to a platform (25m). Climb up to a belay below the big roof on the extreme left edge of the buttress (30m). Traverse left under the roof to a very exposed place on the right wall of Raven's Gully and climb a deep crack to the top (30m).

Raven's Edge (Complete)   170m   VII,7 ★★★

R Anderson and R Milne, 30 March 1996

Start at the foot of Raven's Gully and go right, up a line just right of the edge over-looking Raven's, then left around a projecting rib to a belay at the top of a

Glen Coe Central

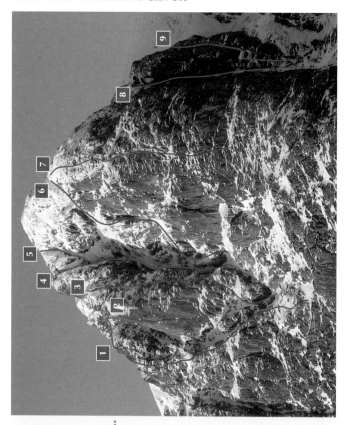

Buachaille Etive Mor North East Face

1 Curved Ridge II/III,3***
2 Agag's Groove VI,6***
3 Shelf Route IV,6**
4 Crowberry Gully, Left Fork IV,5**
5 Crowberry Gully IV,4***
6 North East Zig-Zag III*
7 North Buttress
   (West Route) IV,4***
8 Raven's Gully V,5***
9 Cuneiform Buttress,
   Ordinary Route IV,5

shallow left-facing corner (55m). Climb up left, then down to a thin traverse leading to the foot of the corner, 6m above the gully (15m). Go up to the roof, step down to traverse the wall, then go up left to the foot of the 'open book' corner, which is climbed to a belay at its top (35m). Ascend a corner above and traverse left beneath the roof (possible thread-belay). Continue around the edge to a better placed thread-belay (35m). Climb the deep crack up left (30m) followed by a short wall.

Cuneiform Buttress, Ordinary Route   135m   IV,5
JR Marshall, DN Mill and GJ Ritchie, 15 December 1957
Start at the lowest rocks near the foot of Raven's Gully and climb to a broad terrace. From its right end climb a short steep pitch followed by grooves to another broad ledge beneath the vertical upper section of the cliff. Traverse right around an exposed edge onto the West Face. Climb an obvious shelf then turn towards the centre of the cliff, which is climbed to the top. A right-hand start (*M Hind and R Webb, 2 January 2003*) climbs the obvious right-hand fault to the terrace, 60m, IV,4.

Cuneiform Buttress Direttissima   220m   VII,6
E Brunskill and S McFarlane, 12 December 2002
A serious direct line up the prominent shelf system on the West Face. From the terrace climb out right and straight up a steep groove (Ordinary Route goes up and left) to a cave (30m). Go right to a groove and climb this for 5m. Move right to another groove and climb this to a small ledge (35m). Climb the chimney above (45m). Continue up the chimney-line, then make a serious traverse 10m right to an obvious ledge (35m). Climb two detached flakes and the wall above (10m).

The Long Chimney   135m   IV ★★
R Smith and D Leaver, 15 December 1957
Follow the Ordinary Route to the broad terrace, then traverse hard right and climb the long obvious shallow chimney.

Cuneiform Corner   60m   IV,4
A Paul and D Sanderson, 17 March 1979
To the right of Raven's Gully is a large buttress (Cuneiform Buttress) which overlooks Great Gully. Midway up this buttress, an obvious icefall/corner is followed in two pitches to a terrace, from where a traverse right into Great Gully can be made.
    Note It is possible to continue to the summit by following steep corners/ grooves and icy walls above the traverse-line for another 170m (*III, P Moores and C Butler, February 1983*).

Glen Coe Central

Great Gully   360m   II/III ★

N Collie, 1894

The first deep gully to cross the path about 20 minutes from Lagangarbh. It is some-times confused with easier gullies further west. Early in the season it can give sev-eral hundred feet of ice, but generally banks out with frequent and considerable avalanche danger.

Ephemeron Gully   340m   IV,4 ★

KV Crocket, A Walker and P Craig, 28 December 1985

To the right (west) of Great Gully is Great Gully Buttress. The next buttress to the right is Broad Buttress. This route is immediately on the right (west) side of Broad Buttress and follows a line of icy grooves. Descent can be made by Broad Gully to the right or over the top of Lagangarbh Buttress.

LAGANGARBH BUTTRESS

The most westerly buttress on the North Face of Buachaille Etive Mor (approx. GR 222548). Its West Face overlooks Coire na Tulaich.

Lagangarbh Chimney   60m   III,4 ★★

On the West Face of Lagangarbh Buttress, this climb starts about halfway up the gully to the right of the buttress.

Infected   100m   III

Below Lagangarbh Buttress is a broken buttress, and below this is a shelf. Halfway along this shelf an ice smear sometimes forms. This route follows a prominent right-trending groove just left of the ice smear. Follow the groove right (25m). Climb up to and ascend an icefall (30m). Go up a short wall on the right to easier ground (30m). Ascend a short icefall, going right at the top (15m).

The Dial   85m   III/IV

A Nelson and D Gunn, 16 February 2000

The large slab below and right of Lagangarbh Buttress. Ascend the middle of the slab, aiming for a recess at the foot of a steep section in the corner. Either climb the slab, if formed, or a short steep section followed by an icy groove. This route appears to be in condition quite often and provides a good climb for a short day. Descend to the south.

Coire na Tulaich

This is the coire used by most people in descent from routes on Buachaille Etive Mor. In certain conditions it can hold many ice smears on the side-walls and does have extensive steep ground on all sides.

Sliver   80m   III/IV ★★

D Gunn and A Nelson, 31 December 1999

This climb is high on the north-west-facing side of the coire, beneath the steepest section of the normal descent route, on an obvious wall with icy lines on either side. Start behind a wall formed by a rocky island and follow the rightmost icy line.

Chimney Route   80m   II/III

P Harrop and P Moores, 1995

To the right (west) of the descent col are two buttresses split by a narrow chimney. This is the climb.

Four Feather Falls   120m   III/IV ★★★

'Chalky' White and P Harrop, 27 January 1991

To the left of the buttress containing The Spate a four-fingered icefall can form. Start below the fall in a snow bay and follow a 10m runnel, then grooves, to the base of the icefall (90m). Climb the right-hand icefall.

The Spate   100m   IV,6

A Nelson and P Moores, 13 February 1999

High on the west side of the coire is a buttress with an obvious curving chimney. This route follows that chimney leftwards, with a difficult move over a chockstone at 45m. After the chockstone, step left to an upper chimney, followed by a shelf where a traverse off, up and right is made. This route catches the sun, so start early. Approximates to the summer line of Nobad.

Pick 'n Mix   90m   IV,5/6

A Nelson and P Mills, 5 February 2001

Just after entering the lower narrow section of the coire a wide gully runs up the East Face on the right to the ridge at about 600m. On the right of the gully is a buttress (Creag na Tulaich), about 60m high with a left-facing corner running from bottom to top. This is the climb.

Glen Coe Central

Stob Coire Altruim, 941m   GR 197532

This north-facing crag is gained by a steep pull up from Lairig Gartain and lies on the second of the four tops of Buachaille Etive Mor.

Dalmation Couloir   100m   IV ★★★
GE Little and A Baker, 2 March 1991
Climb the obvious deep chimney in the centre of the buttress.

THE AONACH EAGACH

The Aonach Eagach is the long notched ridge which bounds Glen Coe to the north, applying particularly to the narrow crest extending between Sgor nam Fiannaidh on the west to Am Bodach at the east end. The Glen Coe flank of this ridge is steep and complex, very rocky and seamed by many gullies.

The Aonach Eagach Traverse   3km end to end   III ★★★
In good weather and good conditions the ridge gives a very fine winter expedition. Speed is essential if the party is to avoid benightment. The normal route is from east to west, which gives one the advantage of 100m less to climb. The best starting point is from near the white cottage at Allt-na-Reigh. Parking is available just down the road (GR 173567). A track leads up, crossing the stream, into the coire to the east of Am Bodach, from where easy slopes lead leftwards to the top (943m). Alternatively one may continue directly up the ridge from the start. Not advised in descent.

The descent from Am Bodach to the west can be quite difficult: go slightly right then back left and down a gully-crack. The most interesting section of the ridge is between Meall Dearg (953m) and Stob Coire Leith (940m), particularly a very narrow pinnacled section and an awkward slabby descent beyond it.

It must be pointed out that there is no safe descent from the ridge on the Glen Coe (south) flank of the ridge between the two end peaks of Am Bodach and Sgorr nam Fiannaidh. Very many accidents, some fatal, have occurred on these difficult and craggy slopes. It is best to continue to the end of the ridge and descend from Sgor nam Fiannaidh to the saddle between it and the Pap of Glen Coe. The recommended route is to follow the pathlines shown on the Harvey Glen Coe map towards GR 110586, where the plantation meets the public road. It is very useful to leave a vehicle in this vicinity (without blocking gates) and another at the eastern end of the ridge. One other reasonable descent is due south from the summit of Sgorr nam Fiannaidh. Steep snow or scree slopes lead to a narrow path running down to the Clachaig road junction with the main road. This descent is unrelentingly steep and bad for the knees, but might save on the walk back for the car. The descent alongside Clachaig Gully, directly towards the hotel, should be avoided as it is extremely loose. With care it may be possible to descend towards Loch Leven in a northerly direction at a number of points along the ridge.

Aonach Eagach – South Flank

These two fine cascade ice climbs (below) form on the south flank of the Aonach Eagach below the 'Pinnacles' of that route during sustained freezing conditions. A small parking area at GR 153572 or the bigger one 500m to the west should be used. Climb the hillside due north to the foot of the route. Blue Riband is the obvious steep cascade with a pillar of ice at its base. The ice to its left is yet to be climbed, even after the fantastic cascade climbing of 2010.

Blue Riband   600m V,5 ★★★
J MacKenzie and G Rooney, 18 February 1979
Climb a series of steep ice pitches interspersed with easier sections to below a steep cascade (320m). There is a possible escape from this point. Climb the icefall (35m), then the right branches of the gully to another steep ice pitch (150m). Ascend the slightly overhanging ice (10m) and easier ground (150m) to the top.

Findlay's Tail   130m IV ★
P Moores and A Paul, 27 January 1996
This route is a further 100m right (east) of Blue Riband and forms an obvious ice sheet. Descent by abseil is recommended.

In sustained freezing conditions many cascade ice routes form on the south flank of Am Bodach just above the road near the lay-by at GR 171569. These can provide many pitches of climbing at grades III–V with virtually no walk in. Higher up, and directly above the lay-by, is a very obvious vertical chimney called **The Slit**. *The crags to the right of this have two outstanding climbs linking together icicles and blobs of ice that form in exceptional conditions.*

Liquidation   40m VI,6
D MacLeod and D King, 8 January 2010
The left-hand and slightly more continuous line of ice.

Frozen Assets   40m VII,7
D MacLeod and S Wood, 9 January 2010
The right-hand line of ice daggers climbed with a gentle touch.

Aonach Eagach South Flank

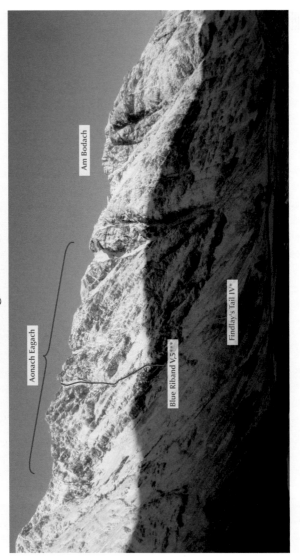

Aonach Eagach

Am Bodach

Blue Riband V,5***

Findlay's Tail IV*

HAUNT OF THE RAVEN by Hamish MacInnes

When I was asked to do a short piece for this guidebook, I thought, 'What the Hell...?' Who wants to read personal crap about what happened to someone who may have misread the guidebook or was too ambitious? Then I had second thoughts – why not? I'm sure Iain Clough would have gone for the idea – giving climb descriptions a human touch. What really evolves when you convert the written word into vertical action, and all the other factors come into play? To put it another way – what happens when the budgie hits the fan?

I am more in sympathy with two pals, John MacSnorrt and Wullie Flyte, in the poem, 'The Conquest of Buachaille Etive', by EA Balfour – John McSnorrt is a rough, tough mountaineer; Wullie more genteel. Upon bagging the summit Wullie exclaimed:

Peak upon peak sae fair and grand,
Like elfin towers in fairyland...'.
MacSnorrt said: 'Dinna be sae fulish,
There's naethin' there but Ballachulish.

My brief contribution is a tale of three climbers, John Cullen, Charlie Vigano of the Creagh Dhu and myself, who in the early 1950s attempted the first winter ascent of Raven's Gully on Buachaille Etive Mor; Raven's is a gash on the side of North Buttress, a prodigious prop of solid porphyry which sweeps up from the Moor of Rannoch to the very summit of the Buachaille. The gully is an annex on the right of this, wet and dripping in summer, frigid in winter when adorned with the white fangs of icicles.

'Ye can't come up here Jimmy!' Two black angry acrobatic residents screamed at us as we roped up at the first obstacle, the overhanging pitch 4. In those days climbing gear was scarce, and the Glasgow shipyards were our source of hardware. For clothing there was the 'Barras', where you didn't ask questions and watched your small change. The week before, one-piece flying suits were loss leaders – ex RAF, insulated and only £1.50 each. They sported numerous pockets, two of which were on the lower outer legs of the suit, excellent for an aviator's map and notebook, but useless on upside-down moves on the aforementioned pitch 4, where I did lose some loose change.

Raven's is a climb that grabs attention, where each succeeding pitch feels harder than the last. Thus engaged, the day slipped by and shadows began to crowd the defile. It was on the last pitch that the budgie, if not a raven, hit the proverbial fan. I had run out most of our 160ft-long rope when it jammed.

Cascade ice on Blue Riband

I tried to descend but it was too dangerous and there were no belays. It was almost dark and I wasn't dressed for the occasion, having only a thin ex-WD anorak over an old summer shirt. I untied and continued, soloing up steep ice, eventually coming to a halt in a short step called the Corkscrew, aptly named. I jammed myself in this enclave with one crampon jammed in an iced crack and my other foot on the wall on my right. It was now about 4pm and very dark, but I could shout to my two friends ensconced under the overhanging walls at the bottom of Raven's Direct Finish, then also unclimbed. This was their belay point. I envied their flying suits, which they now wore. I had left mine to be hauled up at the top of my pitch as it was too bulky to climb in, as I had discovered lower down.

Fortunately we had mentioned to Bill Smith, also of the Creagh Dhu, where we were going. Bill retorted: 'Well when I go down to the Clachaig Inn tonight I won't be looking up at the Buachaille for your lights.' But he did, and saw John and Charlie's distress signal. Eight hours later I heard a cry from above, it was Bill with a posse of top climbers including Jimmy Marshall. I still feel a coldness in my spine when I think of that wonderful day.

Glen Coe Central

Heading for the Aonach Eagach

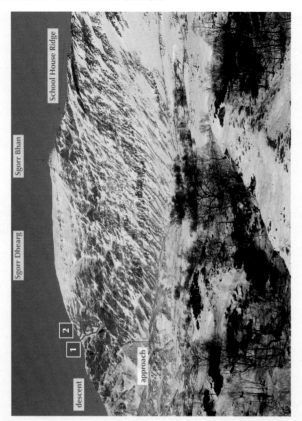

Sgorr Dhearg
East Face

1 Sardines IV,4
2 Hide and Seek V,6

OUTLYING AREAS

BEINN FHIONNLAIDH, 959M   GR 095498, SHEET 50, OS 1:50,000

Access from the south via Glen Creran off the A828 (GR 007460, Sheet 50).

Rapunzel   350m   IV ★★★

A deep chasm splits the South Face of the mountain. Being at such a low altitude and facing south, a good hard frost is needed to provide decent conditions. A route of great variety, similar to Dalness Chasm. When the gully splits take the right fork.

BEINN A'BHEITHIR

The School House Ridge (south-east ridge) of Sgorr Dhearg to .947 (GR 063562 Sgorr Bhan) above the Ballachulish school (GR 080578) via the right of way to Glen Creran is an interesting 580m of grade II under snowy conditions, and is a worthwhile poor-weather route when conditions are hazardous on surrounding peaks.

There are two routes on the North East Face of this peak overlooking the village. The large **Central Gully** gives a climb of II/III if icy, with a steep central pitch and an avoidable cascade lower down. The watercourse to its left **is Dog Leg Gully**, a 200m grade III* in icy conditions finishing up a short chimney to gain the ridge (D Gunn and A Nelson, 1997).

On the left of the East Face is a gully (NN065 559) at 700m which readily forms ice in cold conditions. **Hide and Seek** (200m, V,6) climbs the steep entry pitch on ice, then the right ice branch into a cul-de-sac at 120m. Mixed climbing up and right on a ledge and up an obvious left-facing corner (crux) leads to a terrace, which is followed horizontally left for 80m to easy ground. **Sardines** (200m IV,4) follows the left-hand branches of the main gully on continuous ice to emerge on the ridge, which can be descended to the left (D King and A Spink, 20 March 2006).

Sgorr Dhonuill

The Dragon's Tooth   700m   II ★★

Start from the Ballachulish Hotel. Foot access is by the minor road at GR 044594. Above Gleann a Chaolais and the Dragon's Tooth golf course is a peak variously

SGORR DHONUILL

known as the Dragon's Tooth or Fairy Peak, more appropriately called Sgor a Chaolais. The ridge going south from the top of this tooth to its junction with the ridge leading to the summit of Sgorr Dhonuill (GR 040555) gives an interesting scramble with atmosphere. To gain the ridge go up the good access path from the top left of the glen (Eastern Coire) to above the forest, and gain the nose from here. A grade II snow gully further up the coire also gives access, and it is possible to gain the tooth more steeply from the Western Coire. When going south along the ridge a vertical downwards step will be reached. Turn this on the east side or abseil.

Two climbs on the granite crag at NN033 555 have been recorded.

Thirty Nine Steps   90m   IV,6
S Kennedy and A Nelson, 18 February 1995
The corner-line left of the steep wall. Climb the corner for 10m and traverse left along a ledge to another steep corner. Climb this, move back right and follow a chimney to a ledge (45m). Climb a groove a few metres to the left, which leads into the main corner-line. Follow this to the top (45m).

Peekaboo   70m   VIII,8 ★★
D King and M Pescod, 10 January 2008
The obvious undercut steep wall. Pull through the overhang and climb the wall on good cracks, then trend right to a sloping ledge. Pull back onto the vertical wall and head left on tenuous hooks to a big spike around to the left. Another few moves gain a big ledge (30m). Traverse horizontally right under the obvious corner to the rightmost (bottomless) chimney. Climb this with an overhang at the top (40m).

Sgor na h-Ulaidh, 994m   GR 111518

Glen Coe Outlying

This fine but remote peak lies to the west of Bidean and has several easy climbs on the North Face of the mountain. The conspicuous deep gully directly below the summit gives three or four good pitches and is called **Red Gully**, III**.

Note This is a difficult mountain to descend from in poor visibility.

Fresh snow on The Dragon's Tooth

A'CHAILLACH SOUTH EAST FACE   GR 184570

Red Funnel Gully   **200m   III,3 ★**
R Baillie, H MacInnes and party, 1964
Interesting for an easy day after heavy snow. It overlooks the road through the gorge
at the top of the glen on the Aonach Eagach side and follows the left fork of the
steepest gully, finishing near a prominent rocky nose.

SRON NA LAIRIG   GR 163535

A prominent rocky spur overlooking the head of Lairig Eilde and leading up onto
the south-east ridge of Stob Coire Sgreamhach gives a fine climb, 300m, I/II**. The
approach up the Lairig is quite long but gentle. The lower part is best avoided on the
left, but higher up it narrows to a fine crest. A good primer for the Aonach Eagach.

GLEN ETIVE

Dalness Chasm   **400m   IV ★★★**
H MacInnes and C Williamson, February 1979
This obvious watercourse lies opposite the first cottage down Glen Etive at GR
196520, some 6.5km from the main road. A tremendous climb, although rarely in
condition. Follow the main stream line, with one big pitch, until the triple fork is
reached. Take the right fork by steep short pitches.
          Central Fork (V,5 ★★★)   **Left Fork (V,5 ★★★)**

Glen Ceitlein Slabs   GR 164464, Sheet 50, 1:50,000 OS Map

A large area of slabs which readily forms ice in a good freeze. Access is gained by
parking on the Glen Etive road at GR 136468 and following the well-marked tracks
into Glen Ceitlein. The slabs face west and form the east bank of a prominent gully.
Walk up the glen and turn uphill just beyond a low crag, after about 600m.

The Fall Line   **220m   III ★★**
S Kennedy and A Paul, 14 February 1991
On the approach to the main slabs a considerable icefall sometimes forms on the right,
400m before reaching the slabs. Climb the icefall and a deep narrow chimney above.

Glen Coe Outlying

359

Whore's Apron   310m III ★★
S Kennedy and D Ritchie, 10 February 1991
Climb the main icefall direct towards the left side of the slabs.

Beinn Trilleachan – Etive Slabs   GS 0944, Sheet 50, OS 1:50,000

After several days of hard frost, water smears running down the slabs begin to freeze. Two climbs have been made. The first, **Frozen Ba's**, IV,5*, follows an ice smear near the right side of the main slabs, and then tackles roofs and mixed ground above. The second, **Winter Dan**, IV,5**, takes a much thicker line of ice up the subsidiary buttress just up and to the right of the main slabs. Worth a look for a short day.

Ben Starav – Stob Choire Dheirg, 900m   GR 137427

The massive hill of Ben Starav is found at the bottom of Glen Etive, opposite Beinn Trilleachan on the other side of Loch Etive. There are a few climbs, but only the best is described here. It offers a grand day in a rarely visited coire. Park at GR 137469 and follow the track across the river past Coileitir and the path up the west bank of the Allt nam Meirleach. The climb is on the central of three broken buttress on the east ridge of Stob Choire Dheirg.

Hidden Ridge   200m III/IV,4 ★★
GE Little and D Saddler, 25 January 1986
The central buttress forms into a narrow and pinnacled ridge. Start up an open gully on the right of the foot of the buttress to a block-belay (60m). The short steep groove above forms the crux, and leads to the top of the buttress which now forms a ridge. Follow the ridge over two pinnacles to the summit.

STOB A'GHLAIS CHOIRE, 996m   GR 240516

Well seen from the Kingshouse, the North East Face of this mountain appears to be seamed with steep gullies and ridges. On closer inspection the angle relents. However, the routes are all worthwhile for climbers searching for easier ascents away from the crowds. Access is governed by the amount of water in the River Etive. When the river is low it is possible to cross at a number of spots, either before or after Coupall Bridge (GR 243543), and skirt the foot of Creag Dhubh. Allow 1½ hours for either approach. In descent the coire south-east of the summit of Stob a'Ghlais Choire can be taken. Care should be exercised on these slopes after strong winds or snowfalls, as windslab avalanches may be present. A longer but more satisfying end to a climb would involve ascending both Creise, 1110m (GR 238507), and Meall a'Bhuiridh, 1108m (GR 251503). A descent could then be made through the ski area to the north.

The nature of all the gullies will vary depending on the amount of snow build-up. They will all be easy, grade I or II. The ridges which separate the gullies are worthy of inspection, and will provide steeper mixed climbing at grade II/III. Also, the right-hand skyline will provide an interesting route of ascent, with more difficulty nearer the top. Of particular interest to the climber is the following route.

Inglis Clark Ridge   140m   III ★
R Napier and S Downie, March 1987
In the centre of the North East Face is a broad V-shaped buttress just left of Number Five Gully, the top of which is a flat-topped tower. Start at the right-hand end of the ridge, 30m up Number Five Gully. Follow grooves and some steep ice pitches (crux) to a broad terrace (35m). Ascend to the rock tower and climb it on the right to a wall (65m). Traverse left (5m) along the wall, and then up right by blocks and a right-angled corner-chimney to the top of the tower.

The ridge (Sron na Creise), which drops off of the north end of Stob a'Ghlais Choire, has two icefalls which form low down on its left side (GR 242525).

King's Tear   170m   III/IV,4 ★★
P Moores and W Samuels, 4 January 1997
The right-hand icefall via the steepest ground.

The Weep   250m   II/III
P Harrop, S Kennedy and D Sinclair, 5 January 1997
The left-hand icefall.

Glen Coe Outlying

BEINN UDLAIDH, 840M   GR 274330, SHEET 50, OS 1:50,000

This low-lying cliff is included in this guide due to its proximity to Glen Coe and its collection of quality winter climbs. Being at such a low altitude a prolonged good solid frost is required to harden up the springs which flow down the cliff and produce the climbs. A small selection of the more popular routes are described.

Access to the cliff is by driving down Glen Orchy to the entrance of Glen Orchy

BEINN UDLAIDH

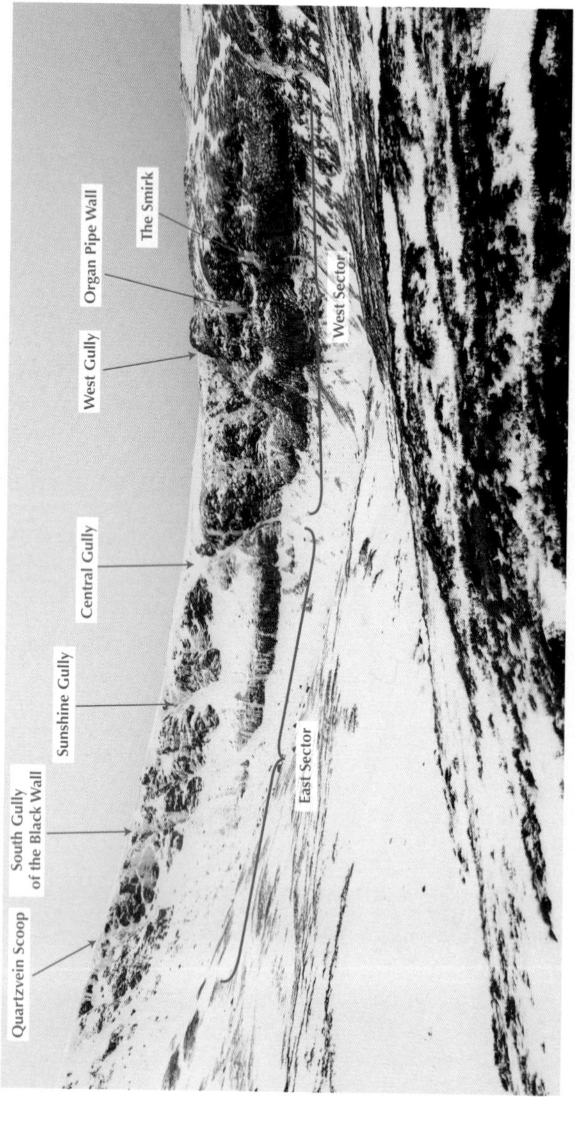

Quartzvein Scoop

South Gully of the Black Wall

Sunshine Gully

Central Gully

West Gully

Organ Pipe Wall

The Smirk

West Sector

East Sector

Cascade-style climbing on Quartzvein Scoop

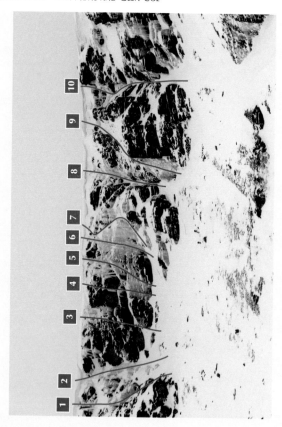

Beinn Udlaidh – East Sector (left side)

1 Ice Crew III,3**
2 Quartzvein Scoop IV,4***
3 Captain Hook VI,6***
4 Cut-throat VI,6***
5 The Croc V,5**
6 Peter Pan Direct V,5***
7 Land of Make Believe II**
8 South Gully of Black Wall IV,4***
9 Green Eyes IV,4*
10 Ramshead Gully III*

Farm, where limited roadside parking can be found. This is where the Allt Daimh joins the River Orchy. Tracks and paths are followed, first over fields and then through forestry in a south-easterly direction for about an hour uphill to the foot of the cliffs. The climbs are described from left to right. Descent is by going either left or right along the top of the cliffs until easy ground leads back into the coire basin.

Zigzag Gully 90m II

A Agnew and J Jewel, 14 November 1970
The leftmost side of the cliffs, with one possible ice pitch at half-height.

Ice Crew 90m III,3 ★★

I Duckworth and N Morrison, February 1980
Close to the left and parallel to Quartzvein Scoop.

Quartzvein Scoop 90m IV,4 ★★★

D Evans, A Gray and A Shepherd, 1979
A steep diagonal line immediately left of the steep Black Wall.

Captain Hook 75m VI,6 ★★★

D Cuthbertson and C Calow, January 1980
Ascends the funnel-shaped cascade in the centre of the Black Wall.

Cut-throat 75m VI,6 ★★★

D Cuthbertson, R Duncan, R Young and C Calow, January 1980
The obvious icicle which is often not complete and may require a free pull on occasions.

The Croc 75m V,5 ★★

A Barton, D Evans and JG Fraser, January 1979
Climb the ice streak on the right-hand part of the Black Wall. A traverse in from the left can be made if the start is not complete.

Peter Pan Direct 85m V,5 ★★★

D Claxton, I Duckworth, A Kay and N Morrison, 1 January 1982
Climb the right hand of two obvious icefalls directly to the top.

Land of Make Believe 90m II ★★

N Morrison and M Orr, 29 December 1979
Start below and right of Peter Pan Direct and follow a zig-zag line of least resistance to the top through spectacular country.

Glen Coe Outlying

Beinn Udlaidh – East Sector (right side)

1 Ramshead Gully III*
2 Ramshead Buttress IV,4
3 Sunshine Gully III,3***
4 Behind the Sun VII,7
5 Central Gully II
6 Junior's Jaunt IV,5**

South Gully of Black Wall
120m   IV,4 ★★★

R McGowan and G Skelton, 30 November 1969
The first obvious gully to the right of the ice-draped Black Wall.

Green Eyes
120m   IV,4 ★

I Duckworth and JG Fraser, 29 December 1979
The ice line on the left of the buttress right of South Gully of the Black Wall.

Ramshead Gully
120m   III ★

GH Caplan and ID Crofton, 4 December 1976
To the right of South Gully is a steep rocky buttress, and Ramshead Gully is on its right. Exit right at the top.

Ramshead Buttress
120m   IV,4

I Duckworth and JG Fraser, January 1980
The open buttress right of Ramshead Gully is climbed by an ice cascade to the right-hand end of a large ledge at halfway. Finish up to the right.

Sunshine Gully
90m   III,3 ★★★

E Fowler, F Jack, R McGowan and G Skelton, 14 November 1970
Midway between South Gully of Black Wall and Central Gully. It appears as a left-trending ramp and can contain plenty of ice.

Behind the Sun
30m   VII,7

A Turner and D MacLeod, 26 February 2010
The overhanging wall of the lower tier is climbed by linked icicles up and left before breaking through the roof at the far left end on icicles with the character of a continental route.

Central Gully
180m   II

J Buchanan, J Forbes and G Skelton, 29 December 1968
The long left-trending gully in the centre of the coire. In lean conditions it can contain four ice pitches.

Junior's Jaunt
80m   IV,5 ★★

P Bilsborough, I Duckworth, N Morrison and W Woods, 24 February 1979
Climbs the prominent cascade which starts 45m up the right wall of Central Gully. Short, hard and technical.

Beinn Udlaidh
West Sector

1 Central Gully II
2 Junior's Jaunt IV,5**
3 Doctor's Dilema IV,4**
4 Junior's Jangle IV,4*
5 White Caterpillar III,3*
6 West Gully III**
7 Sidestep III,3
8 Hobo III,3
9 Organ Pipe Wall V,5**
10 Quintet IV,4

Doctor's Dilema   180m   IV,4 ★★
I Duckworth and M Firth, 1978
On the buttress to the right of Central Gully. Climbs the prominent wide central series of cascades. Starts up left of the toe of the buttress.

Junior's Jangle   90m   IV,4 ★
JG Fraser and N Morrison, 30 December 1979
Start a little way up West Gully and follow a series of corners to the right of centre of the buttress on the left.

White Caterpillar   105m   III,3 ★
G Skelton and W Woods, 30 December 1978
Begin halfway up West Gully and go left on a wide ramp of ice until it is possible to climb up right to a similar ramp going left again and on to the top. A more direct line avoids the moves up right (IV,4).

West Gully   180m   III ★★
The obvious right-trending gully.

Sidestep   180m   III,3
N Morrison and R Stewart, 27 January 1979
Some 150m to the right of West Gully is a deep chimney leading to below an obvious cascade. Climb the buttress left of the chimney to a snowfield, followed by easier climbing up left to the top. It is also possible to finish up Hobo, making a more direct line.

The next three routes start from within the hidden deep chimney.

Hobo   165m   III,3
I Duckworth and G Skelton, 1979
From the bay below the ice cascades go left and climb an obvious turfy fault.

Organ Pipe Wall   75m   V,5 ★★
R Duncan and JG Fraser, 27 January 1979
Climbs the obvious cascade directly by a central groove and wall.

Quintet   120m   IV,4
I Duckworth, JG Fraser, A Pettit and W Woods, January 1980
Ascend the right-hand side of the cascade.

Glen Coe Outlying

The Smirk   90m   V,5 ★★★

R Duncan and JG Fraser, 27 January 1979

The prominent steep chimney-gully on the right-hand side of the West Wall. The left fork or direct finishes are possible. Slow to come into condition.

Steep featured ice on The Smirk

APPENDIX A
Accommodation for climbers

The accommodation shown represents the wide selection available. Many are self-catering and this offers a really flexible accommodation option for winter climbers, allowing early starts and late finishes that cannot often be achieved in standard B&Bs, guest houses or hotels. Most of the accommodation shown is run by independent owners, many of whom are outdoor folk who understand the need for good drying rooms, clean kitchens and warm beds. Using these establishments will help the local economy and people.

Thanks for your support.

Alan Kimber
Previous author of this guide
Proprietor of Calluna Bunkhouse and West Coast Mountain Guides

Calluna, Fort William	(01397)700451	www.fortwilliamholiday.co.uk
Achintee Hostel, Fort William	(01397) 702240	www.achinteefarm.com
Ben Nevis Inn, Fort William	(01397) 701227	www.ben-nevis-inn.co.uk
Glen Nevis Youth Hostel, Fort William	(01397) 702336	www.glennevishostel.co.uk
Fort William Backpackers	(01397) 700711	www.fortwilliambackpackers.com
Chase the Wild Goose Hostel, Banavie	(01397) 748004	www.great-glen-hostel.com
Bank St Lodge, Fort William	(01397) 700070	www.bankstreetlodge.co.uk
Corrie Doon, Banavie	(07767) 062730	www.banavie.com
Kingshouse Hotel, Glencoe	(01855) 851259	www.kingy.com
Glencoe Youth Hostel	(01855) 811219	www.syha.org.uk/hostels/highlands/glencoe.aspx
Red Squirrel Campsite, Glencoe	(01855) 811256	www.redsquirrelcampsite.com
Glencoe Independent Hostel	(01855) 811906	www.glencoehostel.co.uk
Clachaig Hotel and Chalets, Glencoe	(01855) 811252	www.clachaig.com
The Inchree Centre, Onich	(01855) 821287	www.inchreecentre.co.uk
Corran Bunkhouse, Onich	(01855) 821000	www.corranbunkhouse.co.uk
Farr Cottage, Corpach	(01397) 772315	www.farrcottage.com
The Smiddy Bunkhouse, Corpach	(01397) 772467	www.highland-mountain-guides.co.uk
Blackwater Hostel, Kinlochleven	(01855) 831253	www.blackwaterhostel.co.uk
Grey Corrie Lodge, Roybridge	(01397) 712236	www.roybridgehotel.co.uk
Aite Cruinnichidh, Roy Bridge	(01397) 712315	www.highland-hostel.co.uk
Station Lodge, Tulloch, Roybridge	(01397) 732333	www.stationlodge.co.uk

APPENDIX B

Index of routes: Ben Nevis area

APPENDIX C

Index of routes: Glen Coe area

LISTING OF CICERONE GUIDES

For full information on all our British and international guides, please visit our website: www.cicerone.co.uk.

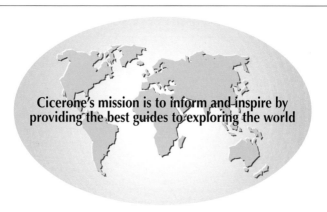

Cicerone's mission is to inform and inspire by providing the best guides to exploring the world

Since its foundation 40 years ago, Cicerone has specialised in publishing guidebooks and has built a reputation for quality and reliability. It now publishes nearly 300 guides to the major destinations for outdoor enthusiasts, including Europe, UK and the rest of the world.

Written by leading and committed specialists, Cicerone guides are recognised as the most authoritative. They are full of information, maps and illustrations so that the user can plan and complete a successful and safe trip or expedition – be it a long face climb, a walk over Lakeland fells, an alpine cycling tour, a Himalayan trek or a ramble in the countryside.

With a thorough introduction to assist planning, clear diagrams, maps and colour photographs to illustrate the terrain and route, and accurate and detailed text, Cicerone guides are designed for ease of use and access to the information.

If the facts on the ground change, or there is any aspect of a guide that you think we can improve, we are always delighted to hear from you.

Cicerone Press
2 Police Square Milnthorpe Cumbria LA7 7PY
Tel: 015395 62069 Fax: 015395 63417
info@cicerone.co.uk www.cicerone.co.uk